Pope Leo I, W Bright

Select sermons of S. Leo the Great on the incarnation

Pope Leo I, W Bright

Select sermons of S. Leo the Great on the incarnation

ISBN/EAN: 9783741191695

Manufactured in Europe, USA, Canada, Australia, Japa

Cover: Foto ©Lupo / pixelio.de

Manufactured and distributed by brebook publishing software (www.brebook.com)

Pope Leo I, W Bright

Select sermons of S. Leo the Great on the incarnation

PREFACE

TO THE SECOND EDITION.

For a general survey of the career of Pope Leo the Great, and for an estimate of his character and of his place in ecclesiastical history, the reader may be referred to the article on "Leo I." in the "Dictionary of Christian Biography," by the Rev. C. Gore, Principal of Pusey House, Oxford; with which may be compared the volume entitled "Leo the Great," contributed by the same author to the S. P. C. K. series of "The Fathers for English Readers."

Something, however, may here be said, by way of introduction to the consideration of S. Leo's position as a preacher and as a controversial theologian, in reference to that commanding personality which Cardinal Newman has aptly characterised by the word "majestic." Leo is the first of four Popes who, even if their lot had been cast in secular life, would have made their mark as great men: the three others, it need not be said, being the first and seventh Gregories and the third Innocent. It is significant that when, on the vacancy of the Roman see in 440, he was absent in Gaul on a high political mission, there was no question of a contested election; the Roman clergy and laity waited tranquilly through forty days for the return of the only ecclesiastic who could be seriously thought of as successor to Sixtus III. There is something of the Aristotelian μεγαλοψυχία in Leo, as he ascends the throne which was called "par excellence," Apostolical; he does not think of evading the task imposed upon him; he has a grave confidence that it is the task for him, that he is the man for it, and that he will be divinely enabled to satisfy its requirements. Authority, so to speak, comes natural to him; his temperament, for instance, is the very opposite to that of Gregory of Nazianzus; it has a certain affinity to that of Basil, but there is in it much more of the simply imperial element, in contrast to that sensitiveness and tenderness which lends so pathetic a charm to the story of the great primate of Cappadocia. If we think of comparing Leo with Athanasius, we find that while he lacked those opportunities of confessorship which were so splendidly used by him who stood "against the world," he was also less fully and conspicuously "royal-hearted"[1] in many-sidedness and far-reaching insight, in depth and massiveness of thought, in balance and harmony of various excellences, in the qualities of a moral centre of union, in the noble affectionateness which kindles and perpetuates loyalty. We think of Leo as of a public personage always; he does not seem to have needed an "interior;" he is absorbed in the work of government, and of government as carried on by the application of a few simple methods.

[1] Newman, in Lyra Apostolica, p. 118.

Preface.

Unity, discipline, obedience to ecclesiastical rule, conformity to orthodox standards, are dominant ideas with him; he does not care, apparently, to balance them by other considerations; it is not much in his line to appreciate difficulties, or to place himself at other persons' standpoints; he has little of that Pauline spirit which can become all things to all men, and even weak with the weak; his character is of the type which secures admiration and reverence, but fails, on the whole, to call forth actual love. The faults which cannot but be discerned in what we may call his Papal policy,—the hasty injustice and absolutism with which he treated so eminent a bishop as Hilary of Arles,[1]—the employment of a worthless Western emperor as the instrument for enforcing his own supremacy throughout the West,[2]—the persistence with which, in spite of evidence which must have been familiar to one who had been in the service of the Roman Church from the time of Pope Zosimus,[3]

---

[1] Tillemont repeatedly says that he was "prévenu contre S. Hilaire," "less of a judge than of a partisan." "It would be difficult," he adds, "to excuse this holy Pope for the charges which he brings against a bishop whose sanctity is so well acknowledged, if we did not every day feel in ourselves the effects of that unfortunate weakness which makes us take our suspicions for proved facts, and believe too easily the evil which is reported to us of others, especially when they have wounded us in regard to pretensions which we think just and wellfounded," (xv. 78—87.) Tillemont indicates clearly enough that, in his opinion, S. Leo had "overstepped the bounds of the canons."

[2] "Epist." xi. (July 8, 445.) Tillemont speaks of this rescript with measured severity, xv. 83, 441. Its language presupposes the corrupt Roman reading of the sixth Nicene canon, which Leo's legate produced at Chalcedon,—whereupon the true text was read.

[3] S. Augustine mentions "Leo the Acolyth" as the bearer of a letter from Rome in 418, Ep. cxci. 1.

he went on claiming the warrant of the Nicene Council for an appellate jurisdiction in his own see,[1] —such things are too clear proofs that he did not rise above the temptations which beset men born to rule, and that the spirit of that lordly verse,

"Tu regere imperio populos, Romane, memento,"[2]

was mingled in his mind with a sincere acceptance of that traditionary Roman belief in the rights of the "Cathedra Petri," to which he gave an emphasised expression and a considerably extended scope.[3]

It would be most unjust to ignore the moral eminence which the inchoate Papacy of that age attained through its high-souled representative. Dean Milman may somewhat overstate the case when he says that "on the throne of Rome alone, of all the greater sees, did religion maintain its majesty, its sanctity, its piety;" for Flavian of Constantinople was undoubtedly a pious prelate, who had shown at his accession that he would not buy support by base means. But Milman adds that "the world would not be inclined rigidly to question pretensions supported," in Leo's case, "by such conscious power or by such singular and unim-

---

[1] True copies of the Nicene canons, containing nothing about appeals to Rome, were sent to Rome in November of 419. The Sardican canons on such appeals could not, then, after this, be honestly adduced by any Roman ecclesiastic as Nicene. Yet Leo does, in effect, so adduce them in a synodical letter to Theodosius, Oct. 13, 449, Epist. xliv. 3.

[2] See Milman, Hist. of Latin Christianity, i. 230, "Leo was a Roman in sentiment," &c. Compare Gore's Leo the Great, p. 101.

[3] This will appear to be the case if his language is compared with that of Innocent I., who had "Papal ideas" in his mind, and in whose language Hallam sees the germ of "the system of Bellarmine," Middle Ages, ii. 228.

peachable virtue, and by such inestimable benefits conferred on Rome, on the empire, on civilisation. Once" (i.e. in 452) " Leo was supposed to have saved Rome from the most terrible of barbarian conquerors; a second time" (in 455) "he mitigated the horrors of her fall before the king of the Vandals. During his pontificate" (440—461) " Leo is the only great name in the empire; it might seem also in the Christian world."[1]

II.

The following specimens of his Sermons[2] for the sacred seasons of Christmas, Epiphany, Passion-tide, Easter, Ascension, and Whitsuntide—which may with sufficient accuracy be described as "on the Incarnation"—will be best introduced by another quotation from the same vivid and vigorous writer.

"He was the first of the Roman Pontiffs whose popular sermons have come down to posterity. The bishops of Constantinople seem to have been the great preachers of their city. . . . Leo, no doubt, felt his strength: he could cope with the minds of the people, and make the pulpit what the rostrum had been of old. His sermons singularly contrast with the florid, desultory, and often imaginative and impassioned style of the Greek preachers. They are brief, simple, severe; without fancy, without metaphysic subtlety, without passion: it is the Roman

---

[1] Milman, i. 228.

[2] Sozomen's statement (vii. 19,) that in his own time there was no public preaching at Rome, must be a gross exaggeration. Tillemont says that Leo in his sermons speaks as if preaching were a recognised duty of "popes, as well as of other bishops," xv. 417.

Censor animadverting with nervous majesty on the vices of the people; the Roman Prætor dictating the law, and delivering with authority the doctrine of the faith. They are singularly Christian—Christian as dwelling almost exclusively on Christ, His birth, His Passion, His Resurrection: only polemic so far as called upon by the prevailing controversies to assert with especial emphasis the perfect Deity and the perfect Manhood of Christ."[1]

Dean Milman adds that there is nothing of a "cultus sanctorum" in these discourses; and it has been well remarked that although he ascribes great efficacy to "the patronage, prayers, or merits of the saints," yet he says nothing about "invoking" them, and " he very zealously guards the prerogative of Christ as the real source of merit."[2] The practical bent of his mind, alike as pastor and as Church ruler, appears in those earnest exhortations to moral watchfulness and active piety which repeatedly occur in his preaching on the events of our Lord's earthly life, but naturally take a more urgent tone in the series of his twelve Lenten Sermons. Again and again he seems to say, "If you call yourselves Christians, take care to act out your Christianity: do not rest until your faith has become a transforming principle in your lives.[3] The Eternal Son of God really became man for you, died for you, rose again for you, went up on

---

[1] Milman, i. 233.

[2] Dict. Chr. Biogr. iii. 670.

[3] "As in faith lies the motive of works, so in works lies the strength of faith," Serm. de Collect. v. 2. See de Collect. iv. 1, that God can be denied by deeds as well as by words, and that many who retain belief have lost charity.

high to intercede for you : do you be real in your devotion to His service. You have been admitted to the highest spiritual privileges :[1] remember the grave responsibilities which they involve. You are constantly exposed to the crafts of the Tempter :[2] take care not to be overcome for want of vigilance. Forewarned, forearmed : the time is short, the work to be done in it is momentous :[3] keep clear of seducing influences ; be strict in self-examination,[4] diligent in prayer, observant of fasts, open-handed in almsdeeds ;[5] but amid all these good activities, beware of a self-complacency which would forfeit grace,[6] and of the self-confidence which goes before a fall ;[7] hold fast to the true faith in a Divine and human Saviour, but see to it that your faith is active through love ;[8] and never lose heart in your efforts to acquire that purity

---

[1] Leo's "sacerdotalism" is quite consistent with a pointed comment on 1 S. Peter ii. 9, " Ut præter istam specialem nostri ministerii servitutem, universi spiritales et rationabiles christiani agnoscant se .... sacerdotalis officii esse consortes," de Natal. ips. iv. 1 ; cp. de Quadr. x. c. 1, that not only the clergy, but " omne corpus ecclesiæ," ought to be holy, so that God's temple " in omnibus lapidibus speciosum, et in tota sui parte sit lucidum."

[2] " Ille cui sanctificatio nostra supplicium est," de Jej. x. mensis, vii. c. 2 ; cp. de Quadr. xi. c. 3.

[3] " Non enim dormientibus provenit regnum cœlorum," in Epiph. v. c. 3.

[4] "Circumspiciat se omnis anima Christiana, et severo examine cordis sui interna discutiat." De Quadr. i. c. 5 ; cp. de Quadr. iii. c. 1, " Scrutetur quisque conscientiam suam."

[5] See Sermon xvi. in this volume, c. 5, and de Quadr. vi. c. 2, de Collectis, vi. c. 2, de Jej. x. mensis, i. c. 2. In the latter passages he dwells on the common humanity of all men, "una est divitum pauperumque natura" .... "unus enim nos Conditor finxit."

[6] Serm. in Epiph. viii. c. 3, de Quadr. iv. c. 3.

[7] De Quadr. v. c. 3.

[8] De Quadr. vii. c. 2.

which, as long as it is sought for, will assuredly be obtained."[1]

Leo's exhortations may be said to revolve in a narrow circle; there are certain things which he is bent on bringing home to the consciences of his flock; he is quite indifferent as to repeating himself, if thereby he can deepen the impression. The general brevity of his sermons may indicate this practical determination; their style is terse, succinct, antithetical, —hardly ever diffuse, for he means to say what will stick and be remembered; their condensation has a peculiar energy and intensity, and their stately rhythm a masterful impressiveness; we feel that the great Pope's voice, as it rang through the pillared naves of the patriarchal basilicas, must have been fraught with solemn power for Roman auditors, who might hardly have appreciated the homely confidential simplicity and the versatile sympathetic self-adaptation with which S. Augustine had poured forth his stores of thought and knowledge, and feeling and experience, into the minds of the Church-people of Hippo.

III.

The work of Leo as a controversial theologian was to guard against the Eutychian reaction from Nestorianism; in other words, to vindicate the reality

---

[1] A sentence well worth remembering, in Serm. de Quadr. xii. c. 1. After quoting "Blessed are the pure in heart," he adds, "Quamvis enim scriptum sit, 'Quis gloriabitur castum se habere cor, aut mundum se esse peccato?' (Prov. xx. 9,) non tamen desperanda est apprehensio puritatis, quæ dum semper petitur semper accipitur."

and permanence of the human nature in Christ, as altogether consistent with the singleness of His Divine personality. Herein consists the value of Leo's "Christological" writings. Modern tendencies, indeed, run sometimes into a Nestorian, sometimes into a purely Humanitarian direction; they have little affinity to Apollinarianism or to Eutychianism. It is, therefore, all the more opportune for us to have our attention directed to a canonised Doctor, who, while insisting, in accordance with the needs of his time, on the truth of our Lord's Manhood, never for a moment forgot the higher aspect of the "mystery of godliness," or failed to contend for His original Divinity. Hence it is that Leo has been called "the final defender of the truth of our Lord's Person against both its assailants;"[1] and there was a substantial warrant for the acclamations of the Council of Chalcedon, which united his name with that of the great opponent of Nestorius: "Leo and Cyril have taught alike!"[2] And in days when a mysticism which would disintegrate Christianity is too often mistaken for "spiritual theology," it is well to be reminded by such teaching as Leo's that the spirit and power of the Faith are bound up with the literal and bodily human life, the death, and the resurrection, of the Incarnate Son of God.

It must be owned that Leo's tone with regard to heretics in general is severe and unconciliatory: it

---

[1] Wilberforce on the Doctrine of the Holy Eucharist, p. 246. Compare Serm. iv. in this volume, c. 4.
[2] Mansi, Concil. vi. 792. In the year before, he had proposed as a test of Anatolius' orthodoxy, *either* Cyril's second letter to Nestorius, *or* his own Tome; Ep. lxx.

unites the sternness of the ecclesiastical magistrate with the warmth of the polemic theologian. He does not sufficiently distinguish between the heretic and the heresy. We cannot imagine him as qualifying his denunciations of the Manichean sect, whose propagandism in Rome excited with too good cause his alarm and indignation, by such a touching disclaimer as S. Augustine prefixes to a criticism of the Manichean "Epistle of the Foundation:" it was not in him to say, "*Illi* in vos sæviant qui nesciunt cum quanta difficultate sanetur oculus interioris hominis, ut posset intueri solem suum!"[1] In one of his Lenten discourses he breaks forth against the Eutychians in general as "filii diaboli atque discipuli, repleti inspiratione viperea:"[2] in another, for Passiontide, he refers to the "viperea hæreticorum colloquia," and adds, "tot species habent diaboli, quot simulacra mendacii."[3] And although he usually speaks of Eutyches himself with some degree of indulgence, as of one who had erred through "ignorance" or "inexperience," rather than through "craftiness,"[4] yet occasionally he seems to think that the "inconsiderate old man" had actually contemplated, and committed himself to, this or that inference from his denial of the Two Natures: and perhaps the most telling passage on the logical results of Eutychianism is that in which he contends that if our Lord had *not* a human nature, then either His humiliations and sufferings must be regarded as illusory, which is Docetism,—or they must be attributed to an inferior Godhead, which

---

[1] S. Aug. c. Epist. Manich. c. 2. [2] Serm. de Quadr. ii. c. 3.
[3] De Pass. xviii. c. 5. [4] Epist. xxx. c. 1.

is the theory of Arius, "whose perversity is greatly assisted by this" (Eutychian) " impiety."[1] In all that Leo writes upon the momentous issue raised by this controversy, we see how intensely he feels that it is not " some little bit (portiuncula) of our faith, some comparatively obscure point, which is being assailed :"[2] it is " the peerless mystery (singulare sacramentum) of man's salvation" which is at stake, when the Christ is not recognised as a Second Adam. It is this intense conviction which gives such glow and energy to the famous 28th Epistle, or " Tome of S. Leo," which should be compared with the 59th, to the clergy and people of Constantinople, written in the March of 450; the 124th, to the monks of Palestine, who were being drawn into an Eutychianising movement, in the summer of 453; the 139th, to Juvenal, Patriarch of Jerusalem, on Sept. 4, 454; and the 165th, sometimes called "the Second Tome," in which Leo exhorts his imperial namesake not to let the Eutychian question be reopened, Aug. 17, 458, i.e., nine years and two months after the first or principal Tome. In these letters he borrows matter,—sometimes from the Tome, sometimes from Sermons, by way of enforcing and illustrating the doctrine of the " Two Natures:" he repeatedly, and as it were in the same breath, lays stress on that unity of our Lord's Person, the " solidity" of which " cannot be broken up by any division :"[3] he explains that " it matters not from which substance Christ is named, since, all separation being excluded, and the unity of person remaining, the selfsame is both whole Son of

---

[1] Epist. lix. c. 3.   [2] Epist. xxx. c. 2.
[3] Epist. cxxiv. c. 7.

man because of the flesh, and whole Son of God because His Godhead is one with the Father:"[1] he insists that "whosoever questions the real assumption of our humanity by the Son of God, in the womb of a Virgin of David's lineage, neither acknowledges the Bridegroom nor understands the bride" (the Church);[2] and that to assign to each of Christ's natures the attributes belonging to it is not to "double the Person" in Whom both are combined.[3] He could adduce in the appendix to Ep. 165 a number of Fathers who supported his contention, beginning with S. Hilary, who in his second book on the Trinity had set forth the principle of the sanctification and "ennobling" of man through the self-humiliation of Him "at Whose voice archangels and angels tremble:" had declared that he who did not own Christ as true Man, no less than true God, knew nothing of his own spiritual life; and, further on, that while the selfsame was God and Man, the sayings relating to Deity must be discriminated from those relating to Manhood. If, in one or two passages from S. Gregory Nazianzen, Leo relied (for he knew no Greek) on an inexact Latin translation, he might have borrowed more than he did both from this Father and from S. Athanasius. He quotes a few words from the latter's Epistle to Epictetus, which he sent in 452 to Julian of Cos with the well-merited eulogy, " He set forth the Incarnation so luminously and carefully, that even in the persons of the heretics of that age he has defeated Nestorius and Eutyches."[4] Five passages are cited from S. Ambrose, and five as from

[1] Epist. cxxiv. c. 7.
[2] Epist. lix. c. 4.
[3] Epist. cxxiv. c. 6.
[4] Epist. cix. c. 3.

Preface. xv

S. Augustine, including one from the retractation of the Gallic monk Leporius: the fourth from Augustine begins explicitly enough; " Let us acknowledge *geminam substantiam Christi*, the Divine, wherein He is equal to the Father, the human, wherein the Father is greater: but Christ is both (*utrumque*) at once, not two, but one."[1] S. Chrysostom's homilies on "the Cross and the Robber," and on the Ascension, are laid under contribution; but it was specially to Leo's purpose to quote Cyril of Alexandria. The last of his four Cyrilline extracts is a "locus aureus" indeed: it includes nearly the whole of the second Epistle to Nestorius, which had been so expressly sanctioned at Ephesus, and afterwards at Chalcedon. He does not here quote any ante-Nicene writer; but in a famous passage of the Tome he had almost reproduced the very words of Tertullian,[2] and he might well have appealed to the authority of S. Irenæus, whose language repeatedly anticipates the requirements of later controversy when he excludes a Docetic view of Christ's manhood, or a quasi-Cerinthian division of His personality, and insists (as, indeed, Justin had done before him,) that Christ *is* the Word, or Son of the Father, Who "became the Son of Man, that through Him we might receive the adoption, humanity[3] carrying, and holding, and embracing the Son of

---

[1] S. Aug. in Jo. Evan. Tract. lxxviii. 3.

[2] "Salva igitur proprietate utriusque naturæ et substantiæ," &c., Ep. xxviii. c. 3; compare Tertull. adv. Praxeam, 27, " Et adeo salva est utriusque proprietas substantiæ," &c. Tertullian goes on to speak of Christ's flesh as "sitiens sub Samaritide, flens Lazarum," &c.; comp. Ep. xxviii. c. 4.

[3] Iren. iii. 16. 3; "Homine," used for manhood. See below, Note 36.

God ;" that " His only-begotten Word . . . . Who became flesh, is Himself Jesus Christ our Lord, Who suffered for us, and rose again . . . and in all respects is man . . . . and therefore is 'summing up' man into Himself, the invisible being made visible, and . . . . the Word man ;"[1] "the Son of God . . . . Who is also the Word of the Father, having become incarnate in man, and fulfilling all the dispensation in regard to man"[2] . . . . " for it was necessary that the Mediator between God and men should, by His proper relationship to both, bring both together into friendship and concord, and present man to God, while He made God known to men :"[3] or again, " If He did not receive the substance of flesh from a human being, He neither was made man nor the Son of man. . . . . If He had taken nothing from Mary, He would not have availed Himself of food . . . . nor have hungered after fasting . . . . nor have wept over Lazarus, nor sweated great drops of blood ; nor have said, ' My soul is exceeding sorrowful ;' nor, when His side was pierced, could there have come forth blood and water ; for all these are tokens of the flesh."[4] Any one who may be so disposed to ask whether the language of the Tome, with its " technical" precision as to the " one Person in two Natures," does not represent an absolute growth in the substance of the idea which it professes to exhibit, would do well to consider what the typical theologian of the second century, in these and similar passages, lays down as " de fide," or, indeed, what the martyr-bishop of the beginning of that century asserts in a

[1] Iren. iii. 16. 6. [2] Ib. iii. 17. 4.
[3] Ib. iii. 18. 7. [4] Ib. iii. 22. 1, 2.

Preface. xvii

single letter as to "our God, Jesus the Christ, Who was conceived in the womb by Mary, and is God in man, Son of man and Son of God,"[1] and whether the natural sense of their words falls short of implying what is affirmed by Leo, or by Theodoret, whose Dialogues, especially the second, may well be studied together with the Tome.[2]

The circumstances under which the Tome was written, and under which it was received at Chalcedon, are sufficiently explained in the Notes. It was practically suppressed by Dioscorus at the Council of the "Latrocinium,"[3] but soon afterwards it was widely circulated, and cordially accepted in the East;[4] and the 68th Epistle in the Leonine series is a letter from three Gallic bishops, who in the summer of 450 acknowledged that "special embodiment of his teaching," and sent their own copy to receive corrections or additions from his hand. A few weeks before the Council of Chalcedon, Eusebius, Archbishop of Milan, writing to Leo in the name of his synod, welcomed the Tome as "shining with the full simplicity of the faith, irradiated with the declarations of Prophets, the authority of Evangelists, and the testimonies of Apostolic teaching," and in complete accordance with the meaning of their own S. Ambrose in his book on the mystery of the Incarnation;[5] and soon afterwards

---

[1] S. Ignatius, ad Eph. 18, 7, 20. See also Trall. 9, Smyrn. 1.
[2] See a summary of the Dialogues in Later Treatises of S. Athanasius (Lib. Fath.) pp. 177—227.
[3] Mansi, vi. 972. Leo applies the term "latrocinium" not to this council itself, but to its proceedings: "in illo Ephesino non judicio, sed latrocinio," Ep. xcv. 2, (July 20, 451.)
[4] Leo, Epist. lxxxviii. 3; Mansi, vi. 953.
[5] Ep. xcvii. 2.

forty-four Gallic bishops assured Leo that throughout Gaul the Tome had been received "just like a creed."[1] A Council at Rome under Pope Gelasius anathematised every one who questioned "a single iota" in the Tome,[2] which was naturally adopted as a test of orthodoxy by all who, in the East or in the West, adhered to the dogmatic standard of the Fourth Œcumenical Council. It did not, indeed, disarm the objections of the Monophysites. Photius describes the replies made by Catholic divines to their objections.[3] The Ecclesiastical History of John of Ephesus shows that on one occasion their bishops protested that while the breath was in their nostrils, their lips should never cease to anathematise "the Synod" (of Chalcedon) "and Leo's letter:"[4] and Gibbon tells us how, when a patriarch imposed by Justinian on the Alexandrians began "to read the Tome of S. Leo," he was interrupted by "a volley of curses, invectives, and stones."[5] A touching contrast to such wild scenes was presented for centuries by many a church in Italy and Gaul, where the Tome supplied lessons for the services of Advent.

It is hoped that the present translation, which has in this edition been substituted for the Latin text, and illustrated, like the Sermons, with notes, designed specially for theological students, may be found useful for private reading, especially in seasons which

[1] Ep. xcix. 2.
[2] Mansi, viii. 148.
[3] Biblioth. 225, 228. Leo complains that the Tome had been mistranslated. Ep. cxxiv. 1.
[4] John of Eph., Eccl. Hist. E. Tr. by Dean Payne Smith, p. 39.
[5] Gibbon, vi. 60.

commemorate the Incarnation of our Lord. Part of the Epistle was translated in the writer's "History of the Church from the Edict of Milan to the Council of Chalcedon :" and a version of the whole of it, excepting the last chapter, had previously been embodied in Dr. Neale's "History of the Alexandrian Patriarchate." This version, however, is somewhat too literal to be satisfactory. In some instances, I have followed the rendering in Dr. Heurtley's recently published translation. To conclude with the simple and impressive words of Tillemont: "Je pense que rien n'a rendu S. Léon si célèbre, et n'a tant contribué à lui attirer la vénération de toute l'Eglise."[1]

CHRIST CHURCH,
Dec. 3, 1885.

[1] Tillemont, xv. 541.

CONTENTS.

SERM.		PAGE
I.	CHRISTMAS	1
II.	CHRISTMAS	5
III.	CHRISTMAS	11
IV.	CHRISTMAS	19
V.	EPIPHANY	26
VI.	EPIPHANY	29
VII.	PASSION-TIDE	35
VIII.	PASSION-TIDE	40
IX.	PASSION-TIDE	45
X.	PASSION-TIDE	52
XI.	PASSION-TIDE	58
XII.	PASSION-TIDE	65
XIII.	EASTER	73
XIV.	EASTER	79
XV.	ASCENSION	87
XVI.	ASCENSION	91
XVII.	WHITSUNTIDE	97
XVIII.	WHITSUNTIDE	103
	THE TWENTY-EIGHTH EPISTLE, OR THE "TOME"	109
	NOTES	125
	INDEX	244

SERMONS ON THE INCARNATION.

SERMON I.

CHRISTMAS.

SERM. 21. In Nativitate Domini, I. *Salvator noster.*

OUR Saviour, dearly beloved, was born to-day: let us rejoice! For it is not right that sadness should find a place among those who are keeping the birthday of Life, which swallows up the fear of mortality, and bestows on us gladness on account of the promise of eternity. No one is shut out from the participation of this cheerfulness; all have one common cause of gladness. For as our Lord, the destroyer of sin and death, finds no one free from guilt, so is He come to set all free. Let the saint exult, for he draws nigh to the palm; let the sinner rejoice, for he is invited to forgiveness; let the Gentile be inspired, for he is called unto life. For, according to that fulness of time which the Divine counsel in its inscrutable depth ordained, the Son of God took on Him the nature of mankind in order to reconcile it to its Maker, that the devil, the inventor of death, might be conquered through that very nature which had been conquered by him. And this conflict, which He entered upon for our sakes, He waged upon a principle of great and wondrous equity; inasmuch as the Almighty Lord does battle with our cruel enemy not in His own Majesty, but in our lowliness, opposing him by the very same form and the very same nature, as sharing indeed in our mortality, but free from every kind of sin. For *this* Nativity has no concern with what we read in regard to all men, " No one is clean from defilement, not even an infant, whose life on earth is but one day old."[1] And thus, no element derived from carnal passion or from the "law of sin" passed or flowed into this peerless Nativity. A Virgin of the royal stock of David is chosen to become with child of a sacred seed, and to conceive a divine and human Offspring, first in soul and then in body.[2] And lest, in ignorance of the Divine counsel, she should tremble at the unwonted result, she learns by conversing with an Angel what is to be wrought in her by the Holy Spirit. Nor does she, who is soon to be the Mother of God,[3] believe that she is losing her honour. For why should she be hopeless of becoming a Mother in a new way, when she has a promise that "the power of the Highest"[4] will effect it? She believes, and her faith is confirmed by the further evidence of a miracle which comes first; Elizabeth is endowed with unexpected fruitfulness, that as God had given conception to a barren woman, there might be no doubt that He would give it to a Virgin.

[1] Job xiv. 4, LXX. See Note 1.　　[2] See Note 2.
[3] See Note 3.　　[4] S. Luke i. 35.

2. Accordingly, God, the Word of God, the Son of God, Who "in the beginning was with God, by Whom all things were made, and without Whom was nothing made,"[1] in order to deliver man from eternal death, became Man; in such wise humbling Himself to assume our lowliness without lessening His own Majesty, that, remaining what He was, and putting on what He was not,[2] He united the true "form of a servant"[3] to that form in which He was equal to God the Father, and combined both natures in a league so close, that the lower was not consumed by receiving glory,[4] nor the higher lessened by assuming lowliness. Accordingly, while the distinctness of both substances is preserved,[5] and both meet in one Person, lowliness is assumed by majesty, weakness by strength, mortality by eternity; and in order to discharge the debt of our condition, the inviolable nature is united to the passible, and very God and very Man are combined in our one Lord: so that, as the appropriate remedy for our ills, one and the same "Mediator between God and men" might from one element be able to die, and from the other to rise again. With good reason, then, did virginal purity receive no damage from giving birth to Salvation; for honour was preserved while fruit was brought forth. Therefore, dearly beloved, for "Christ, the Power of God and the Wisdom of God,"[6] such a Nativity as this was befitting, whereby He might at once concur with us in Manhood, and excel us in Godhead. For unless He were very God, He would

---

[1] S. John i. 1, 3.
[2] See Note 4.
[3] Phil. ii. 7.
[4] See Ep. xxviii. 4, below.
[5] See Note 5.
[6] 1 Cor. i. 24.

not bring us healing;[1] unless He were very Man, He would not supply an example. Therefore do the Angels at our Lord's birth exult, as they sing, "Glory be to God on high," and proclaim "peace on earth to men of good will."[2] For they see the Heavenly Jerusalem being constructed out of all the nations of the world; and how greatly ought men in their low estate to be gladdened by this ineffable work of Divine loving-kindness, when it affords such joy to Angels in their high dignity?

3. Let us, then, dearly beloved, render thanks to God the Father, through His Son, in the Holy Spirit,[3]—to Him Who on account of His great mercy wherewith He loved us, has had pity upon us, and "when we were dead in sins has quickened us together with Christ,"[4] that in Him we might be a new creation and a new handywork. Let us therefore "put off the old man with his deeds,"[5] and having obtained a share in Christ's birth, let us renounce "the works of the flesh." Acknowledge, O Christian, thine own dignity; and having been "made partaker of the Divine nature,"[6] do not by degeneracy of conduct return to thine old meanness. Bethink thee of what a Head and of what a body thou art a member. Remember that thou hast been "rescued from the power of darkness,"[7] and translated into the light and kingdom of God. By the Sacrament of Baptism thou wast made "a temple of the Holy Spirit;"[8] do not by evil deeds drive away from thyself so great an inmate, and subject thyself again to the service of the devil. For thy

---

[1] See Note 6. Cf. Serm. iv. c. 3.   [2] S. Luke ii. 14.
[3] See Note 7.   [4] Eph. ii. 5.   [5] Col. iii. 9.
[6] 2 S. Pet. i. 4.   [7] Col. i. 13.   [8] 1 Cor. vi. 19.

ransom[1] is the Blood of Christ: for He will judge thee in truth Who redeemed thee in mercy, Who with the Father and the Holy Spirit reigneth for ever and ever. Amen.

SERMON II.

CHRISTMAS.

SERM. 23. In Nativitate Domini, III. *Nota quidem.*

YOU well know, dearly beloved, and have frequently heard, the things which belong to the sacred observance[2] of this day's solemnity; but as this visible light affords pleasure to uninjured eyes, so do sound hearts receive perpetual joy from the Nativity of the Saviour, on which we must never be silent, though we cannot set it forth as it deserves. For we believe that text, "Who shall declare His generation?"[3] to refer not only to that mystery wherein the Son of God is co-eternal with the Father, but also to this birth whereby "the Word was made flesh." Accordingly, God, the Son of God, equal and of the same nature from the Father and with the Father, Creator and Lord of the universe, in His entireness present everywhere, and in His entireness transcending all things, did, in the order of the times which run their course by His own appointment, choose to Himself this day whereon to be born of the Blessed Virgin Mary for the world's salvation; His Mother's honour being preserved through-

---

[1] See Serm. viii. 4.   [2] See Note 8.   [3] Isa. liii. 8.

out, who, as she ceased not to be a Virgin by bringing forth, so had not ceased to be a Virgin by conceiving;[1] "That it might be fulfilled," as the Evangelist says, "which was spoken by the Lord through" Isaiah "the Prophet; Behold, a Virgin shall conceive in her womb, and bear a Son, and they shall call His Name Emmanuel, which being interpreted is, God with us."[2] For this wondrous child-bearing of the Holy Virgin did bring forth as her offspring one Person, truly human and truly Divine;[3] because both substances did not in any such sense retain their properties, as that there could be in them a difference of persons; nor was the creature in such wise taken into fellowship with the Creator, that He should be the Inhabitant and it the habitation; but in this way, that the one nature should be united to the other.[4] And although the nature which is assumed is one, and that which assumes is another, yet both these diverse ones meet[5] in so close an union, that it is one and the same Son Who calls Himself inferior to the Father in that He is very Man, and declares Himself equal to the Father in that He is very God.

2. This union, dearly beloved, whereby the Creator and the creature are combined, could not be discerned and understood by the blinded Arians,[6] who, not believing the only-begotten Son of God to be of the same glory and substance with the Father, called the Son's Godhead inferior, deriving their arguments from those words which are to be referred to that "form of a servant" which the same Son of God would show us not to exist in Him as belonging to another and a

---

[1] See Note 9.　　[2] S. Matt. i. 22.　　[3] See Note 10.
[4] See Note 11.　　[5] "Convenit."　　[6] See Note 12.

different person, and therefore with the same "form" says, "The Father is greater than I," as with the same He says, "I and the Father are one."[1] For in the form of a servant, which He assumed at the close of ages for our restoration, He is inferior to the Father; but in the form of God, in which He existed before the ages, He is equal to the Father. In human lowliness He was "made of a woman, made under the law;"[2] remaining, in Divine Majesty, the Word of God, "by Whom all things were made." Therefore He Who in the form of God made man, in the form of a servant was made Man; but both acts belonged to *God* in regard to the power of that which assumed, both to *Man* in regard to the lowliness of that which was assumed.[3] For both natures retain their own properties without defect;[4] and as the form of God does not annul the form of a servant, so the form of a servant does not lessen the form of God. Accordingly, this sacred fact of strength united with weakness permits us to call the Son inferior to the Father, in that He has the same nature of man with ourselves; but the Godhead, which in the Trinity of the Father, and the Son, and the Holy Spirit, is One, excludes all notion of inequality. For in the Trinity the external existence has nothing temporary, the nature nothing dissimilar; the will therein is one, the substance is the same, the power is equal, and there are not three Gods, but one God;[5] because, where no diversity can exist, the unity is true and inseparable. Accordingly, in the entire and perfect nature of very Man was born

---

[1] S. John xiv. 28; x. 30. See Note 13.　　[2] Gal. iv. 4.
[3] See Serm. viii. 1.　　[4] In Ep. xxviii. 3.
[5] See Note 14, and Serm. xviii. 1.

very God, entire in what was His own, entire in what was ours. Now we call those things our own which the Creator formed in us from the beginning, and which He took on Himself in order to repair them. For of those things which the deceiver brought in, and which man, being deceived, admitted, there was not a vestige in the Saviour;[1] nor did it follow from His submitting to a fellowship in human infirmities, that He became a partaker in our transgressions. He took on Him the form of a servant without the defilement of sin, exalting what was human, not lessening what was Divine; for that "emptying of Himself,"[2] whereby the Invisible made Himself visible, was the condescension of pity, and not the defect of power.

3. In order, therefore, that we might be recalled to eternal bliss from the bonds in which we were born, and from our wanderings in the paths of this world, He Himself descended to us, unto Whom we could not ascend; for although there was in many men a love of truth, yet amid the variety of uncertain opinions men were cheated by the craft of deceitful demons, and human ignorance was drawn by a falsely-called science into diverse and contrary conclusions. But to end this mocking sport, wherein captive souls were at the beck of the insulting enemy, the Law's teaching sufficed not, nor could our nature be restored by the Prophets' exhortations alone; but a real redemption had to be superadded to moral instructions, and a stock tainted from the beginning required to pass through a new birth, and start afresh. For those who had to be reconciled a Victim had to be offered, which should be both associated to our race and un-

---

[1] See Note 15.   [2] Phil. ii. 7, ἑαυτὸν ἐκένωσε.

touched by our contamination; that this purpose of God, whereby it was His pleasure that the sin of the whole world should be effaced by Jesus Christ's Nativity and Passion, might extend itself to the ages of all generations, and that we might not be unsettled, but rather confirmed, by ordinances varying according to the character of the times, since in no age has there been any alteration in the faith whereby we live.[1]

4. Let us, then, hear no more of the complaints of those who, carping with profane murmurs at the Divine dispensations, cavil at the lateness of our Lord's Nativity, as though that which was effected in the last age of the world had no beneficial effect on former times. For the Incarnation of the Word caused that to be done which was done; and the mystery of man's salvation was never at a standstill in any remote period. What the Apostles proclaimed, the Prophets heralded; nor was that too late in being accomplished which was always believed. In fact, by this delay[2] of the work of our salvation, God's wisdom and benignity made us more capable of receiving His call; that so what had for so many ages been fore-announced by many signs, many voices, and many mysteries, might not be misapprehended in these days of the Gospel; and that the Nativity of a Saviour, which was to exceed all miracles and all the measure of man's understanding, might produce in us a faith all the more steadfast, in proportion as its antecedent proclamation had been of older date and greater frequency. It was not, then, by a new-made plan, nor by a tardy compassion, that God

[1] See Note 16.   [2] See Note 17.

took thought for human interests; but from the foundation of the world it was one and the same cause of salvation which He established for all men. For the grace of God, by which the whole body of the Saints has always been justified, was not begun by the birth of Christ, but enlarged; and this mystery of great loving-kindness, with which the whole world has now been filled, was so effective in its types, that they who believed in it as promised have not attained to less than they who received it as bestowed.

5. Wherefore, dearly beloved, since it is by manifest loving-kindness that such great riches of Divine goodness have been poured out upon us, so that, in order to invite us to life eternal, not only have the beneficial examples of those who went before lent their aid, but also the Truth Itself has appeared in visible bodily presence, it is with no dull or carnal gladness that we ought to celebrate the day of our Lord's Nativity. And we shall each of us celebrate it worthily and heartily, if every one recollects of what body he is a member, and to what a Head he is joined, lest as an ill-fitting joint he adhere not to the sacred building. Consider, dearly beloved, and thoughtfully ponder, according to the light given by the Holy Spirit, Who it is Who has taken us into Himself, and Whom we have taken to ourselves; for as the Lord Jesus was made our flesh by being born, so have we too been made His Body by being born again. Therefore are we both members of Christ, and the temple of the Holy Spirit; and on this account the blessed Apostle says, "Glorify and carry God in your body:"[1] Who, while presenting to us the

---
[1] 1 Cor. vi. 20. See Note 18.

pattern of His own gentleness and lowliness, infuses into us the same power wherewith He redeemed us, as He Himself, our Lord, promises: "Come unto Me, all ye that labour and are heavy laden, and I will refresh you. Take My yoke upon you, and learn of Me, for I am meek and lowly of heart, and ye shall find rest unto your souls."[1] Let us, then, take on us that yoke—not a heavy nor painful one—of the Truth which guides us, and be like to His lowliness, to Whose glory we desire to be conformed; while He assists and leads us on to His promises, Who according to His great mercy is able to efface our sins, and to perfect His own gifts in us, even Jesus Christ our Lord, Who liveth and reigneth for ever and ever. Amen.

SERMON III.

CHRISTMAS.

SERM. 26. In Nativitate Domini, VI. *Omnibus quidem.*

THERE are certainly no days nor times, dearly beloved, in which the birth of our Lord and Saviour from a Virgin Mother does not present itself to the minds of the faithful, while meditating on the things of God; so that, when the soul is lifted up to do homage to its Maker, whether it be employed in the sighs of supplication, or in joyful bursts of praise, or in the offering of sacrifice,[2] its spiritual insight takes

[1] S. Matt. xi. 28.   [2] See Note 19.

hold of nothing more frequently or more trustfully than the fact that God, the Son of God, begotten of the co-eternal Father, was also Himself born of a human birth. But this Nativity, adorable in heaven and on earth, is brought before us by no day more clearly than by this, which, while a fresh light is beaming in the natural world, brings home to our perceptions[1] the brightness of the wondrous mystery. For not only into our remembrance, but in some sense into our very sight, returns that conversation of the Angel Gabriel with the awe-struck Mary, and that conception from the Holy Spirit, as marvellous in being promised as in being believed. For to-day the Maker of the world was brought forth from the Virgin's womb, and He Who formed all natures became the Son of her whom He created. To-day the Word of God has appeared in the garb of flesh, and that which was never visible to men's eyes begins to be even subject to the touch of their hands. To-day the shepherds learned from Angelic voices that a Saviour was born in the essence of our flesh and soul; and among the prelates of the Lord's flock a form has been arranged for proclaiming the good tidings on this day, so that we too say with the host of the heavenly army,[2] "Glory be to God on high, and on earth peace to men of good will!"

2. Although therefore that infancy, to which the majesty of the Son of God refused not to stoop, advanced with increasing years to full-grown manhood; and, since the triumph of the Passion and Resurrection was completed, all the acts of that lowliness, which was put on for our sakes, have passed away; yet

[1] "Ingerit."   [2] See Note 20.

does this day's festival renew for us the sacred beginnings of the life of Jesus, born of the Virgin Mary; and while we adore our Saviour's birth, we are found to be celebrating our own origin. For the generation of Christ is the starting point of the Christian people, and the birthday of the Head is the birthday of the body. Although each of those whom He has called has his own sphere, and all the children of the Church are distinguished by succession of times, yet the whole number of the faithful, sprung from the font of Baptism,[1] as they are crucified with Christ in His Passion, and raised to life in His Resurrection, and placed at the Father's right hand in His Ascension, so are born with Him in His Nativity. For every one of the believers in any part of the world who is regenerated in Christ has the line of that old nature in which he was born, cut short, and passes by a second birth into a new man; nor is he now reckoned as belonging to the stock of his natural father, but as an offshoot of the Saviour, Who became the Son of Man for this end, that we might be able to be sons of God. For unless He had come down to us by His condescension, no man by any merits of his own could have attained to Him. On this point, therefore, let not earthly wisdom bring any darkness over the hearts of those who are called; nor let the dust of earthly thoughts, which is soon to return to the depths, lift up itself against the loftiness of the grace of God. That which was arranged before the endless ages was accomplished in the world's closing period; prefigurative signs came to an end, and in the presence of realities law and prophecy became truth: that

---

[1] See Note 21. Comp. Serm. ix. c. 6.

Abraham might become a father of all nations, and in his seed might be given to the world the promised blessing; and the character of Israelites might not belong only to those whom flesh and blood had begotten, but the whole body of the adopted ones might come into possession of the inheritance prepared for the children of faith.[1] Let no idle questionings produce clamorous misrepresentation; nor let human reason criticise the carrying out of a Divine work. With Abraham we believe God, and "stagger not through unbelief," but "know with full assurance that what the Lord has promised, He is able also to perform."[2]

3. Therefore, dearly beloved, there is born, not from fleshly seed, but from the Holy Spirit, a Saviour Who could not be held under condemnation for the primæval transgression.[3] Whence the very greatness of the gift bestowed exacts from us a reverence worthy of its own splendour. For to this end, as the blessed Apostle teaches, "have we received, not the spirit of this world, but the Spirit which is from God, that we may know the things which have been freely given to us by God;"[4] Whom we cannot otherwise devoutly worship than by offering to Him that which He bestows. But in the treasury of the Lord's bounty what can we find so appropriate, in honour of the present festival, as that peace which was the first thing proclaimed by the choir of Angels at the Lord's Nativity? For it is peace which brings forth the children of God, which is the nurse of affection and the mother of unity, the repose of the blessed and the

[1] See Note 22.   [2] Rom. iv. 20, 21.
[3] See Serm. i. c. 1.   [4] 1 Cor. ii. 12.

home of eternity; of which the peculiar work and special benefit is, that it joins to God those whom it separates from the world. Whence the Apostle stirs us up to seek for this blessing, when he says, "Being therefore justified by faith, we have peace with God."[1] In this brief sentence is comprehended the effect of nearly all the commandments; because where true peace shall be found, no virtue can be absent. But what is it, dearly beloved, to have peace with God, except to say "I will" to what He commands, and "I will not" to what He forbids? For if human friendships require likemindedness, and demand similarity of wills, and opposite characters can never attain to a lasting concord, how will he be a partaker of Divine peace who is pleased with what displeases God, and longs to delight himself in things whereby he knows that God is offended? This is not the mind of the children of God, nor is such the wisdom that is received by those whom His adoption has ennobled. Let the chosen and royal race correspond to the dignity of their regeneration.[2] Let them love what their Father loves, and have no feelings out of harmony with their Maker; lest the Lord say once more, "I have begotten and raised up children, but they have spurned Me. The ox has recognised his owner, and the ass his master's crib; but Israel hath not known Me, and My people hath not understood Me."[3]

4. Great is the sacredness of this gift, dearly beloved; and this grant exceeds all others, that God calls man His son, and man calls God his Father: for by these names we feel and learn what the affec-

---

[1] Rom. v. 1.   [2] Serm. i. c. 3.   [3] Isa. i. 3.

tion is that ascends to so great a height. For if, in the case of a natural descent and an earthly stock, the sons of noble parents are degraded by evil and vicious conduct, and unworthy descendants are put to shame by the very illustriousness of their ancestors; to what end will they come who do not fear, out of love for this world, to be struck off the roll of the lineage of Christ? But if it is a matter for praise among men that the honour of the fathers should receive new splendour in the offspring, how much more glorious is it that those who are born of God should shine forth after their Maker's image, and exhibit in themselves Him Who gave them birth, as our Lord says, "Let your light so shine before men, that they may see your good works, and glorify your Father Who is in heaven."[1] We know indeed, as John the Apostle says, that "the whole world is placed under the malignant one;"[2] and the devil and his angels in their plottings strive by numberless temptations to effect this object; that man, while striving after things heavenly, may be either terrified by adversity or corrupted by prosperity. But greater is He Who is within us than he who is against us; and those who have peace with God, and are always saying to their Father, with their whole hearts, "Thy will be done," can be overcome in no struggles and harmed by no conflicts. For when we by our own confessions accuse ourselves, and refuse the assent of our mind to carnal appetites, we do indeed stir up against ourselves the hostility of him who is the author of sin; but inasmuch as we are submissive to God's grace, we establish an indestructible peace with Him,

---

[1] S. Matt. v. 16.   [2] 1 S. John v. 19, ἐν τῷ πονηρῷ κεῖται.

so that we are not only subjected to our King by obedience, but united to Him by our own determination. For if we think as He thinks, if we will what He wills, and condemn what He condemns, then, as He has enabled us to will,[1] He will also enable us to act, that so we may be co-operators in His works, and with exulting faith take up the prophet's word, "The Lord is my light and my salvation; whom then shall I fear? The Lord is the defender of my life; of whom shall I be afraid?"

5. Let those then, who "have been born, not of blood, nor of the will of the flesh, nor of the will of man, but of God,"[2] offer up to their Father the concord of "peace-making children;"[3] and let all the members of the adopted family meet in the First-born of the new creation, Who "came not to do His own will, but the will of Him that sent Him."[4] For it is not those who are unlike and discordant, but those who think the same things and love the same things, that the Father in His favour has adopted as His heirs. Those who have been refashioned after one likeness ought to have a conformity of soul. Our Lord's birthday is the birthday of peace, for so says the Apostle: "He Himself is our Peace, Who has made both one;" for "whether we be Jews or Gentiles," "through Him we have access by one Spirit unto the Father;"[5] through Him Who before that day of His Passion, which He chose beforehand by a voluntary appointment, instructed His disciples by this lesson above all others, in that He said: "My peace I give to you, My peace I leave to you." And

---

[1] See Note 23.   [2] S. John i. 13.   [3] S. Matt. v. 9.
[4] S. John vi. 38.   [5] Eph. ii. 14—18; 1 Cor. xii. 13.

lest, under a general phrase, it should not be clear what kind of peace He calls His, He added, "Not as the world giveth, give I unto you."[1] The world, He means, has friendships of its own, and brings many hearts together by a perverted love. Even in vicious courses there are congenial spirits, and likeness of desires produces harmony of feelings. And if some persons happen to be found who take no pleasure in what is wicked and base, and exclude from the bond of their love associations which are unlawful, yet even they, if they are Jews, or heretics, or Pagans,[2] do not belong to God's peace, but to the world's. Whereas the peace of spiritual and Catholic persons, which comes from heaven, and leads to heaven, will not have us to be united in any sort of fellowship with the lovers of this world, but to resist all hindrances, and wing our way from pernicious pleasures to true joys, as our Lord says: "Where thy treasure is, there will thy heart be also."[3] That is, if what thou lovest is beneath, thou wilt descend to the depths; if above, thou wilt attain the heights; and thither may we, being one in will and mind, and united in faith, hope, and love, be carried and led onward by the Spirit of peace; for "whosoever are led by the Spirit of God, they are the sons of God,"[4] Who reigneth with the Son and the Holy Spirit, for ever and ever. Amen.

[1] S. John xiv. 27.
[2] See Note 24.
[3] S. Matt. vi. 21.
[4] Rom. viii. 14.

SERMON IV.

CHRISTMAS.

SERM. 28. In Nativitate Domini, VIII. *Cum semper.*

WHILE we are exhorted, dearly beloved, by all the Divine oracles, to be always rejoicing in the Lord, yet are we beyond doubt more abundantly excited to spiritual gladness on this day, when the mystery of our Lord's Nativity is gleaming more brightly over us ; so that, recurring to that ineffable condescension of the Divine mercy, wherein the Creator of men was pleased to become Man, we may be found in His nature Whom we adore as in our own. For God, the Son of God, the Only-begotten from the everlasting and unbegotten Father, everlastingly remaining in the form of God, and possessing, apart from all change and all time, the privilege of being nothing else than the Father is,[1] took the form of a servant without any detriment to His own majesty, that He might advance us to what was His, not degrade Himself into what was ours.[2] Wherefore both the natures, retaining their own properties, have been brought into so close a fellowship of union, that whatever therein belonged to God is not disjoined from Manhood, while whatever belonged to Man is not divided from Godhead.

2. Accordingly, dearly beloved, now that we are celebrating the birthday of our Lord and Saviour, let us have thoroughly true ideas as to the child-bearing of the Blessed Virgin, so as to believe that at no point of time was the power of the Word absent from

[1] See Note 25.   [2] Ep. xxviii. 3.

the flesh and soul which she conceived;[1] and that the temple of Christ's body was not first formed and animated, to be afterwards claimed for Himself by its Inhabitant on His arrival, but it was through Him and in Him that a beginning was given to a new Man, so that in one and the same Son of God and man, there was Godhead "without mother" and Manhood "without father."[2] For the Virgin, having been made fruitful by the Holy Spirit, brought forth, without a trace of corruption, at once the offspring of her race and the Maker of her stock. Wherefore also the same Lord, as the Evangelist mentions, asked the Jews "whose Son" they had learned from the authority of Scripture that "the Christ" should be: and when they replied that the tradition was that He was to come of David's seed, He said, "How then doth David in spirit call Him his Lord, saying, The Lord said unto my Lord, Sit Thou on My right hand, until I make Thy foes Thy footstool?"[3] Nor could the Jews solve the question proposed to them, because they understood not that in the one Christ, according to prophecy, were both the blood of David and the Divine nature.

3. But the majesty of the Son of God, Who is equal to the Father, when clothing itself with the lowliness of a servant, neither feared diminution nor needed increase; and by the sole power of Godhead could effect that operation of its own mercy, which it was bestowing[4] on the restoration of man, so as to rescue from the yoke of a dreadful tyrant the creature formed after God's image. But since the devil had

---

[1] See Note 26.
[2] Heb. vii. 3.
[3] S. Matt. xxii. 42, ff.
[4] "Impendebat."

not so proceeded by sheer force against the first man, as to draw him over to his own side without consent of his free-will, therefore in such sort were that voluntary sin and that hostile design to be destroyed, as that the gift of grace should not clash with the rule of justice. Accordingly, amid the universal ruin of the whole human race, there was but one remedy which, under the mysterious law of the Divine procedure, could come to the aid of the prostrate; and that was, if some son of Adam could be born, unconnected with original transgression,[1] and innocent, who could benefit the rest both by his example and by his merit. But as natural generation did not allow of this, and the offshoot of a vitiated root could not be without that seed of which Scripture says, "Who can make him clean who was conceived of impure seed? is it not Thou Who art alone?"[2] the Lord of David became the Son of David, and from the fruit of the promised sprout arose an unvitiated offspring, by the combination[3] of two natures into one Person; so that by the same conception and the same child-bearing was born our Lord Jesus Christ, in Whom were present both very Godhead for the performance of miracles, and very Manhood for the endurance of sufferings.[4]

4. Let the Catholic Faith, therefore, dearly beloved, contemn the vagaries of noisy heretics, who, deceived by the vanity of this world's wisdom, have departed from the Gospel of truth, and, being unable to apprehend the Incarnation of the Word, have made to themselves matter for blindness out of the very cause

[1] "Prævaricationis." Cp. Serm. i. c. 1. [2] Job xiv. 4, Vulg.
[3] "Conveniente;" so Serm. ii. c. 1. [4] Ep. xxviii. 4.

of illumination. For, having reviewed the opinions of well-nigh all misbelievers—opinions which even rush into a denial of the Holy Spirit[1]—we are assured that hardly any one has gone astray unless he has failed to believe the reality of two natures in Christ, and at the same time to acknowledge one Person. For some have ascribed to our Lord mere manhood;[2] others, mere Godhead. Some have said that there was in Him, indeed, true Godhead, but only the semblance of flesh.[3] Others have declared that He took on Him true flesh, but had not the nature of God the Father; and, attributing to His Godhead what belonged to the human essence, have invented for themselves a greater and a lesser God, whereas in true Godhead there can be no gradation, because whatever is less than God is not God.[4] Others, knowing that there is no interval between the Father and the Son, have yet, from inability to understand the unity of Godhead except in the sense of unity of Person, asserted that the Father was the same as the Son, so that to be born and bred up, to suffer and die, to be buried and rise again, belonged to the selfsame (Father,) Who sustained throughout the characters both of the Man and of the Word.[5] Some have thought that the Lord Jesus Christ had a body not of our substance, but composed of higher and subtler elements.[6] Some, again, have supposed that in Christ's flesh there was no human soul, but that the functions of a soul were discharged by the Word's Godhead itself. And their folly passed into this form, that they admitted the existence of a soul in

[1] See Serm. xvii. c. 4.   [2] See Note 27.   [3] See Note 28.
[4] See Note 29.   [5] See Note 30.   [6] See Note 31.

our Lord, but said that His soul was without a mind, because Godhead alone was sufficient to the Man for all purposes of reason. At last these same men dared to aver, that a certain part of the Word had been converted into flesh; so that amid the manifold variations of one dogma, not only was the nature of the flesh and soul dissolved, but even the essence of the Word Himself.[1]

5. There are also many other portentous falsities, with the enumeration of which I must not fatigue the attention of your Charity. But after diverse impieties, which have been mutually connected by the affinity which exists between manifold blasphemies,[2] these following are the errors which I warn your dutiful and devout minds most especially to avoid. One, invented by Nestorius, attempted some time ago to raise its head, but not with impunity. Another, asserted by Eutyches, has lately broken out, and deserves to be condemned with similar abhorrence. For Nestorius dared to call the Blessed Virgin Mary the Mother of a man only, so that no union of the Word and the flesh should be believed to have been effected in her conception and child-bearing, on the ground that the Son of God did not Himself become Son of Man, but, purely of His good pleasure, took a created man as His associate.[3] This statement could nowise be tolerated by Catholic ears, which were so possessed with the true Gospel as to be absolutely assured that there was no hope of salvation for mankind, unless He Himself were the Virgin's Son Who was the Creator of His Mother. But Eutyches, the profane assertor of the more recent impiety, did indeed con-

[1] See Note 32.   [2] See Note 33.   [3] See Note 34.

fess an union of two natures in Christ, but affirmed that union to have had this effect, that of the two there remained but one, while the essence of the other ceased to exist; which annihilation,[1] in fact, could only take place either by destruction or by separation.[2] Now this is so inimical to sound faith, that it cannot be received without ruin to the Christian name. For if the Word's Incarnation consists in a union of the Divine and human natures, but by this very combination what was twofold became single, then Godhead alone was born of the Virgin's womb, and alone, under an illusory semblance, underwent bodily nourishment and growth; and,—to pass over all the changes of human life,—Godhead alone was crucified, Godhead alone died, Godhead alone was buried; so that, according to those who think thus, there is no reason to hope for a resurrection, and Christ is *not* "the firstborn from the dead;"[3] for if there had not been one who could be put to death, there was none who had a right to be raised to life.

6. Far from your hearts, dearly beloved, be the pestilent falsehoods inspired by the devil! and while you know that the Son's everlasting Godhead did not, while with the Father, go through any process of increase, consider thoughtfully that to the same nature to which in Adam it was said, "Earth thou art, and to earth shalt thou go," in Christ it is said, "Sit Thou on My right hand." According to that nature wherein Christ is equal to the Father, the Only-begotten was never inferior to the Father in majesty: nor is it a temporary glory which He possesses with the Father, seeing that He is on that very right hand of the

[1] "Finiri."   [2] See Note 35.   [3] Col. i. 18.

Father, of which it is said in Exodus, "Thy right hand, O Lord, is become glorious in power;"[1] and in Isaiah, "Lord, who hath believed our report? and to whom has the arm of the Lord been revealed?"[2] Therefore the Manhood,[3] taken into the Son of God, was so received from the very outset of its bodily existence into the unity of Christ's Person, that it was neither conceived without the Godhead, nor brought forth without the Godhead, nor nourished without the Godhead. *He* was one and the same, both in working miracles and in suffering insults; through human infirmity He was crucified, dead, and buried; through Divine power He was raised up on the third day, ascended into heaven, sat down on the right hand of God the Father, and in the nature of Manhood received from the Father what in the nature of Godhead He Himself also bestowed.

7. While you meditate on these things, dearly beloved, with devout hearts, be ever mindful of the precept of the Apostle, who admonishes us all when he says, "Beware lest any spoil you through philosophy and vain deceit, after the tradition of men, and not after Christ: for in Him dwelleth all the fulness of the Godhead bodily, and ye have been filled up in Him."[4] He said not "spiritually," but "bodily," that we may understand the substance of the flesh to be real, where the indwelling of the fulness of Godhead is bodily; by which indwelling, in truth, is the whole Church also filled, which, cleaving to the Head, is the body of Christ, Who liveth and reigneth with the Father and the Holy Spirit, God for ever and ever. Amen.

[1] Exod. xv. 6.
[2] Isa. liii. 1.
[3] See Note 36. Cp. Ep. xxviii. 3.
[4] Col. ii. 8, ff.

SERMON V.

EPIPHANY.

SERM. 31. In Solemnitate Epiphaniæ, I. *Celebrato.*

THE last holy day which we celebrated was the day on which a pure Virgin brought forth the Saviour of mankind. And now, dearly beloved, the venerable festival of the Epiphany[1] gives us a continuation of joys, so that among these kindred solemnities, with their holy rites[2] in close proximity, our heartiness of rejoicing and fervour of faith may be kept from becoming languid. For the salvation of all men is interested in the fact, that the infancy of the Mediator between God and men was already manifested to the whole world while it was still detained in an insignificant little town. For, although He had chosen out the Israelitish nation, and one family of that nation, from which to take on Him the nature of universal humanity, yet it was not His will that the beginnings of His early life should be concealed within the narrow limits of His Mother's abode; but as He was pleased to be born for all, He willed to be speedily recognised by all. Accordingly, there appeared to three[3] Magi a star of unparalleled brilliancy, that, being brighter and lovelier than the other stars, it might easily attract to itself the eyes and minds of those who gazed at it, and so they might at once observe that what seemed so strange was not without a meaning. Therefore He Who vouchsafed the sign

---

[1] See Note 37.   [2] "Sacramenta."   [3] See Note 38.

gave intelligence to those who saw it; and that which He made them understand He made them seek after; and He, when sought, presented Himself to be found.

2. The three men follow the leading of the heavenly light, and accompanying with fixed gaze the indications given by its guiding brightness, are led by the splendour of grace to the recognition of the truth, after having supposed that the birth of a King, which was signified to them by their natural thoughts,[1] must be inquired for in a royal city. But He Who had taken on Him the form of a servant, and had come not to judge, but to be judged, chose beforehand Bethlehem for His Nativity, Jerusalem for His Passion. Herod, indeed, hearing that a prince of the Jews was born, suspected a successor, and was terror-struck; and having plotted the death of the Author of salvation, He falsely engaged to do Him homage. How happy would he have been if he had imitated the faith of the Magi, and turned into a religious act what he was designing as a fraud! O blind impiety of foolish jealousy, that thinkest that a Divine plan is to be disturbed by thy madness! The Lord of the world, Who bestows an eternal kingdom, is not seeking a temporal one.[2] Why dost thou attempt to overturn the immutable order of things appointed, and to anticipate the deed of other men? Not to thy time does Christ's death belong. First must the Gospel be founded; first must the kingdom of God be preached; first must healings be vouchsafed; first must miracles be done. Why wouldest thou have that for thine own crime, which is to be the work of others? and while

[1] See Note 39.   [2] See Note 40.

thou art not to have the perpetrating of this wickedness, why precipitate on thyself alone the guilt of desiring it? By this design thou gainest nothing, performest nothing. He Who by His own will was born, will die by the power of His own fiat. Therefore the Magi accomplish their desire, and being guided by the same star, reach a Child, the Lord Jesus Christ. In the flesh they adore the Word; in infancy, Wisdom; in weakness, Power; in man's true nature, the Lord of Majesty. And to manifest the sacred import of their faith and intelligence, they bear witness by gifts to what they believe in their hearts. They offer frankincense to the God, myrrh to the Man, gold to the King,[1] consciously venerating the Divine and the human nature brought into unity; because, while the substances had their own properties, there was no diversity in power.[2]

3. But after the Magi had returned to their own country, and Jesus had been removed into Egypt in consequence of a Divine warning, while Herod thinks over the matter, his frenzy blazes forth; yet all in vain. He commands all the infants in Bethlehem to be killed, and as he knows not which infant to dread, he directs a general sentence against the age which he suspects. But what the impious king takes out of the world, Christ places in heaven; and to those on whom as yet He bestows not His redeeming blood, He even now grants the dignity of martyrdom.[3] Lift up, then, dearly beloved, your faithful minds to the radiant grace of the everlasting light, and, venerating the sacred acts done in order to man's

---
[1] See Note 41. [2] See Note 42.
[3] See Note 43.

salvation,[1] apply your earnest heed to the things which took place in your behalf. Love pure chastity, for Christ is a Son of virginity. "Abstain from fleshly lusts, which war against the soul," as the blessed Apostle, present by his words, as we read, exhorts us.[2] "In malice be children,"[3] for the Lord of glory conformed Himself to mortal infancy. Follow after that humility which the Son of God was pleased to teach His disciples. Clothe yourselves with the strength of patience, that in it you may be able to "make your souls your own;"[4] for He Who is the redemption of all is Himself the courage of all. "Set your affection on things above, not on things on the earth."[5] Walk on firmly in the path of truth and life. Let not earthly things be a hindrance to you for whom heavenly things have been prepared; through our Lord Jesus Christ, Who with the Father and the Holy Spirit liveth and reigneth for ever and ever. Amen.

SERMON VI.

EPIPHANY.

SERM. 36. In Solemnitate Epiphaniæ, VI. *Dies.*

THE day on which Christ, the Saviour of the world, first appeared to the Gentiles is to be reverenced by us, dearly beloved, with sacred honour; and we ought

---

[1] See Note 44. [2] 1 S. Pet. ii. 11. [3] 1 Cor. xiv. 20.
[4] See Note 45. [5] Col. iii. 2.

to feel this day in our hearts those joys which were in the breasts of the three Magi, when, being urged onwards by the sign and leading of a new star, they adored the visible presence of that King of heaven and earth, in the promise of Whom they had believed. For that day has not in such a sense run its course, as that the mighty work which was then revealed has passed away, and nothing has come down to us but the report of what was done, for faith to receive and memory to celebrate; since, through the multiplied bounty of God, even our own times have daily experience of whatever belonged to those earliest days. Therefore, although the narrative of the Gospel readings[1] does specially review those days in which three men, who had been neither taught by the preaching of Prophets nor instructed by the testimony of the Law, came from the remotest part of the East in order to know God, yet do we see this same event even now taking place, both more manifestly and to a wider extent, in the illumination of all who are called. For the prophecy of Isaiah is being fulfilled, who says, "The Lord hath made bare His holy arm in the sight of all nations, and all nations of the earth have seen the salvation which is from the Lord our God." And again: "And they who were not told of Him shall see, and they who have not heard shall understand."[2] Wherefore, when we see men given to worldly wisdom, and far away from the confession of Jesus Christ, being led out of the depth of their error, and called to acknowledge the true light, it is beyond doubt the splendour of Divine grace which is at work; and whatever of new light

---

[1] See Note 46. [2] Isa. lii. 10, 15.

appears in darkened hearts is gleaming from the rays of that same star, that, having touched souls by its own brightness, it may both impress them by the miracle, and by its guidance bring them on to worship God. But if we would fain see, with careful intelligence, how even that triple kind of gifts is offered by all who come to Christ with the steps of faith, is not the same offering being performed in the hearts of true believers? For he brings forth gold from the treasury of his soul, who owns Christ as King of all things; he offers myrrh, who believes that God's Only-begotten Son united to Himself man's true nature; and he venerates Him with a kind of frankincense, who confesses Him to be in no wise inferior to the Father's majesty.

2. When we have thoughtfully looked at these points of comparison, dearly beloved, we find that Herod's character also is not absent. For the devil himself, as he was then Herod's secret instigator, so is now too his unwearied imitator. For he is tortured by the calling of all Gentiles, and agonized by the daily destruction of his own power; grieving that he is everywhere forsaken, and the true King in all places adored. He prepares deceits, he feigns agreements, he breaks forth into slaughter; and in order to make use of that remnant of men whom he still deceives, he burns with envy in Jews,[1] he plots by craft in heretics, he is kindled with ferocity in Pagans.[2] For he sees how invincible is the power of the eternal King, Whose own death has extinguished the power of death; and therefore he has put in force his whole art of doing mischief against those who

[1] See Note 47.   [2] See Note 48.

serve the true King, hardening some by their inflated pride in knowledge of the law, depraving others into a frenzy of persecution. But this madness of this Herod is being overcome and crushed by Him Who crowned even little ones with the glory of martyrdom, and infused into His faithful ones so unconquerable a love, that they are bold to say in the Apostle's words,[1] "Who shall separate us from the love of Christ? shall tribulation, or distress, or persecution, or famine, or nakedness, or peril, or sword? As it is written, For Thy sake are we killed all the day long; we are counted as sheep for the slaughter. But in all these things we overcome[2] by reason of Him that loved us."

3. We do not believe, dearly beloved, that this fortitude was necessary for those times alone, in which the kings of the world, and all secular powers, used to rage with bloodthirsty impiety against the people of God, because they thought that it would conduce to their chiefest glory, if they could take away from the earth the Christian name: not knowing that the Church of God was being enlarged by their frantic cruelty, because amid the punishments and deaths of blessed martyrs, those who were thought to be diminished in number were multiplied by their example.[3] At length, so greatly has our faith been indebted to the onslaughts of persecutors, that the royal sovereignty has no greater adornment than that the lords of the world are the members of Christ; nor do they glory so much in having been born in imperial dignity, as they rejoice in having been born

---

[1] Rom. viii. 35.   [2] "Superamus."
[3] See Note 49.

again in baptism.[1] But seeing that the storm of those former whirlwinds has sunk to rest, and our conflicts have long ago ceased, and a kind of tranquillity seems to smile upon us, we must watchfully guard against those dangers which spring from the repose of peace itself.[2] For the adversary, who in open persecutions was ineffective, is venting his fury by hidden arts of mischief, in the hope that, as he has not crushed us by the stroke of affliction, he may cast us down by a fall through pleasure. Accordingly, as he sees that the faith of princes withstands him, and that the indivisible Trinity of the One Godhead is not less heartily worshipped in palaces than in churches, he grieves that the shedding of Christian blood is forbidden; and as he cannot obtain our death, he attacks our manner of life. For the terror of proscriptions he substitutes the fire of avarice, and corrupts by covetousness those whom he failed to break down by losses. For that malice which is habituated to a long exercise of its own wickedness has not laid aside its hate, but turned its ability to the object of subduing to itself the minds of the faithful by allurements. It inflames those with appetites whom it cannot distress by tortures; it sows discord, kindles anger, sharpens tongues, and, lest the more cautious spirits should withdraw themselves from unlawful knaveries, it presents opportunities for the perpetration of misdeeds. For this is what it aims at as the fruit of all its treachery—that he who is not honoured by the sacrificing of sheep and rams, and by the burning of incense,[3] should get homage done him by means of any crime.

[1] See Note 50.   [2] See Note 51.   [3] See Note 52.

4. Our peace then, dearly beloved, has its own perils; and in vain do men make themselves comfortable on the score of their religious liberty, while they make no stand against vicious desires. It is the quality of men's deeds that shows their hearts; it is the character of their acts which exposes the form of their minds. For there are certain men, as the Apostle says, who "profess that they know God, but who in works deny Him."[1] For the guilt of denying Him is really incurred, when that good thing which the voice is heard to speak of is not retained in the conscience. It is true that the frailty of man's nature does easily glide on into transgression; and as there is no sin without enjoyment, men quickly acquiesce in deceitful pleasure. But let us have recourse, against carnal desires, to spiritual protection; and let the mind which has a knowledge of its God, turn away from the foe's counsels, who would persuade it to its ruin. Let it profit by God's long-suffering; and let not a persistency in doing wrong be cherished, just because vengeance is delayed. Let not the sinner be at ease on the score of impunity; for if he shall have lost the time of repentance, he will have no place of forgiveness, as the Prophet says: "For in death no man remembereth Thee, and who shall give Thee thanks in the pit?"[2] But if a man finds by experience that it is hard to correct and recover himself, let him flee to the clemency of God his Helper, and entreat that the bonds of evil habit may be broken by Him Who "raises up all those that fall, and lifts up all who are crushed."[3] The prayer of one who makes his confession will not be void, for God will in mercy

[1] Titus i. 16.   [2] Ps. vi. 5. See Note 53.   [3] Ps. cxlv. 14.

"fulfil the desire of them that fear Him;"[1] and as He has given the source from which we were to seek, He will give what is sought; through our Lord Jesus Christ, Who liveth and reigneth with the Father and the Holy Spirit, for ever and ever. Amen.

SERMON VII.

PASSION-TIDE.

SERM. 56. De Passione Domini, V. Preached on Sunday. *Creator*.

CHRIST, the Creator and Lord of all things, after His unparalleled birth from the holy Virgin, after the homage done to His cradle by the confession of the Magi, and after the manifold teaching of His heavenly speech, and the various healings of disease effected by the mandate of His powerful word, consummates the economy of all sacred events[2] and of all mighty works by the Passion through which we are saved. And so it is, dearly beloved, that the true ground and principal cause of Christian hope is the Cross of Christ, which, although it be "to the Jews a stumbling-block, and to the Greeks foolishness," is yet "to us the power of God, and the wisdom of God."[3] Wherefore at all times, indeed, ought this supreme and mightiest mystery of the Divine mercy to be retained in all its dignity in our hearts; but at this time it demands to be more vividly felt in the heart, and more clearly discerned by the mind, seeing that all the work of

---
[1] Ps. cxlv. 19.   [2] "Sacramentorum."   [3] 1 Cor. i. 23, 24.

our salvation is being brought home to us, not only by the recurrence of the time, but also by the course of Gospel readings. Let then the imaginations of impious men have no place among us; let not our healthy and sound intelligence be so corrupted either by Jewish stumbling or Gentile scoffing, as that what was done for us, not only in lowliness but in majesty, should seem either impossible in regard to man, or unworthy in regard to God. It befits us to receive both truths, to believe both; for, except by means of both, no one can be saved. For God, being righteous and merciful, did not make such use of the rights of His own will as to exert for our restoration the mere power of His benignity; but since the consequence of man's committing sin had been that he became "the slave of sin,"[1] therefore in such wise was healing bestowed on the sick, in such wise reconciliation on the guilty,[2] in such wise redemption on the captives, that a righteous sentence of condemnation should be annulled by a righteous work on the part of a Deliverer. For if Godhead by itself were to stand forth in behalf of sinners, the devil would be overcome rather by power than with reason. And again, if the mortal nature by itself were to undertake the cause of the fallen, it would not be released from its condition, because it would not be free from its stock. Therefore it was necessary that both the Divine and human substances should meet in our Lord Jesus Christ, that our mortal nature might, through the Word made flesh, receive aid alike from the birth and passion of a new Man.

2. So, while the blindness of the Jews does not see

[1] S. John viii. 34.   [2] See Note 54. Compare Serm. iv. c. 3.

what is Divine in Christ Jesus, and the wisdom of the Gentiles contemns what is human; while the former speak depreciatingly of the Lord's glory, and the latter put on airs of pride about His lowliness;[1] we adore the Son of God, alike in His own might and in our infirmity; nor are we ashamed of the Cross of Christ; nor do we, amid the voices of gainsayers, doubt either as to His Death or His Resurrection. For that which draws the scorners into unbelief is the very thing which guides us into faith; and that which in their case is the occasion of confusion, is in ours the very cause of piety. So, after our Lord had warned His disciples to contend by watchful prayer against the force of urgent temptation, He prayed to the Father, saying, "Father, if it be possible, let this cup pass from Me; nevertheless, not as I will, but as Thou wilt."[2] The first petition belongs to weakness, the last to strength. From what belonged to us, He wished for one thing; from what belonged to Himself, He chose another. For the Son, equal to the Father, was not ignorant that all things are possible to God; nor had He descended into the world to take up the Cross without His own will, so that some disturbance of His design should make Him suffer this collision of opposite feelings.[3] But that the distinction between the nature which was taken up and that which took it up might be manifest, in regard to what was human, He longed for the exertion of Divine power; in regard to what was Divine, He had respect to man's case. Accordingly, the lower will gave way to the higher; and it

[1] See Note 55. [2] S. Matt. xxvi. 39.
[3] See Note 56.

was soon shown what can be prayed for by one in distress, and what ought not to be granted by the Healer. For since "we know not what to pray for as we ought,"[1] and it is good for us that what we wish should, for the most part, not take place, when we seek for what will hurt us, our good and righteous God is merciful in refusing it.[2] Therefore, when our Lord had by a threefold prayer settled the mode of putting right our own will, He said to His disciples, still weighed down by sorrow, "Sleep on now, and take your rest. Behold, the hour is at hand, and the Son of Man will be delivered into the hands of sinners. Rise up, let us go. Behold, he is at hand who will betray Me."[3]

3. But while our Lord was actually uttering these words, those whom He had referred to rushed upon Him, and a band came together with swords and staves to seize Christ, following as their leader Judas Iscariot, who, by the distinction of his perfidy, had won the pre-eminence in this deed. From this man was withheld no condescension, lest some vexation should give him a motive for crime; but he was inflamed by the fiery breath of him to whom he had voluntarily offered his services, and he found a chief corresponding in character to his own mind. Deservedly, as the prophet also had foretold, was "his prayer turned into sin;"[4] for when the enormity was consummated, his very conversion was so perverse that he sinned even in repenting. Thus the Son of God allows impious hands to be laid upon Him, and that which is wrought by the fury of savage

---

[1] Rom. viii. 26.
[3] S. Matt. xxvi. 45, 46.
[2] See Note 57.
[4] Ps. cix. 7.

men is completed by the power of the Sufferer. For this was that sacred work[1] of great loving-kindness, which Christ was pursuing amid those injuries; for if He had repelled them by a display of power and by manifest strength, He would have only been performing what was Divine, not curing what was human. But amid all the outrages contumeliously and wantonly offered to Him by the frenzy of people and of priests, our stains were being washed out, our offences expiated. For the nature which in us was ever guilty and captive, in Him suffered as innocent and free; that in order to "take away the sin of the world," that Lamb might offer Himself as a Sacrifice, Who might both be united to all men by bodily substance, and distinguished from all by spiritual origin. Let this be enough, dearly beloved, to be imparted to your ears to-day. Let the rest be deferred to Wednesday;[2] your prayers being aided by the Lord, Who will deign to grant that what we promise we may fulfil; through the same our Lord, Whose are honour and glory for ever and ever. Amen.

[1] "Sacramentum."   [2] See Note 58.

SERMON VIII.

PASSION-TIDE.

SERM. 62. De Passione Domini, XI.   Preached on Sunday.
Desiderata.

LONGED for by us, dearly beloved, and an object of desire to the whole world, the festival of our Lord's Passion[1] has come, and suffers us not to be silent, amid our exulting bursts of spiritual joy. For although it is difficult to discourse often on the same subject worthily and appropriately, yet in regard to so great a mystery of the Divine mercy, a priest is not free to withhold from the ears of the faithful people the sermon which is their due. For the subject itself, from the very fact of its being unspeakable, supplies the ability to speak: nor can we be at a loss for something to say on a matter for which what is said can never be sufficient.[2] Well, then, may our human weakness sink under God's glory, and ever find itself inadequate to the exposition of the works of His mercy. Well may our thoughts be oppressed, our capacity come to a stand, our utterance fail; good is it that we should feel how imperfect are even our right thoughts about the majesty of the Lord. For since the Prophet says, "seek the Lord and be strengthened, seek His face evermore,"[3] no one ought to presume that he has found the whole of what he is seeking, lest by ceasing to advance he fail to come near. And among all the works of God, by which man's admiration, kept on the stretch, is wearied,

[1] See Note 59.   [2] See Note 60.   [3] Ps. cv. 4.

what is there which so greatly at once delights and transcends our mental gaze, as the Passion of our Saviour? As often as we think, to the best of our power, about His omnipotence, which belongs to Him as of one co-equal essence with the Father, the lowliness which we see in God amazes us more than the power; and we find it harder to grasp the "emptying" of the Divine majesty[1] than the carrying up on high of the "form of a servant." But it helps us greatly in understanding, if we remember that although the Creator is one, and the creature another,—the inviolable Godhead one, and the passible flesh another,—yet the two distinct substances concur in one Person,[2] so that, alike in infirmities and in mighty acts, the contumely and the glory belong to One and the same.[3]

2. By this rule of faith, dearly beloved, which we have received in the very opening of the Creed by the authority of Apostolic teaching,[4] while we call our Lord Jesus Christ the only Son of God the Father Almighty, we also confess Him, the self-same, as born, from the Holy Spirit, of the Virgin Mary;[5] nor do we go astray from His majesty when we believe Him to have been crucified, dead, and raised again the third day. For all acts which belong to the God or the Man, were at once accomplished by manhood and Godhead;[6] so that, while the impassible is present in the passible, neither can strength be affected amid

---

[1] See Serm. ii. c. 2.
[2] "Concurrat." See Serm. i. c. 2, and Ep. xxviii. 3, "coeunte:" Serm. ii. c. 1, "convenit."
[3] See Serm. ii. c. 2; Ep. xxviii. 3.
[4] See Note 61.
[5] See Note 62.
[6] See Note 63.

weakness, nor weakness overcome amid strength. Deservedly was the blessed Apostle Peter praised on his confession of this union; who, when our Lord asked what His disciples understood concerning Him, with all speed anticipated the voices of them all, saying, "Thou art the Christ, the Son of the living God." Which indeed he saw, not by flesh and blood explaining it (for their interposition might have been a hindrance to the inward eyes,) but by the very Spirit of the Father working in his believing heart; so that, being prepared for the government of the whole Church,[1] he might first learn what he had to teach, and on account of the firmness of that faith which he was to proclaim, might hear it said, "Thou art Peter, and upon this rock I will build My Church, and the gates of hell shall not prevail against it."[2] Accordingly, the strength of Christian faith, which, being built on an impregnable rock, fears not the gates of death, confesses one Lord Jesus Christ, both very God and very Man : believing the same to be the Virgin's Son Who is the Maker of His Mother;[3] the same to have been born in the close of ages, Who is the Creator of times; the same to be Lord of all power, and one of the race of mortals; the same to have "known no sin," and to have been sacrificed for sinners "in the likeness of sinful flesh."[4]

3. And that He might loose mankind from the bonds of deadly transgression, He concealed from the devil's fury the power of His own Majesty, and opposed him in the infirmity of our lowliness. For if the cruel and proud enemy could have known the

[1] See Note 64.
[2] S. Matt. xvi. 16.
[3] See Ep. xxviii. 4.
[4] 2 Cor. v. 21; Rom. viii. 3.

plan of God's mercy, he would rather have set himself to soften the minds of the Jews into gentleness, than to kindle them into unrighteous hatred; lest he should lose the dominion over all his captives, while attacking the freedom of One Who owed him nought.[1] So was he cheated by his own malice: he brought on the Son of God a punishment which was to be turned to the healing of all the sons of men. He shed righteous blood, which was to be both a ransom and a cup[2] for the reconciliation of the world. What the Lord chose according to the purpose of His own will, that He took upon Him. He submitted Himself to the impious hands of infuriate men, who, while busy with their own wickedness, were doing the behest of the Redeemer. And even towards His slayers so strong was His feeling of tenderness, that in His prayer to the Father from the Cross, He asked not that He should be avenged, but that they should be pardoned, saying, "Father, forgive them, for they know not what they do."[3] And the might of that prayer had this result, that the hearts of many of those who said, "His blood be on us and on our children," were converted to repentance by the preaching of Peter the Apostle, and in one day "about three thousand" Jews were baptized; and they all became "of one heart and of one soul,"[4] prepared already to die for Him Whose crucifixion they had demanded.

4. To this pardon the traitor Judas could not attain. For the son of perdition, at whose "right hand the devil stood," passed away into despair, before Christ fulfilled the mystery of general redemption. For after

---

[1] See Note 65.
[2] See Note 66.
[3] S. Luke xxiii. 34.
[4] Acts ii. 41; iv. 32.

the Lord had died for all[1] the ungodly, perhaps even this man might have obtained healing, if he had not hurried to the halter.[2] But in that malignant heart, now given to thievish fraud, now busy with a parricidal bargain, there had never settled down any of the proofs of the Saviour's mercy. He had received with his impious ears the words of the Lord, when He said, "I came not to call the righteous, but sinners,"[3] and, "The Son of Man is come to seek and save that which was lost:"[4] but he had not understood the clemency of Christ, Who was not only wont to heal bodily infirmities, but also to cure the wounds of sickly souls, saying to the paralytic, "Son, be of good cheer, thy sins are forgiven thee;"[5] and saying also to the adulteress who was brought before Him, "Neither will I condemn thee; go, and sin no more;"[6] so as to show through all His acts that in that Advent of His He came as Saviour of the world, not as Judge. But the impious traitor, far from understanding this, rose up against himself, not with the just sentence[7] of a penitent, but with the frenzy of a lost man: so that having sold the Author of life to murderers, he increased his own damnation by sinning even in his death.

5. Therefore has that which was done against our Lord Jesus Christ by false witnesses, by cruel rulers, by impious priests, using the ministry of a cowardly governor,[8] and the attendance of an ignorant cohort, been in all ages a matter to be at once detested and embraced. For as the Cross of our Lord, in regard

---

[1] See Note 67.   [2] See Note 68.   [3] S. Matt. ix. 13.
[4] S. Luke xix. 10.   [5] S. Matt. ix. 2.   [6] See Note 69.
[7] Cp. 2 Cor. vii. 11.   [8] See Note 70.

to the mind of the Jews, was cruel, so in regard to the power of the Crucified it is marvellous. The people rages against One, and Christ has mercy on all. What is inflicted by ferocity is welcomed by free will, so that the audacity of the crime accomplishes the work of the eternal Will. Wherefore the whole order of events, which the Gospel narrative goes through so fully, is in such a manner to be received by the ears of the faithful, that while we entirely believe in the acts which were performed at the time of our Lord's Passion, we are to understand that in Christ was not only remission of sins accomplished, but also a pattern of righteousness displayed. But, that this may by the Lord's help be more carefully discussed, let this part of the discourse be reserved for Wednesday. God's grace, we hope, will be present, to enable us, by your prayers, to fulfil our promise; through our Lord Jesus Christ, Who with the Father and the Holy Spirit reigneth for ever and ever. Amen.

SERMON IX.

PASSION-TIDE.

SERM. 63.   De Passione Dom. XII.   Preached on Wednesday.
Gloria.

THE glory of our Lord's Passion, dearly beloved, on which we promised to speak further to you to-day, is pre-eminently wonderful in regard to that mysterious humiliation which has both redeemed and taught us all; so that from the same quarter whence a ransom was given, might righteousness also be received. For the omnipotence of the Son of God, wherein through identity of essence He is equal to the Father, could have rescued mankind from the devil's tyranny by the simple mandate of His own will, had it not been in the highest degree consonant to the Divine operations that the hostility of our wicked foe should be conquered by that which it had conquered, and our natural freedom be restored through that very nature through which our general captivity had been brought about.[1] Now, by the Evangelist's language, "the Word was made flesh and dwelt among us," and the Apostle's, "God was in Christ reconciling the world unto Himself,"[2] it has been shown that the Only-begotten Son of the most high Father entered into so close a fellowship with human lowliness, that having taken upon Him the substance of our flesh and soul, He remained one and the same Son of God, exalting what was ours, not what was His;[3] for it was weakness that was uplifted, not strength; so that when the creature was united to its Creator, nothing Divine should be wanting to the assumed element, nothing human to the assuming one.

2. This design of God's mercy and justice, though overshadowed in previous ages by certain veils, was yet not so much hidden as to be closed to the understanding of holy men, who lived praiseworthy lives from the beginning even to our Lord's Advent. For the salvation which was to come in Christ was pro-

[1] See Serm. vii. c. 1.   [2] 2 Cor. v. 19.
[3] See Note 71.

mised both by the words of prophets and the significancy of events, and was obtained not only by those who preached it, but by all those who believed the preachers. For it is one faith which justifies the Saints of all times;[1] and to the self-same hope of the faithful pertains all that either we acknowledge to have been done, or our fathers hailed as to be done, by the Mediator between God and men, Jesus Christ. Nor is there any distinction between Jews and Gentiles; for, as the Apostle says, "circumcision is nothing, and uncircumcision is nothing, but the keeping of the commandments of God;"[2] which, if we keep them with integrity of faith, make us true sons of Abraham,[3] that is, complete Christians, as the same Apostle says: "For whosoever of you have been baptized into Christ, have put on Christ. There is no Jew nor Greek, there is no bondman nor free, there is no male nor female, for ye are all one in Christ. And if ye are Christ's, then are ye Abraham's seed, and heirs according to the promise."[4]

3. There is therefore no doubt, dearly beloved, that the human nature was taken by the Son of God into so close a connection, that not only in that Man Who is "the First-born of the whole creation," but also in all His Saints, Christ is one and the same;[5] and as the Head cannot be disjoined from the members, so neither can the members from the Head. For although it belongs not to this life, but to the life eternal, that God should be "all in all,"[6] yet even

---

[1] See Serm. ii. c. 4.
[2] 1 Cor. vii. 19.
[3] See Serm. iii. c. 2.
[4] Gal. iii. 27—29.
[5] See Note 72.
[6] 1 Cor. xv. 28.

now is He the inseparable Inhabitant of His Temple, which is the Church, according to His own express promise,—" Lo, I am with you all days, even unto the end of the world."¹ In conformity with which the Apostle says, " He is the Head of the body, the Church ; Who is the beginning, the First-born from the dead, that in all things He might be holding the pre-eminence ; for it seemed good that in Him should all fulness dwell, and that through Him should all things be reconciled in Him."²

4. Now what else is conveyed to our hearts by these and by more testimonies besides, than that we should be thoroughly renewed after the image of Him Who, abiding in the " form of God," was pleased to be the form of " sinful flesh ?"³ For He, without any fellowship with sin, took on Him all the infirmities which come from sin, so that He lacked not the sensations⁴ of hunger and thirst, of sleep and weariness, of sorrow and weeping, and endured the cruellest pains, even to the extremity of death. For no one could be loosed from the nets of mortality, unless He in Whom alone⁵ the nature of all men was innocent allowed Himself to be put to death by the hands of the ungodly. Wherefore the Son of God, our Saviour, ordained for all who should believe in Him both a mystery and an example ;⁶ that they might take hold of the former by new birth, and follow the latter by imitation. For this is what the blessed Apostle Peter teaches us, saying, " Christ suffered for us, leaving you an example that you should follow

---

¹ S. Matt. xxviii. 20. ² Col. i. 18—20.
³ Cp. Rom. viii. 3. ⁴ See Note 73.
⁵ See Serm. i. c. 1. ⁶ See Note 74.

in His steps, Who did no sin, neither was guile found in His mouth; Who, when He was reviled, reviled not again; when He suffered, He threatened not, but gave Himself up to him that judged Him unjustly;[1] Who Himself bore our sins in His own body on the tree, that we being dead to sins, should live unto righteousness."

5. As then there is no one among believers, dearly beloved, to whom the gifts of grace are denied, so there is no one who does not owe obedience to Christian discipline. For although the harshness of the symbolic law has been abolished, yet the benefits of voluntary obedience have increased, as John the Evangelist says, "The law was given by Moses, but grace and truth came by Jesus Christ."[2] For everything connected with the law in the earlier times, in respect either to the circumcision of the flesh, or the diversities of victims, or the observance of the Sabbath, bore witness to Christ, and spoke of Christ's grace beforehand. And He "is the end of the law,"[3] not by making void its significances, but by fulfilling them. And although He Himself is the Author alike of old things and of new, yet He changed the ordinances connected with prefigurative promises, because He brought the things promised to effect, and caused the announcements to cease, since He, so announced, had come. But in regard to moral precepts, no decrees of the older Testament were set aside,[4] but many were enlarged by the Gospel teaching, that they might be more perfect and luminous,

---

[1] See Note 75.
[2] S. John i. 17.
[3] Rom. x. 4.
[4] See Note 76.

as giving salvation, than they had been as promising a Saviour.[1]

6. So then, all those things which the Son of God both did and taught for the reconciliation of the world, we do not simply know of by the history of past events, but feel even now by the power of present operations. He it is Who, having been brought forth by the Holy Spirit from a Virgin Mother, by the same inspiration makes fruitful His undefiled Church, so that through the baptismal child-bearing[2] is produced an innumerable multitude of children of God, of whom it is said, "who were born, not of blood, nor of the will of the flesh, nor of the will of man, but of God." He it is in Whom the seed of Abraham is blessed by the adoption of the whole world to sonship, and the patriarch becomes "a father of nations,"[3] while the promised sons are born, not carnally, but by faith. He it is Who, making no exception of any nation, forms out of every people under heaven one flock of holy sheep, and daily performs what He had promised in the words, "And other sheep I have, which are not of this fold; them also I must bring, and they shall hear My voice, and there shall be one flock[4] and one Shepherd." For although it is to blessed Peter in the first instance[5] that He says "Feed My sheep," yet the care (of the sheep) actually belonging to all shepherds is under the direction of the one Lord; and those who come to the Rock He nourishes in such pleasant and well-watered pastures, that numberless sheep,

---

[1] See Note 77. [2] See Serm. iii. c. 2.
[3] Gen. xvii. 5. [4] "Grex." S. John x. 16.
[5] "Principaliter." See Serm. viii. c. 2.

strengthened with the fatness of love, hesitate not themselves to die for the Name of the Shepherd, even as the good Shepherd was pleased to lay down His life for the sheep. He it is in Whose suffering not only the glorious courage of martyrs has a share, but also the faith of all who are new-born in their actual regeneration. For while they renounce[1] the devil, and believe in God; while they pass from the old life into the new; while the image of the earthly man is laid aside, and the form of the Heavenly taken up; there takes place a certain appearance of death, and a certain likeness of resurrection; so that he who is taken up by Christ and "takes up Christ" is not the same after the laver as he was before Baptism, but the body of the regenerate becomes the flesh of the Crucified.[2]

7. This, dearly beloved, is "the change from the right hand of the Highest,"[3] "Who worketh all in all," so that in the case of every faithful man we may, through the character of a good life, understand Him to be the author of pious works: giving thanks to the mercy of God, Who so adorns the whole body of the Church by innumerable bestowals of spiritual gifts, that by the rays of one light the same splendour is everywhere manifest, nor can the good desert[4] of any Christian be aught else than the glory of Christ. This is that "true light which" justifies and "enlightens every man."[5] This is that which "rescues us from the power of darkness, and translates us into the kingdom of the Son of God."[6] This is that which

---

[1] See Note 78.
[3] Psalm lxxvii. (or lxxvi.) 10; LXX. Vulg.
[5] S. John i. 9.
[2] See Note 79.
[4] See Note 80.
[6] Col. i. 13.

through newness of life elevates the desires of the soul, and quenches the appetites of the flesh. This is that whereby the Lord's Passover is legitimately celebrated "in the unleavened bread of sincerity and truth;"[1] while, after the leaven of the old malice has been cast away, the new creature is exhilarated[2] and fed from the Lord Himself. For the participation of the Body and Blood of Christ effects nothing else than this, that we pass into That which we receive,[3] and, as we have died with Him, and been buried with Him, and raised up with Him, so we bear Him throughout, both in spirit and in flesh, as the Apostle says: "For ye are dead, and your life is hid with Christ in God; for when Christ, your life, shall appear, then shall ye also appear with Him in glory;"[4] Who, with the Father and the Holy Spirit, liveth and reigneth for ever and ever. Amen.

SERMON X.

PASSION-TIDE.

SERM. 64. De Passione Dom. XIII. Preached on Sunday. *Omnia.*

TRUE it is, dearly beloved, that all times give to Christian minds opportunity for meditating on the mystery of our Lord's Passion and Resurrection; nor is there any duty of our religion whereby we do not

---

[1] 1 Cor. v. 8.   [2] "Inebriatur." Cf. Psalm xxii. 5, Vulg.
[3] See Note 81.   [4] Col. iii. 3.

celebrate alike the reconciliation of the world and the assumption of human nature in Christ. But now it is right that the universal Church should be instructed by a fuller understanding, and enkindled with a more fervent hope, at a time when the dignity of these events is so brought out by the recurrence of the hallowed days, and by the pages of Gospel truth, that we ought rather to honour the Lord's Passover as present than remember it as past. Let not then the gaze of our faith go astray in any point from those things which belong to the Cross of Jesus Christ, and let us not receive with listless ears any one of these facts which are brought to mind by the Gospel narrative: so that, whereas there have not been wanting, and are not now wanting, those who attack the reality of our Lord's Incarnation, and affirm that when in the womb of the Virgin Mother Mary the Word was made flesh, and was born as an Infant, and advanced by bodily growth to the age of full manhood, and was crucified, dead, and buried, and rose again the third day, all this was indeed done in the form of our likeness, but not in the nature of our flesh :[1] we, in no point departing from the testimonies of Evangelists and Apostles, may be confirmed by the intelligence of those whose assured experience[2] has informed us, and may be able piously and firmly to say that we ourselves have in them been instructed, that what they saw we have seen, what they learned we have learned, and what they touched we have handled. And just because we are not deceived as to our Lord's birth, we are not disturbed as to His Passion.

2. For we know, dearly beloved, and confess with

[1] See Serm. iv. c. 4, 5.   [2] See Note 82.

our whole heart, that the Godhead of the Father, and the Son, and the Holy Spirit, is one,[1] and the essence of the everlasting Trinity is consubstantial, in no wise divided, in no wise diverse, because it is at once apart from all time, at once immutable, at once never ceasing to be what it is. Now, in this ineffable Unity of the Trinity, whose works and judgments are in all points done in common,[2] it was the Person of the Son in particular Who undertook the restoration of mankind; that since it is He by Whom "all things were made, and without Whom nothing was made," and Who animated with the breath of rational life man formed from the earth's clay, He, the selfsame, might restore to its lost dignity our nature which had been cast down from the citadel of immortality, and as He had been its founder, might be also its restorer, in such a way directing His design to its accomplishment, as to employ rather just reason than forcible power for the destruction of the devil's sovereignty.[3] Since then the universal posterity of the first man had fallen down pierced at once by the same wound,[4] nor could any good deserts of saints overcome the law whereby death was brought upon it, there came from heaven the one only Physician, often heralded by many signs, and long promised by prophetic assurances, who, remaining in "the form of God," and losing nought of His own majesty, was to be born in the nature of our flesh and soul, without the contagion of the primeval offence. For the Son of the Blessed Virgin was the only one born without sin; not external to mankind, but unconnected with

[1] See Serm. ii. c. 2.   [2] See Note 83.
[3] See Serm. vii. c. 1.   [4] See Serm. i. c. 1.

their guilt; in Whom there could be both the perfect innocence and the true nature of the man made after God's image and likeness, since of Adam's progeny there was but one in whom the devil had nothing that he could call his own. And while venting his fury against Him Whom he held not under the law of sin, he lost the rights of his impious sovereignty.[1]

3. For the shedding of righteous blood for the unrighteous was so potent in the way of privilege, so rich in the way of ransom, that if the whole body of the captives had believed in their Redeemer, not one would have been detained in the tyrant's bonds. For, as the Apostle says, "where sin abounded, grace did much more abound."[2] And when those who were born under a pre-existing law of sin received the power of being born again unto righteousness, the grant of freedom became more valid than the debt of servitude. What hope, then, do they leave to themselves in the protecting power of this mystery, who deny the reality of human substance in the body of our Saviour? Let them say by what sacrifice they have been reconciled, by what blood redeemed![3] Who is it that "offered Himself for us, an offering and a sacrifice to God for a sweet-smelling savour?" Or what sacrifice was ever more sacred than that which the true High Priest, by the immolation of His own flesh, laid on the altar of the Cross?[4] For although "in the sight of the Lord the death" of many a saint was "precious,"[5] yet in no case was the slaughter of an innocent man the propitiation for a

---

[1] See Serm. viii. c. 3.
[2] Rom. v. 20.
[3] See Ep. xxviii. 5.
[4] See Note 84.
[5] Ps. cxvi. 15.

world. Righteous men did not give crowns, but received them; and from the endurance of the faithful sprang, not gifts of righteousness, but examples of patience. For in each case, each man's death stood alone, nor did any one by his death pay the debt of another; for among the sons of men our Lord Jesus was the only one in Whom all were crucified, all died, all were buried, and all raised; of Whom He Himself said, "When I shall be lifted up, I will draw all things unto Me."[1] For true faith, which justifies ungodly men, and creates righteous ones, being attracted to One Who shares its nature, obtains salvation in Him in Whom alone man finds himself innocent: and as "there is one Mediator between God and men, the Man Christ Jesus,"[2] by His sharing man's nature man attained to the peace of God, having a full right to glory in His power, Who having done battle with the proud foe in the infirmity of our flesh, bestowed His victory on those in whose body He triumphed.

4. Since, then, in our Lord Jesus Christ, the true Son of God and man, we acknowledge a Divine nature from His Father, and a human substance from His Mother; although there is but one Person of God the Word and of the flesh, and both essences have acts in common,[3] yet must we take notice of the character of the works themselves, and discern, by the gaze of a pure faith, to what heights the lowliness of infirmity is promoted, and to what depths the loftiness of power stoops down: what it is which the flesh does not without the Word, and what it is which the Word effects not without the flesh.[4] For without

---

[1] See Note 85.
[2] 1 Tim. ii. 5.
[3] See Serm. viii. c. 2.
[4] See Note 86.

the power of the Word, the Virgin would neither conceive nor bear; and without the reality of the flesh, the Infant would not lie wrapt in swathing bands. Without the power of the Word, the Magi would not adore a Child made known to them by a new star; and without the reality of the flesh, there would be no command to remove into Egypt the Child Whom Herod was desiring to kill. Without the power of the Word, the Father's voice sent forth from heaven would not say, " This is My beloved Son, in Whom I am well pleased:"[1] and without the reality of the flesh, John would not bear witness, " Behold the Lamb of God, behold Him Who taketh away the sins of the world."[2] Without the power of the Word, there would not take place the recovery of the weakly and the revival of the dead; and without the reality of the flesh, He would not need food after fasting, nor sleep after weariness. Lastly, without the power of the Word, the Lord would not declare Himself equal to the Father;[3] and without the reality of the flesh the Selfsame would not call the Father greater than Himself;[4] while the Catholic Faith[5] accepts both statements and defends both, believing the one Son of God to be both Man and the Word, according to the distinctness of the Divine and the human substance. Much is there, dearly beloved, which we might take out of the whole body of the Scriptures in order to expound this faith which we preach: for nothing is oftener presented to us in the Divine

---

[1] S. Matt. iii. 17. [2] S. John i. 29.
[3] S. John x. 30. See Serm. ii. c. 1.
[4] S. John xiv. 28. See Note 13.
[5] See Note 87.

oracles, than the Son of God, as touching His Godhead, everlasting from the Father, and the Selfsame, as touching the flesh, born in time from His Mother. But lest the attention of your Charity be wearied, we must put an end to this day's sermon, that we may reserve for Wednesday what has to be added ; by the aid of our Lord Jesus Christ, Who with the Father and the Holy Spirit liveth and reigneth for ever and ever. Amen.

SERMON XI.

PASSION-TIDE.

SERM. 66. De Passione Domini, XV. *Evangelica.*

THE course of Gospel-readings, dearly beloved, which has laid open the history of our Lord's Passion, is so well known to the universal Church by general and frequent listening, that each of you can recall the order of events as if it had passed under your own eyes. And they are to be regarded as having made no slight progress, who entertain no doubt as to what they have heard, so that even if they cannot, as yet, clearly apprehend some Scriptural mystery, they still most firmly believe that in the Divine books there is no falsehood.[1] Since, then, it is to a pure faith that the fulness of understanding has been promised, let vigorous and illuminated

[1] See Note 88.

minds lift themselves up to obtain the teaching of the Holy Spirit, and not be content to know the order of what was done, without also looking into the actual ground of the loving-kindness bestowed upon them: so that human nature may love its Maker the more for knowing how much He has loved it. For God had no reason, save His own goodness, for showing us mercy; and the second birth of men is more wonderful than their first estate. For it is a greater thing that in the last ages God restored what had perished, than that in the beginning He made what was not.[1] And so, after we had lost, by our first parents' transgression, the freedom of natural innocence, no good deserts of the saints who lived before Christ could of themselves regain it. For the doom pronounced against the transgressors held in its gripe the whole race of their captive posterity; and no one was exempt from condemnation, because no one was free from sin. But the Saviour's redeeming grace, while " destroying the work of the devil,"[2] and breaking the bonds of sin, arranged in such sort the mystery of its great loving-kindness, that while the pre-ordained full number of generations should run its course to the end of the world, the renewal of man's origin should reach backward to all ages by the justifying power of a common faith.[3] For the Incarnation of the Word, and the putting to death of Christ, and His resurrection, became the salvation of all the faithful: and the blood of one Righteous Man has bestowed on us, who believe that it has been shed for the reconciliation of the world, that very thing which it conferred

[1] See Note 89. [2] 1 S. John iii. 8. [3] See Serm. ii. c. 4.

on the fathers, who believed that in like manner it was to be shed.

2. There is nothing, therefore, dearly beloved, in the Christian religion which contradicts the ancient types; nor did the righteous men of the earlier times ever hope for salvation save in the Lord Jesus Christ. Varied, indeed, were the Divine arrangements, according to the counsel of the Divine will; but both the testimonies of the Law, and the oracles of prophecy, and the offerings of victims, shed their light on the self-same point. For such was the fitting mode of instructing that people,—that they should receive those things as overshadowed which they could not apprehend if unveiled; and that thus the Gospel should have greater authority with them, after it had been ministered to by those pages of the Old Testament, with all their signs and mysteries, of which our Lord declared that He was "not come to destroy the Law, but to fulfil it."[1] Let not, then, the Jew think that he gains anything by his carnal lingering on the surface of the letter, and by being convicted of opposition to those Scriptures which with us enjoy their true dignity; while we are both instructed by predictions and enriched by fulfilments. For, since the Lord says, "When I shall be lifted up, I will draw all things unto Me," there remained nought of the teachings of the Law, nought of the prophetic types, which did not wholly pass over into the ordinances of Christ.[2] With us is the seal of circumcision, the hallowing of chrism,[3] the consecration of priests; with us the purity of sacrifice, the reality of baptism, the dignity of the temple; so that the heralds rightly ceased to speak

---

[1] S. Matt. v. 17.   [2] See Serm. ix. c. 5.   [3] See Note 90.

on the arrival of what they heralded. Nor is reverence for the promises made void, because the fulness of grace has been manifested. But since, as the Apostle says,[1] "blindness in part has taken place in Israel, nor are they the children of the promise who are children of the flesh," the ineffable mercy of God has made for itself a people of Israel out of all nations, and, softening the stony hardness of Gentile hearts, has raised up "out of stones" true children of Abraham:[2] so that, when all are "concluded under sin,"[3] those who were born carnally may be born again spiritually; and it matters not whom any one had for his father, since, through the common confession of our faith, the font of Baptism makes all innocent, and the election of adoption confirms them as heirs.

3. For what else has the Cross of Christ done, and is doing, than this—that by the abolition of enmities the world is reconciled to God, and through the sacrifice of an immolated Lamb all things are recalled to true peace? But he is not in concord with God, who dissents from that profession which he uttered at his regeneration;[4] and being unmindful of his compact with God, is shown to cling to what he renounced, while he is found to go back from what he believed. For vainly does he take to himself the name of Christian, and to no purpose does he think that he is celebrating the Lord's Paschal feast, who does not believe that Jesus Christ rose again in that flesh wherein He was born, and suffered, and died, and was buried; and who does not confess that the first-fruits of our nature were raised to life in Him. Let him, then,

---

[1] See Rom. xi. 25; ix. 8.
[2] S. Matt. iii. 9.
[3] Gal. iii. 22.
[4] See Serm. ix. c. 6.

who truly venerates our Lord's Passion so look at the Crucified Jesus with the eyes of his heart, as to be assured that his own flesh is the flesh of Jesus. Let the earthly nature "tremble" when its Redeemer is put to death; let the "rocks" of unbelieving minds be burst open; and let those who were weighed down by the "sepulchres" of mortality shake off the mass of obstacles, and leap forth. Let there now appear in "the holy city,"[1]—that is, in the Church of God,—tokens of the coming resurrection; and let that which is to be wrought on bodies take place in hearts. To none of the weak has the victory of the Cross been denied, nor is there any one to whom the prayer of Christ cannot bring help. If that prayer was beneficial to so many who raged against Him, how much more helpful is it to those who are being converted to Him? Ignorance has been removed, difficulty modified, and that "fiery sword" by which the land of life was shut in has been quenched by the sacred blood of Christ. Before the true Light the gloom of the old night has given way. The Christian people is invited to the riches of Paradise; and to all the regenerate has been laid open a path of return to the lost Country, if only no one causes that way to be closed against himself, which could be opened to the faith of the robber.[2]

4. While, then, dearly beloved, we are celebrating the ineffable mystery of the Paschal festival, let us acknowledge, by the teaching of God's Spirit, of what a glory we have been called to partake, and into what a hope we have entered. Nor let us be so engrossed, either in the way of anxiety or of pride, with

[1] See S. Matt. xxvii. 51—53.   [2] See Note 91.

the business of this present life, as not to be conformed with all our hearts' affections to our Redeemer, and to press on by means of His example. For He neither did nor suffered anything but with a view to our salvation; that the strength which was present in the Head might also be present in the body. For, first of all, that assumption of our nature into Godhead, whereby the Word was made flesh and dwelt among us,—what man, save the unbeliever, did it leave outside its merciful operation? And who is there who has not a common nature with Christ, if[1] he has received Him Who assumed that nature, and is regenerate by that Spirit by Whose agency Christ was born? Further, who cannot recognise in Christ his own infirmities?[2] Who cannot see that the taking of food, the reposing in sleep, the anxiety of sorrow, the tears of pity, belonged to the "form of a servant?" And since that form had to be healed of its old wounds, and cleansed from the filth of sin, in such a way did the only-begotten Son of God become also Son of Man, as to lack neither all the reality of Manhood, nor the fulness of Godhead. As, therefore, that is ours which the Virgin Mother brought forth in union with Godhead, so is that which the impious Jews crucified. Ours is that which lay lifeless in the sepulchre, and which rose again the third day, and which ascended above all the heights of the heavens to the right hand of the Father's majesty; so that if we walk in the way of His commandments, and are not ashamed to confess what He, in the lowliness of a bodily form, bestowed on the work of our salvation, we too may be prompted to a fellowship in

[1] See Note 92.   [2] See Serm. ix., c. 4.

His glory; for that which He gave notice of will be manifestly fulfilled, " Whosoever shall confess Me before men, him will I also confess before My Father Who is in heaven."[1]

5. And this exhortation of ours is aided and furthered by God's grace, which, by the revelation of the truth throughout all churches, has crushed[2] the enemies of the Incarnation of Christ, and of His death and resurrection: so that the faithful in the whole world, being in unity with the authority of the Apostolic faith, might rejoice with us in one burst of gladness, as the blessed Apostle Paul says, " Know ye not, that as many of us as have been baptized in[3] Christ Jesus have been baptized in His death? For we have been buried together with Him, through baptism, in death; that like as Christ rose from the dead through the glory of the Father, so should we also walk in newness of life. For if we have been planted together in the likeness of His death, we shall be also in the likeness of His resurrection; knowing that our old man has been crucified with Him, that the body of sin might be destroyed, and henceforth we might not serve sin. For he who is dead has been justified from sin. Now if we be dead with Christ, we believe that we shall also live with Him,"[4] Who liveth and reigneth with the Father and the Holy Spirit for ever and ever. Amen.

---

[1] S. Matt. x. 32.
[2] See Note 93.
[3] "In Christo Jesu," &c.
[4] Rom. vi. 3—8.

SERMON XII.

PASSION-TIDE.

SERM. 70. De Passione Domini, XIX. *Sacram.*

THE sacred history of our Lord's Passion, dearly beloved, which we have gone through, as usual, in the Gospel narrative, has, I suppose, so fixed itself in the minds of you all, that to every one who has listened the very reading has become a kind of seeing. For true faith has this power, that it is mentally not absent from things in which the body's presence cannot join; and whether the heart of the believer is returning to the past, or reaching onward to the future, his cognizance of the truth is unconscious of intervals of time. So it is that there is present to our thoughts an image of the things done for our salvation; and everything that in those days wrung the disciples' hearts, touches our feelings too. Not that we are either depressed by sadness, or scared by the ferocity of the raging Jews; for even those who were shaken by the greatness of that storm were borne onwards into an unshaken constancy by our Lord's Resurrection and Ascension; but that when we consider what sort of men the people of Jerusalem and the priests were at that time, it is with great mental agitation that we apprehend so dark a deed of impious men. For although our Saviour's Passion had reference to the salvation of mankind, and the bonds of eternal death were broken by our Lord's temporal death, yet what the patience of the Crucified wrought is one thing, what the frenzy of the crucifiers wrought is another. Nor did the compassion and the wrath tend to the same results, inasmuch as by the effusion of the same blood Christ released the world from captivity, and the Jews slaughtered the Redeemer of all.

2. Thus the carnal Israel was hardened by its own malice; and got no benefit from the testimony of the law, nor from the symbolism of mystic rites, nor from the oracles of Prophets, when John declared that the Lord's Passover, which had been kept for so many ages, was fulfilled in Him of Whom he said, with a public attestation, " Behold the Lamb of God, behold Him Who taketh away the sins of the world."[1] Iniquity makes a fight against righteousness, blindness against light, falsehood against truth. But by means of the fierceness of opponents, and of the wickedness of cruel men, Jesus secured the carrying out of an eternal appointment, and so well provided for men by His own death, as not to deny even to His very persecutors the sacred gift[2] of salvation. For He Who had come to give to all believers pardon of all sins, willed not to exclude even Jewish guilt[3] from that universal forgiveness. And therefore while we detest their perfidy, we welcome their faith if they are converted; and, imitating the mercy of our Lord, Who prayed for those by whom He had been crucified, we also join our prayers with blessed Paul the Apostle, and desire that mercy may be obtained by that people, on account of whose "stumbling" we have received the grace of reconciliation: for, as the same

---

[1] S. John i. 29.   [2] "Sacramentum."
[3] See Note 94.

"teacher of the Gentiles" says, "God hath concluded all things in unbelief, that He may have mercy upon all."[1]

3. But what was that which both took away understanding from the Jews, and perturbed the hearts of the wise men of this world, save the Cross of Christ, which caused both the wisdom of philosophers to vanish, and the Israelitish teaching to become dark? For all the thoughts of the human mind were surpassed by the depth of the Divine counsel, when "it pleased God by the foolishness of preaching to save them that believed:"[2] that the very difficulty of believing might make a steadfast faith all the more marvellous. For it was thought illogical and irrational[3] to accept with one's mind the propositions, That the Creator of all natures had been brought forth in the substance of a true Man by a spotless Virgin; that the Son of God, equal to the Father, He Who filled all things, and held the universe in His grasp, had suffered Himself to be seized by the hands of infuriate men, to be condemned by the judgment of unjust men, and after shameful mockeries to be affixed to a Cross. But in all these events are present together the lowliness of man and the loftiness of Godhead; nor does this plan of mercy obscure the majesty of Him Who shows mercy; for ineffable power brought this to pass, that while true Man is in the inviolable God, and true God in the passible flesh, there should be bestowed on man glory through contumely, immortality through capital punishment, life through death. For unless the Word were made flesh, and so firm an union established between the two na-

[1] Rom. xi. 32. [2] 1 Cor. i. 21. [3] See Note 95.

tures, that not even the brief space of death could sever the assumed nature from the assuming one,[1] our mortal being would never have been able to return to life eternal. But in Christ we received a signal assistance indeed; in that the mortal condition was not permanent in that passible nature which the impassible essence had taken to itself; and through that which could not die, that which was dead could be raised to life.

4. In order that we may adhere immovably, dearly beloved, to this sacred fact,[2] we must strive with a great effort both of body and mind; seeing that while it is a very grievous offence to neglect the Paschal festival, it is more dangerous to take our place in Church assemblies while we are not numbered in the fellowship of our Lord's Passion. For since our Lord says, "He that taketh not up his cross, and followeth Me not, is not worthy of Me;"[3] and the Apostle, "If we suffer with Him, we shall also reign with Him;"[4] who does really honour Christ as having suffered, died, and been raised, save he who both suffers, and dies, and rises again with Christ?[5] And indeed in all the children of the Church, these events have already been begun in the very mystery of regeneration, wherein the death of sin is the life of the new-born, and the three days' death of the Lord is imitated by trine immersion;[6] so that, as if by the removal of a burial mound, those whom the bosom of the font received in their old state are brought forth in a new condition by the Baptismal water. But nevertheless,

---

[1] See Note 96.
[2] "Sacramento."
[3] S. Matt. x. 38.
[4] 2 Tim. ii. 12.
[5] See Serm. xiv. c. 3.
[6] See Note 97.

that which has been celebrated in a Sacrament must be fulfilled in practice;[1] and those who have been born of the Holy Spirit must not spend whatever remains to them of bodily life without a taking up of the Cross. For although the strong and cruel tyrant has had the vessels of his ancient plunder torn away from him,[2] through the power of the Cross of Christ, and the sovereignty of the prince of this world has been ejected from the bodies of the redeemed, yet does the same malignant one persist in plotting even against the justified, and in many ways attacks those in whom he does not reign: so that, if he finds any souls negligent and careless, he again entangles them in crueller snares, snatches them out of the paradise of the Church, and brings them into the partnership of his own condemnation. Therefore, when any one feels that he is overpassing the bounds fixed by Christian duty, and that his appetites are tending to what may make him go astray from the straight path, let him have recourse to the Cross of our Lord, and nail to the wood of life the motions of a pernicious will: let him cry out in the prophet's words to the Lord, and say, "Pierce my flesh with nails from the fear of Thee, for I have been afraid of Thy judgments."[3]

5. But what is it to have our flesh pierced with the nails of the fear of God, except to restrain our bodily senses from the allurements of unlawful desire under the fear of the Divine judgment? So that he who resists sin, and mortifies his lusts, that he may not do anything worthy of death, may venture to say with the Apostle, "But God forbid that I should

---
[1] See Note 98.   [2] See S. Luke xi. 21.
[3] Ps. cxviii. (our cxix.) 120, LXX.

glory, save in the Cross of our Lord Jesus Christ, by Whom the world has been crucified unto me, and I unto the world."[1] There, then, let the Christian station himself, where Christ lifted him up with Himself; and to that point let him direct all his life, where he knows that human nature was saved. For the Passion of our Lord is prolonged even to the end of the world: and as in His Saints He is honoured, He is loved, and in the poor He is fed, He is clothed,[2] so in all who suffer for righteousness' sake, He suffers too. Unless indeed we are to think that, since faith has been multiplied all over the world, and the number of the ungodly is diminishing, all persecutions, and all the conflicts which raged against the blessed Martyrs have come to an end; as though the necessity of taking up the Cross had been incumbent on those only, on whom the most atrocious punishments were inflicted in order to overcome their love for Christ. But very different is the experience of pious men who are serving God, and very different the witness borne by the Apostle's declaration, who says, "All who resolve to live piously in Christ Jesus, suffer persecution."[3] By which sentence, he is proved to be sadly lukewarm and indolent who is attacked by no persecution. For none but they who love the world can have peace with it; and there is no fellowship at any time between iniquity and righteousness, no concord of falsehood with truth, no agreement of darkness with light. For although the piety of good men desires bad men to be corrected, and obtains the conversion of many through the grace of a compas-

---

[1] Gal. vi. 14.   [2] See Note 99.
[3] 2 Tim. iii. 12.

sionate God, yet the plottings of malignant spirits against holy men are not at rest, and either by secret craft or open war they assail the purpose of a good will in all the faithful.[1] For to them everything is hostile which is right, everything which is holy; and while they are not free to do more against any one than is permitted by the Divine justice, which is pleased either to rebuke its servants by discipline or to train them by endurance, yet are they at work with the subtlest skill in deceiving, that they may seem to be hurting or sparing men at the good pleasure of their own power. And many—more is the pity—are so befooled by their wicked pretences, that certain persons are both afraid of encountering the hostility of the evil ones, and desirous of enjoying their favour; whereas the good offices of demons are more hurtful to all men than wounds, because it is safer for a man to have earned the devil's enmity than his friendship.[2] Therefore the wise souls, which have learned to fear one Lord, to love one, and to hope in one, have mortified their lusts and crucified their bodily senses, and do not stoop either to dread their foes, or to do them homage. For they prefer God's will even to themselves, and love themselves all the better inasmuch as for the love of God they love themselves *not*. And when they hear it said to them from God, "Go not after thy lusts, and turn away from thy will,"[3] they make a division of their feelings, and distinguish between "the law of the mind"[4] and the law of the body; that they may in certain points deny themselves, losing themselves in regard to what they desire accord-

[1] See Serm. vi. c. 2.
[2] Ecclus. xviii. 30.
[3] See Note 100.
[4] Rom. vii. 23.

ing to the flesh, and finding themselves in regard to what they long for in the spirit.

6. It is, then, dearly beloved, in such members of Christ's body that the holy *Pasch*[1] is lawfully celebrated: and nothing is wanting to those triumphs which our Saviour's Passion has obtained. For in those who, after the Apostle's example, "chastise their body, and subject it to servitude,"[2] the same enemies are being crushed by the same courage, and even now is the world being overcome by Christ. For when the incentives to any vices whatever are conquered by His servants, the strength and the victory belong to Himself.

These things, dearly beloved, which pertain to our fellowship in the Cross, have been, I think, sufficiently imparted to your ears to-day; that the sacred Paschal rite may be lawfully celebrated even in the members of Christ's body. It remains for us to discourse on the mode of gaining a share in the Resurrection. But, lest a prolongation of my sermon should be onerous both to myself and to you, we will defer what we have promised until the Sabbath day.[3] God's grace, we believe, will be present, that our debt may be discharged by His own assistance, Who liveth and reigneth with the Father and the Holy Spirit, for ever and ever. Amen.

[1] See Note 101. [2] 1 Cor. ix. 27. [3] See Note 102.

SERMON XIII.

EASTER.

SERM. 71. De Resurrectione Domini, I. Preached on Holy Saturday, in the Vigil of Easter. *Sermone.*

IN our last sermon, dearly beloved, we brought before you—not inappropriately, I think—the duty of partaking in the Cross of Christ; that the actual life of believers may have within itself a Paschal solemnity,[1] and that what is honoured in the festival may be celebrated in the conduct. And you yourselves have found on trial how useful this is, and have learned from your own devotion how much good is done to minds and bodies by lengthened fasts, more frequent prayers, and more abundant almsgiving. For there is hardly any one who has not made progress in this exercise, and laid up in the secret chamber of his conscience something in which he can rightfully rejoice. But these gains have to be kept by persevering watchfulness, lest, after effort has subsided into indolence, the devil's envy should steal away what the grace of God has bestowed. Since, then, this was what we wished to effect by the observance of the forty days, that we might feel somewhat of the Cross at the time of our Lord's Passion,[2] we must exert ourselves, that we also may be partakers of Christ's Resurrection, and even while we are in this body may pass from death unto life. For to every man who by

---

[1] "Sacramentum."   [2] See Note 103.

some kind of conversion is changed from one thing to another, not to be what he was is an ending, and to be what he was not is a beginning. But it makes a difference, to *what* a man either dies or lives; for there is a death which is a cause of living, and there is a life which is a cause of dying. And nowhere but in this transitory world are both these things sought after; and on the character of acts done in time depend the differences of eternal retributions. We must, then, die to the devil and live to God; we must have no strength left for iniquity, that we may rise again unto righteousness. Let old things sink down, that new may spring up. And since, as the Truth says, "No man can serve two masters,"[1] let our master be, not he that has hurled to ruin those who were standing up, but He that raised up to glory those who were cast down.

2. Since, then, the Apostle says, "The first man is of the earth, earthy; the second man is from heaven, heavenly; as is the earthy, such are they also that are earthy; and as is the heavenly, such are they also that are heavenly; as we have borne the image of the earthy, let us also bear the image of Him Who is from heaven:"[2] we ought greatly to rejoice in this change, whereby we are transferred from earthly meanness to heavenly dignity, through the ineffable mercy of Him Who, in order to advance us to what was His, descended into what was ours; that He might assume, not only the substance, but even the liability of the sinning nature, and Divine impassibility might allow those things to be inflicted on itself, of which human mortality has such miserable experience.

[1] S. Matt. vi. 24.   [2] See Note 104.

Wherefore, lest the troubled minds of the disciples should be tortured by a lengthened grief, He shortened with such wonderful quickness the predicted waiting-time of three days, that by a combination of the last part of the first day and the first part of the third with the whole of the second, some little time might be taken out of the period, while the number of the days remained the same. Accordingly, the Resurrection of our Saviour kept neither His soul waiting long in Hades, nor His flesh in the sepulchre; for the Godhead, which departed not from either portion of the substance of the assumed Manhood,[1] united by its power what by its power it had divided.

3. There followed, therefore, many proofs on which was to be founded the authority of the faith that was to be preached throughout the whole world. And although the rolling away of the stone, the evacuation of the sepulchre, the laying aside of the linen, and the angelic narrators of the whole fact, did abundantly establish the reality of our Lord's Resurrection, yet He manifestly appeared to the sight of the women, and frequently to the eyes of the Apostles; not only talking with them, but also abiding and eating with them, and suffering Himself to be handled with careful and inquisitive touch by those of whom doubt was taking hold. For it was with this intent that He entered in to His disciples when the doors were shut,[2] and gave the Holy Spirit by His breath; and having given them the light of intelligence, opened to them the secrets of Holy Scripture, and again Himself showed the wound in the side, the

---

[1] See Serm. xii. c. 3.   [2] See Note 105.

prints of the nails, and all the signs of His most recent Passion, that the natures of God and Man might be acknowledged to remain in Him distinct, yet without division,[1] and we might in such sense know that the Word is not the same as the flesh, as to confess that the One Son of God is both the Word and the flesh.[2]

4. The Apostle Paul, the " teacher of the Gentiles," dearly beloved, is not out of harmony with this faith, when he says, "Although we have known Christ after the flesh, yet now henceforth know we Him no more."[3] For our Lord's Resurrection was not the end of His flesh, but its change ; nor was its essence consumed by the increase of its power. It was the quality that passed away, not the nature that failed ; and that Body which could be crucified became impassible, that which could be killed became immortal, that which could be wounded became incorruptible. And with good reason is Christ's flesh said not to be known in that state in which it had been known ; for there remained in it nothing passible, nothing weak, so that it might be itself in respect to its essence, and not be itself by means of glory. And what wonder if he declares this concerning the Body of Christ, since he says of all spiritual Christians, "Therefore henceforth we know no man after the flesh." To us, he says, a beginning was made of resurrection in Christ from the moment at which, in Him Who died for all, the type of all our hopes passed on before. We do not hesitate in distrust ; we are not in suspense through doubtful expectation ; but, having received the beginning of the promise, we see already by the eyes of

[1] See Note 106.   [2] Ep. xxviii. 5.   [3] See Note 107.

faith what is to come; and, rejoicing in the promotion of our nature, we already have possession of what we believe.

5. Let us not, then, be occupied with the appearances of temporal things, nor let what is earthly turn our gaze toward itself, away from what is heavenly. Let those things be considered as over and done with, which for the most part are already no more; and let the mind, intent on what is to abide, there fix its desire where what is offered is eternal.[1] For although it is "by hope that we have been saved,"[2] and as yet we carry the corruptible and mortal flesh, yet are we rightly said "not to be in the flesh," if fleshly feelings have no dominion over us;[3] and deservedly do we cease to be named after that thing, the will of which we do not follow. When, then, the Apostle says, "Make not provision for the flesh in its desires,"[4] we do not understand that we are interdicted from those desires which agree with our health, and are demanded by human infirmity. But because we must not obey all desires, nor perform everything that the flesh craves for, we know ourselves to be admonished about the duty of observing the measure of temperance, so as neither to grant what is superfluous, nor deny what is necessary, to that flesh over which the mind is set as a judge. Wherefore the same Apostle elsewhere says, "For no one ever hated his own flesh, but nourishes and cherishes it;"[5] for in truth it is not for viciousness nor for luxury, but for the service which it owes, that it must be supported and cherished: that the renewed nature may keep its own

[1] See Note 108.   [2] Rom. viii. 24.   [3] Ib. 9.
[4] Rom. xiii. 14.   [5] Eph. v. 29.

order; that the lower elements may not perversely and shamefully predominate over the higher, nor the higher succumb to the lower, and through the victory of vices over the mind, servitude take place where sovereignty ought to be.

6. Let, then, the people of God acknowledge themselves to be a new creation in Christ Jesus, and, with souls on the watch, understand by Whom they have been assumed, and Whom they have assumed. Let not the things which have been made new return to the old state which abides not: and let not him "that has put his hand to the plough"[1] give up his work, but fix his attention on what he is sowing, not look back to what he has left. Let no one fall back into the condition whence he rose; but even if through bodily infirmity he still lies sick of some ailments, let him earnestly long to be cured and relieved. For this is the way of salvation, and the imitation of the Resurrection begun in Christ: that since, in the slippery path of this life, divers accidents and falls are not wanting, the steps of the walkers may be transferred from watery places to firm ground. For, as Scripture says, "The steps of a man are ordered by the Lord, and He will delight in his way. When the just man falls, he shall not be overthrown; for the Lord will support him with His hand."[2] This thought, dearly beloved, is to be kept in mind, not for the Paschal solemnity alone, but for the sanctification of our whole life;[3] and to this object ought our present exercise to be directed, that the things which have delighted the minds of the faithful by the experience of a short observance, may pass into habit, may remain invio-

---

[1] S. Luke ix. 62.   [2] Ps. xxxvii. 23.   [3] See Note 109.

late ; and that, if any fault has crept in, it may be destroyed by swift repentance. And since the curing of old diseases is a difficult and tardy process, the fresher our wounds are, let us be quicker in applying remedies; that, continually rising up from all collisions into a sound state, we may be enabled to attain that incorruptible Resurrection, wherein our flesh is to be glorified in Christ Jesus our Lord, Who liveth and reigneth with the Father and the Holy Spirit, for ever and ever. Amen.

SERMON XIV.

EASTER.

SERM. 72. De Resurrectione Domini, II. *Totum*.

THE whole of the sacred Paschal event, dearly beloved, has been presented to us by the Gospel narrative; and our mental hearing has been so well reached through the ear of the flesh, that every one of us can picture to himself the events which occurred. For the context of the Divinely-inspired history has evidently shown us by what impiety our Lord Jesus Christ was betrayed, by what judgment He was condemned, by what cruelty He was crucified, and by what glory He was raised. But we must also add the discourse which is due from us; that as I am conscious that you are asking again, in devout expectation, for the discharge of my usual debt, so the exhortation of the priest[1] may be subjoined to that solemn

[1] See Note 110.

and most sacred reading. Since, therefore, there is no place for ignorance in faithful ears, the seed of the Word, which consists in the preaching of the Gospel, ought to grow in the soil of your heart, that the removal of those thorns and briars which would choke it may give freedom for the plants of devout thought and the shoots of right desire to spring up and bear their fruit. For the Cross of Christ, which was freely endured for the sake of mankind's salvation, is both a mystery and an example:[1] a mystery whereby the power of God is fulfilled, an example whereby the devotion of man is excited. For to men rescued from captivity their redemption grants this further boon, that they may be able to imitate and follow it. For if the wisdom of this world glories so much in its own wanderings, that every one follows the opinions, the conduct, and all the teachings of whomsoever he has chosen for his guide, what fellowship shall we have with the Name of Christ, except that of being inseparably united to Him Who is, as He Himself informed us, "the Way, and the Truth, and the Life,"[2] —that is, the Way of holy living, the Truth of Divine doctrine, and the Life of everlasting blessedness?

2. For when the whole mass of mankind had fallen in its first parents,[3] the merciful God willed in such sort to give aid, through His only-begotten Son Jesus Christ, to the creatures made in His own image, that the restoration of their nature should not be external to that nature, and their second state should be advanced beyond the dignity of their own origin.[4] Happy, if they had not fallen from what God made; but

[1] See Serm. ix. c. 4.
[2] See Note 111.
[3] See Serm. x. c. 2.
[4] See Rom. v. 15.

happier, if they remain in what He re-made! It was much to have received a form from Christ, but it is more to have a substance in Christ.[1] For we were taken up into its own life by that Nature which bends itself to what measures of benignity it chooses, without anywhere incurring the alteration which belongs to changeableness:[2] we were taken up by that Nature which would neither consume what was its own by what was ours, nor ours by its own; which in such sort made, in itself, one Person of Godhead and Manhood,[3] that by due arrangement of infirmities and of powers, neither could the flesh be inviolable by means of the Godhead, nor the Godhead passible by means of the flesh. We were taken up by that Nature which would not break off the shoot of our race from the common line, while at the same time it would bar out the contagion of that sin which passes into all men.[4] Infirmity, it is true, and mortality, which were not sin, but the punishment of sin, were received by the Redeemer of the world, with a view to punishment, that they might be bestowed with a view to ransom. Hence, that which in all men was a transmission of condemnation, is in Christ a mystery[5] of loving kindness. For He, being free from debt, offered Himself to that most cruel creditor,[6] and permitted Jewish hands, doing the devil's service, to torture His immaculate flesh. And it was for this end that He willed His flesh to be mortal up to the Resurrection, that believers in Him might find that persecution could not be invincible, nor death terrible; since, as their fellow-

[1] See Note 112.
[2] See Ep. xxviii. c. 3.
[3] See Serm. ii. c. 1.
[4] Serm. i. c. 1 : x. c. 2.
[5] "Sacramentum."
[6] See Serm. viii. c. 3.

ship in His nature was beyond a doubt, so should be their partaking of His glory.

3. If, then, dearly beloved, we unhesitatingly believe in our hearts what we profess with our lips, then in Christ have we been crucified, have died, have been buried, have also been raised the third day. Whence the Apostle says, "If ye have risen together with Christ, seek those things which are above, where Christ is sitting on the right hand of God. Set your affections on things above, not on things on the earth. For ye are dead, and your life is hid with Christ in God. For when Christ, your Life, shall appear, then shall ye also appear with Him in glory."[1] But that the hearts of the faithful may know that they have that by which they can be raised up to heavenly wisdom, after having despised worldly lusts, our Lord pledges to us His presence, saying, "Behold, I am with you all days, even unto the end of the world."[2] For not in vain had the Holy Spirit said by Isaiah, "Behold, a Virgin shall conceive and bear a Son, and they shall call His Name Emmanuel, which is, being interpreted, God with us."[3] Jesus, then, is fulfilling what properly belongs to His own Name, and He Who ascended into heaven does not forsake His adopted ones.[4] He Who sits at the Father's right hand is the same Who dwells in His whole body; and He Himself strengthens us for patience here below, Who invites us to glory above.

4. We must, therefore, neither play the fool's part among vanities, nor the coward's amid adversities. On one hand deceits flatter us, on the other labours

---

[1] Col. iii. 1—4.　　[2] S. Matt. xxviii. 20.
[3] Isa. vii. 14; S. Matt. i. 23.　　[4] See Note 113.

become heavier. But since "the whole earth is full of the Lord's mercy,"[1] the victory of Christ is ever present with us, that His words may be fulfilled, "Fear not, for I have overcome the world."[2] Whether, then, we are fighting against worldly ambition, or the lusts of the flesh, or the darts of heretics, let us always be armed with the Cross of our Lord. For we do not at any time withdraw from the Paschal feast, if in the sincerity of truth[3] we abstain from the leaven of the old malice. For amid all the changes of this life, which are full of manifold sufferings, we ought to remember the Apostle's exhortation, whereby he instructs us, saying, "Let this mind be in you, which was also in Christ Jesus; Who, being in the form of God, thought it not robbery to be equal with God, but emptied Himself, taking the form of a servant, made in the likeness of men; and found in fashion as a man, He humbled Himself, being made obedient even unto death, and that the death of the Cross. Wherefore God also hath exalted Him, and given Him a Name which is above every name, that in the Name of Jesus every knee should bow, of things in heaven, on earth, and under the earth; and that every tongue should confess that the Lord Jesus Christ is in the glory of God the Father."[4] If, he means, you understand the mystery of great lovingkindness, and attend to what the only-begotten Son of God performed for the salvation of mankind, let this mind be in you which was also in Christ Jesus, Whose lowliness no rich man may despise, no high-born man be ashamed of. For no human felicity, of whatsoever

---

[1] Ps. xxxiii. 5.
[2] S. John xvi. 33.
[3] See Note 114.
[4] Phil. ii. 5—11.

kind, can be advanced to so high a pinnacle, as to think that it has a right to be ashamed of Him Who, continuing to be God, in the form of God, did not think it beneath Him to assume the form of a servant.

5. Do you imitate what He wrought, love what He loved, and, when you find the grace of God in yourselves, love your own nature again in Him. For as He lost not His riches by becoming poor, diminished not His glory by His humiliation, lost not His eternity by His death,[1] so do you also, by the same steps and the same footprints, despise earthly things that you may take hold of things heavenly. For the taking up of the Cross is the putting to death of lusts, the killing of vices, the avoidance of vanity, and the renunciation of every error. For while the immodest, the lustful, the proud cannot celebrate the Lord's Pasch, yet none are more widely separated from this festival than heretics, and above all, those who think wrongly of the Incarnation of the Word, either by diminishing what belongs to the Godhead, or making void what belongs to the flesh. For the Son of God is very God, having from the Father the whole of the Father's being, not subject to time by any beginning, nor to change by any variation;[2] neither divided from the One, nor different from the Almighty, the everlasting Only-begotten of the everlasting Father.[3] And the faithful mind, believing in the Father, and the Son, and the Holy Spirit, must not, in regard to that same essence of one Godhead, either divide the Unity by introducing degrees,[4] or confound the Trinity by

---

[1] See Ep. xxviii. c. 3.
[2] See Note 115.
[3] See Serm. iv. c. 1.
[4] See Note 116.

reducing it to singleness. But it is not sufficient to know the Son of God as in the Father's nature only, unless we recognise Him as in what is ours, while He departs not from what is His. For that "emptying," which He bestowed on the work of man's restoration, was a dispensation of mercy, not a privation of power.[1] For since moreover, from the eternal counsel of God, there was "no other name under heaven given unto men, in which they must be saved,"[2] the Invisible made the visible substance His own, the Timeless the temporal, the Impassible the passible: not that strength should give way amid weakness, but that weakness might be able to pass into strength indestructible.

6. On this account the same festival which is by us called Pasch, is named among the Hebrews *Phase*, that is, *passing-over*, as the Evangelist bears witness and says, "Before the feast of Pasch, Jesus knowing that His hour was come, that He should pass[3] out of this world unto the Father." Now to what nature could that future "passing-over" belong save to ours, since the Father was inseparably in the Son, and the Son in the Father? But since the Word and the flesh are one Person, the assumed is not divided from the assumer, and the honour of being promoted is called a dignifying of the promoter, as the Apostle says in the words just mentioned; "Wherefore God also exalted Him, and gave Him a Name which is above every Name." In which place certainly it is the assumed manhood[4] whose exaltation is set before us; that the same amid whose sufferings the Godhead

---

[1] See Serm. ii. c. 2; Ep. xxviii. c. 3.
[2] Acts iv. 12.
[3] μεταβῇ, S. John xiii. 1.
[4] "Hominis."

remains inseparable, should be coeternal in the glory of the Godhead. In order to this partaking in an ineffable gift, our Lord was Himself preparing for His faithful ones a blessed "passing-over," when, being now close to His approaching Passion, He prayed not only for His Apostles and disciples, but also for the universal Church, and said, " But I am not asking on behalf of these alone, but of them also who shall believe in Me through their word: that they all may be one, as Thou, Father, art in Me, and I in Thee, that they also may be one in Us."[1]

7. Of which unity those will be unable to have any share, who deny the human nature to remain in the Son of God, Who is very God,—assailants of the mystery of salvation, and exiles from the Paschal feast, which they cannot celebrate with us, because they dissent from the Gospel and contradict the Creed.[2] For although they dare to use the Christian name, yet are they repelled by that whole creation which has Christ for its Head; whereas you are with good right exulting, and piously rejoicing in this solemnity, while you accept no falsehood amid the truth, nor are doubtful about Christ's Nativity in the flesh, nor about His Passion and Death, nor about His bodily Resurrection; seeing that you recognise, without any severance of Godhead, a true Christ from the Virgin's womb, a true Christ on the wood of the Cross, a true Christ in the body's sepulchre, a true Christ in the glory of the Resurrection, a true Christ on the right hand of the Father's majesty: "from whence also," as the Apostle says, "we look for the Saviour, our Lord Jesus Christ, Who shall refashion

---

[1] S. John xvii. 21.   [2] See Ep. xxviii. 2.

the body of our lowliness, to become conformed to the body of His glory,"[1] Who liveth and reigneth with the Father and the Holy Spirit for ever and ever. Amen.

SERMON XV.

ASCENSION.

SERM. 73. De Ascensione Domini, I. *Post beatam.*

AFTER the blessed and glorious Resurrection of our Lord Jesus Christ, wherein by Divine power He "raised up in three days" the true Temple of God, which the impious Jews had destroyed, there was this day fulfilled, dearly beloved, that number of forty holy days which had been ordained by a most sacred appointment, and spent in giving us profitable instruction, that while the tarrying of our Lord's corporeal presence is extended by Him to this space, our faith in His Resurrection might be fortified by necessary proofs. For the death of Christ had sorely disturbed the hearts of the disciples, and a kind of torpor of distrust had crept into minds oppressed by sorrow on account of the punishment of the Cross, the yielding up of the spirit, and the burial of the lifeless body. For when the holy women, as the Gospel history has made clear, announced that the stone was rolled away from the tomb, that the body was not in the sepulchre, and that Angels bore testimony that the Lord was alive, their words seemed

[1] Phil. iii. 21.

to the Apostles and disciples to be like "idle tales." And surely this uncertainty, wherein human weakness was wavering, would in no wise have been allowed by the Spirit of truth to exist in the hearts of His preachers, unless the trembling anxiety and inquiring hesitation had laid the foundations of our faith. It was then for our perturbations and for our dangers that provision was being made in the case of the Apostles; we, in those men, were being instructed against the calumnies of the impious and against the arguments of this world's wisdom. We have been taught by their seeing, we have been informed by their hearing, we have been confirmed by their touching. Let us give thanks to the Divine providence, and to that necessary tardiness of our holy fathers. Doubts were felt by them, that no doubts might be felt by us.[1]

2. Those days, then, dearly beloved, which elapsed between the Resurrection and Ascension of our Lord, did not pass away in an inactive course: but in them great and sacred truths were confirmed, great mysteries were revealed. In them is taken away the fear of terrible death, and the immortality not only of the soul, but also of the flesh, is displayed. In them, by means of the Lord's breathing, the Holy Spirit is poured into all the Apostles; and to the blessed Apostle Peter above the rest,[2] after the keys of the kingdom, is entrusted the care of the Lord's flock. In these days, when two disciples are on their road, the Lord associates Himself as a third with them;[3] and in order to clear away all the darkness of

[1] See Note 117. [2] See Serm. viii. c. 2.
[3] S. Luke xxiv. 15.

our uncertainty, the tardiness of those who are quailing and trembling is rebuked. Illuminated hearts receive the flame of faith, and, having been lukewarm, are made to burn while the Lord is "opening the Scriptures." Moreover, "in the breaking of bread the eyes" of those who sit at meat with Him are "opened:" and far happier for them is that opening, whereby the glorification of their nature was displayed to them, than that which befell those first parents of ours, on whom was heaped the confusion of their own transgression.

3. But among these and other miracles, when the disciples were tossed by restless thoughts, and the Lord had appeared in the midst of them and said, "Peace be unto you,"[1] lest that which was floating in their minds should become a permanent opinion,—for they "supposed that they saw a spirit" and not flesh,—He confutes those thoughts which were discordant with the truth, presents to their eyes, amid their doubtings, the marks of the cross abiding in His hands and feet, and invites them to "handle" Him carefully:[2] for to heal the wounds of unbelieving hearts, the traces of the nails and spear were retained, that they might hold fast, not by a doubtful faith, but by a most assured knowledge, the truth that the nature which had lain in the sepulchre would be seated with God the Father on the throne.

4. So, then, through all this period, dearly beloved, which intervened between our Lord's Resurrection and His Ascension, what God's providence was providing for, what it was teaching, what it was bringing home to His servants' eyes as well as hearts was

[1] S. Luke xxiv. 36; S. John xx. 19.   [2] S. Luke xxiv. 39.

this,—that the Lord Jesus Christ, Who was truly born, and suffered, and died, was to be acknowledged as truly raised again. Whence the most blessed Apostles, and all the disciples, who had been both trembling at the result of the crucifixion, and doubtful as to belief in the Resurrection, were so invigorated by the clear vision of the truth, that when the Lord was going up to the height of heaven, they were not only not affected by any sadness, but even filled with a "great joy."[1] And a truly great and ineffable cause of rejoicing it was, when in the presence of a holy multitude the nature of mankind was ascending above the dignity of all celestial creatures, to pass above the Angelic ranks, and to be elevated above the high seats of Archangels, and not to let any degree of loftiness be a limit to its advancement, until it should be received to sit down with the Eternal Father, and associated in the throne with His glory, to Whose nature it was coupled in the Son! Since, then, Christ's Ascension is *our* advancement, and whither the glory of the Head has gone before,[2] thither is the hope of the body summoned, let us, dearly beloved, exult with befitting joys, and rejoice with devout thanksgiving. For to-day have we not only been confirmed in the possession of Paradise, but in Christ have even penetrated the heights of heaven, having won, through the ineffable grace of Christ, richer gifts than we had lost through the devil's envy.[3] For those whom the venomous enemy cast down from the happiness of their first habitation, has the Son of God made of one body with Himself,

---

[1] S. Luke xxiv. 52.   [2] See Note 118.
[3] Cp. Serm. xiv. c. 2.

and placed at the Father's right hand, with Whom He liveth and reigneth, in the unity of the Holy Spirit, God, through all eternity. Amen.

SERMON XVI.

ASCENSION.

SERM. 74. De Ascensione Domini, II. *Sacramentum.*

THE sacred work,[1] beloved, of our salvation, of that salvation which the Maker of the universe valued at the price of His own Blood, was fulfilled, from the day of His corporeal birth even to the issue of His Passion, by means of an economy of humiliation. And although even in "the form of a servant" there gleamed forth many a token of His Godhead, yet properly speaking, His course of action at that time was concerned with proving the reality of the Manhood which He had assumed. But after the Passion, when the bonds of that death were broken, which had exposed its own strength by going to attack Him Who knew no sin, infirmity was turned into that strength, mortality into that eternity, and contumely into that glory, which the Lord Jesus Christ, by "many and manifest proofs,"[2] made clear to the eyes of many, until He carried on into heaven that victorious triumph which He had won over death. As, then, in the Paschal solemnity our Lord's Resurrection was our cause of rejoicing,

---

[1] "Sacramentum."   [2] Acts i. 3.

so is His Ascension into heaven the groundwork of our present joys, while we recall and duly venerate that day, whereon our lowly nature was in Christ advanced above all the host of heaven, above all the ranks of Angels, and beyond the height of all Powers, to sit down with God the Father. By which order of Divine works we have been placed on a sure basis, we have been built up; that the grace of God might become more wonderful, when after the removal from men's sight of the things which were justly felt to claim reverence for themselves, faith did not lose confidence, hope did not fluctuate, love did not wax lukewarm. For in this consists the vigour of great minds, and in this the light of thoroughly faithful souls, unhesitatingly to believe what is not seen by bodily discernment, and to fix the affections on a point to which one cannot raise one's eyes. But whence could this piety spring up in our hearts, or how could any one be justified by faith, if our salvation were centred in those things only which were subject to our gaze? Wherefore also to that man who seemed to be doubtful about Christ's Resurrection, unless he could explore both by sight and touch the traces of the Passion of Christ's own flesh, our Lord said, "Because thou hast seen Me, thou hast believed; blessed are they that have not seen, and yet have believed."[1]

2. Therefore that we, dearly beloved, might be able to take in this blessedness, after all things had been fulfilled which were appropriate to the preaching of the Gospel and the mysteries of the New Testament, our Lord Jesus Christ, being elevated into heaven in

[1] S. John xx. 29.

the presence of His disciples on the fortieth day after His Resurrection, put an end to His corporal Presence,[1] as He was to remain at the Father's right hand until the times Divinely ordained for the multiplying of the Church's children have been completed, and He comes, in the same flesh wherein He ascended, to judge the quick and the dead. Accordingly, that presence of our Redeemer which could be gazed upon was superseded by what was mysterious; and, that faith might be the loftier and firmer, sight was succeeded by doctrine, the authority of which might be followed by believing hearts, illumined by rays from on high.

3. This faith, increased by our Lord's Ascension, and strengthened by the gift of the Holy Spirit, has not been overawed by chains, nor imprisonments, nor banishments, nor famine, nor the sword, nor the teeth of wild beasts, nor punishments invented by the cruelty of persecutors. For this faith, throughout the whole world, not only men, but even women, not only young boys, but even tender maidens, contended even to the shedding of their own blood.[2] This faith has cast out demons, driven away sicknesses, raised the dead. Hence also the blessed Apostles themselves, who, although confirmed by so many miracles, instructed by so many discourses, had yet been scared by the horrors of the Lord's Passion, and had not received without hesitation the truth of His Resurrection, profited so greatly by the Lord's Ascension, that whatever before had caused them fear was turned into joy. For they had lifted up their souls to contemplate fixedly the Divinity of Him that was sitting at the Father's right hand; nor

[1] See Note 119. [2] See Note 120.

were they any longer hindered by the interposition of bodily vision from directing the glance of the mind to that which had neither, in descending, been absent from the Father,[1] nor, in ascending, withdrawn from the disciples.

4. Accordingly, then it was, dearly beloved, that the Son of Man became known as the Son of God in a more transcendent and sacred way, when He betook Himself to the glory of the Father's majesty, and in an ineffable manner began to be more present in His Divinity, when He became farther off in His Humanity. Then did a more instructed faith begin to approach, by the steps of the mind, to the Son as equal to the Father, and not to need any handling of the corporeal substance in Christ, wherein He is inferior to the Father.[2] For, while the nature of the glorified body remained, thither was the faith of believers summoned, where the Only-begotten, equal to the Begetter, might be touched, not by a hand of flesh, but by spiritual understanding. Hence comes that saying of our Lord, after His Resurrection, to Mary Magdalene, when she, representing the Church, was hastening to draw near to touch Him; "Touch Me not, for I am not yet ascended to My Father;"[3] that is, "I will not have thee come to Me corporeally, nor recognise Me by the sensations of the flesh. I am putting thee off to something loftier, I am preparing for thee something greater. When I shall have ascended to My Father, then shalt thou handle Me more perfectly and more truly, being about to apprehend what thou touchest not, and to believe what

---

[1] See Serm. xviii. c. 5.   [2] See Serm. ii. c. 2.
[3] S. John xx. 17. See Note 121.

thou seest not." And when, as the Lord was ascending into heaven, the disciples' eyes were gazing at and following Him with rapt admiration, there stood by them two Angels in garments glittering with a marvellous whiteness, "who also said, Ye men of Galilee, why stand ye gazing into heaven? This Jesus, Who has been taken up from you into heaven, shall so come in like manner as ye have seen Him go into heaven."[1] By which words all the children of the Church were taught that they must believe that Jesus Christ would come visibly in the same flesh wherein He had ascended; and that there could be no doubt of all things being subject to Him Who, from the very beginning of His corporeal birth, had been served by the attendance of Angels. For as it was an Angel who announced to the Blessed Virgin that Christ was to be conceived of the Holy Spirit, so too it was the voice of the heavenly ones that proclaimed Him to the shepherds as born of the Virgin. As the first testimonies, which told that He had risen from the dead, were those of messengers from on high, so it was the services of Angels which proclaimed that He would come in that very flesh to judge the world: that we might understand what mighty Powers will be present with Him when He comes to judge, seeing that such mighty ones ministered to Him even when He came to be judged.

5. Let us then exult, dearly beloved, with spiritual joy, and rejoicing before God with meet thanksgiving, let us freely lift up the eyes of our heart to that height on which Christ is. Let not earthly desires depress the minds that are called upwards;[2] let not perishing

[1] Acts i. 11.   [2] See Note 122.

things occupy those that are chosen beforehand to things eternal; let not deceitful allurements retard those that have entered on the way of truth; and let the faithful so pass through these temporal things, as to know that they are but pilgrims in this world's valley,[1] wherein, even if some conveniences may try to allure us, we must not be so poor-spirited as to embrace them, but brave enough to pass them by. For to this devotedness does the most blessed Apostle Peter incite us; and according to that love which, by his triple profession of love for the Lord, he conceived for feeding the Lord's sheep, he entreats us, saying, "Dearly beloved, I beseech you as strangers and pilgrims, to abstain from fleshly lusts, which war against the soul."[2] And in whose cause do fleshly pleasures make war, save in the devil's, who, when souls are aiming at things above, is glad if he can bind them with the delights of corruptible goods, and lead them away from those seats whence he himself fell? And against his plots every faithful man ought to be wisely on the watch, that he may strike down his enemy from that part which is being attacked. Now nothing is more effectual, dearly beloved, against the wiles of the devil, than a kindly compassion and a bounteous charity, by means of which every sin is either avoided or conquered. But this exalted virtue is not attained until that which is adverse to it is overthrown. Now, what is so hostile to mercy and to works of charity as covetousness, from the root of which shoots up the germ of all evils? And unless it is killed in that which feeds it, it is inevitable that in the soil of that heart, wherein the plant of this evil has gathered

---

[1] See Note 123.   [2] 1 S. Pet. ii. 11.

strength, the thorns and briars of vices should spring up rather than any seed of true virtue. Let us, therefore, dearly beloved, resist this most pestilent evil, and follow after charity, without which no virtue can shine; that through this way of love, whereby Christ descended to us, we also may be able to ascend to Him, to Whom, with God the Father and the Holy Spirit, belong honour and glory for ever and ever. Amen.

SERMON XVII.

WHITSUNTIDE.

SERM. 75. De Pentecoste, I. *Hodiernam.*

THAT this day's solemnity, dearly beloved, is to be venerated among our chiefest festivals, the hearts of all Catholics well know; nor is there any doubt of the amount of reverence due to this day, which the Holy Spirit consecrated by that transcendent miracle of His own bounty. For from that day on which our Lord ascended above the height of all heavens to sit on the right hand of God the Father, this day is the tenth, which, being the fiftieth from His Resurrection, has dawned upon us, on that very day from which it took its origin, containing in itself great mysteries, which belong to sacred facts both old and new; whereby it is most clearly shown that grace was heralded by the Law, and the Law was fulfilled by grace. For as, after the Hebrew people had in old time been delivered from the Egyptians, on the fiftieth day after the sacrificing of the lamb the Law was given on Mount Sinai; so after the Passion of Christ, wherein the true Lamb of God was slain, on the fiftieth day from His Resurrection the Holy Spirit descended on the Apostles and on the believing people: so that the thoughtful Christian may readily acknowledge that the beginnings of the Old Testament were subservient to the outset of the Gospel, and that the second covenant was established by the same Spirit by Whom the first had been ordained.

2. For, as the Apostolic history testifies, "when the days of the Pentecost were completed, and the disciples were all together in the same place, there came suddenly from heaven a sound as of a vehement wind approaching, and it filled the whole house where they were sitting. And there appeared to them, distributed, tongues as of fire,[1] and it sat upon each of them. And they were all filled with the Holy Spirit, and began to speak with other tongues, as the Holy Spirit was giving them utterance."[2] O how rapid is the discourse of wisdom! and where God is the Master, how soon is that learned which is taught! No interpretation was added that they might hear better; they were not familiarised with the words in order to use them, nor had they time given them for study; but by the Spirit of truth "blowing where He willed,"[3] the peculiar languages of the several nations were made common in the mouth of the Church.[4] It was, then, from this day that the trumpet of the preaching of the Gospel gave forth its sound; it was

---

[1] See Note 124.
[2] Acts ii. 1—4.
[3] S. John iii. 8.
[4] See Note 125.

from this day that showers of spiritual gifts,[1] streams of blessings, watered every desert and all the dry ground, for "the Spirit of God was being borne over the waters"[2] in order to "renew the face of the earth;"[3] and new flashes of light were beaming forth to drive away the old darkness, seeing that by the splendour of the radiant tongues was being received that lustrous Word of the Lord, that fiery utterance, wherein were present an illuminating energy and a burning force, to create intelligence and to consume sin.

3. But although, dearly beloved, the appearance of the event was indeed wonderful, nor can it be doubted that, in that exultant choir of all human tongues, the majesty of the Holy Spirit was present, yet let no one fancy that in what was seen by bodily eyes His Divine substance showed itself. For His invisible nature, which He shares with the Father and the Son, did exhibit, by such a manifestation as it pleased, the character of its own gift and work. But it retained within its Divinity that which belonged to its own essence; for as the Father and the Son, so also the Holy Spirit is inaccessible to human eyesight. For in the Divine Trinity there is nothing dissimilar, nothing unequal; and all that can be thought of as pertaining to that substance, admits of no difference in respect to power, glory, and eternity.[4] And while in regard to the distinctness of Person, the Father is one, the Son is another, the Holy Spirit another, yet it is not another Godhead nor a different nature: seeing that, while the Only-begotten Son also is from the Father, the Holy Spirit likewise is the Spirit of

---

[1] "Charismatum." [2] Gen. i. 2.
[3] Ps. civ. 30. [4] See Serm. ii. c. 2.

the Father and of the Son, not like any creature whatsoever, which is the creature of the Father and of the Son, but as living and mighty together with Both, and eternally subsisting from that which the Father and Son are.[1] Wherefore, when our Lord, before the day of His Passion, was guaranteeing to His disciples the coming of the Holy Spirit, " I have yet," said He, "many things to say to you, but you cannot bear them now. Howbeit, when He, the Spirit of truth, is come, He will guide you into all truth. For He will not speak from Himself, but whatever He will hear, He will speak, and will announce to you things to come. All things that the Father hath are Mine: therefore said I, that He shall take of Mine, and shall show it unto you."[2] It is not then that some things belong to the Father, some to the Son, some to the Holy Spirit; but that whatever the Father has, the Holy Spirit also has: nor was this communion ever non-existing in that Trinity, because in the Trinity to have all things is the same as to exist always. In the Trinity let no times, no degrees, no differences, be thought of; and if any one cannot explain, in respect to God, what is, let no one dare to affirm what is not.[3] For it is more excusable not to utter, concerning the ineffable Nature, what is worthy of it, than to give a definition contrary to truth. Therefore, whatever pious hearts can conceive about the everlasting and unchangeable glory of the Father, the same let them understand also about the Son, and about the Holy Spirit, without any severance or difference.[4] For this is the very reason why we confess

[1] See Note 126.
[2] S. John xvi. 12—15.
[3] See Note 127.
[4] See Note 128.

this Blessed Trinity to be One God,—because in these Three Persons there is no diversity of substance, or of power, or of will, or of operation.

4. As therefore we detest the Arians, who insist on making some interval between the Father and the Son, so do we equally detest the Macedonians[1] also, who, although they ascribe equality to the Father and the Son, yet think the Holy Spirit to be of an inferior nature; not considering that they are falling into that blasphemy, which is not to be forgiven either in the present world or in the future judgment, as our Lord says, "Whosoever shall say a word against the Son of Man, it shall be forgiven him; but whosoever speaks against the Holy Spirit, it shall not be forgiven him, neither in this world nor in the world to come."[2] Therefore, if he persist in this iniquity, he is without pardon, because he has excluded from himself Him by means of Whom he might have confessed; nor will he ever attain the remedy of forgiveness, who has not an Advocate to be his patron. For from the Spirit comes the calling on the Father, from Him are the groans of suppliants;[3] "and no one can say that Jesus is the Lord, but by the Holy Spirit," Whose equality in omnipotence and oneness in Godhead with the Father and the Son are most clearly proclaimed by the Apostle when he says, "There are indeed divisions of graces, but the same Spirit. And there are divisions of ministrations, but the same Lord. And there are divisions of operations, but the same God, Who worketh all in all."[4]

5. By these and other proofs innumerable, which

---

[1] See Note 129.
[2] See Note 130.
[3] Rom. viii. 26.
[4] 1 Cor. xii. 3—6.

shine forth in the authoritative record of Divine utterances, let us with one accord be stirred up to reverence for Pentecost, rejoicing in honour of the Holy Spirit, by Whom the Holy Catholic Church is sanctified, and every rational soul penetrated; Who is the Inspirer of faith, the Teacher of knowledge, the Fountain of love, the Seal of chastity, and the Cause of all virtue. Let the minds of the faithful rejoice, because throughout all the world One God, the Father, and the Son, and the Holy Spirit, is praised by an acknowledgment which all tongues render; and because that indication which was given in the form of fire is still continued alike in a work and a gift. For the Spirit of Truth Himself makes the house of His glory to shine with the radiance of His own light, and wills not to have in His temple anything dark or lukewarm.[1] And it is by this aid and teaching that the cleansing power of fasts and alms has been vouchsafed to us. For this venerable day is followed by a customary and most salutary observance,[2] which all holy men have always found most useful to them, and to the diligent performance of which we exhort you with a pastor's earnestness; that if, in the days just preceding, any stain has been contracted through careless negligence, it may be chastened by corrective fasting, and amended by devout piety. On Wednesday and Friday, therefore, let us fast; on the Sabbath, let us all join in keeping vigils with our accustomed devotion: through Jesus Christ our Lord, Who liveth and reigneth with the Father and the Holy Spirit, one God, for ever and ever. Amen.

[1] See Note 131.　　　　[2] See Note 132.

SERMON XVIII.

WHITSUNTIDE.

SERM. 77. In Pentecoste, III. *Hodiernam.*

THIS day's festival, dearly beloved, which is venerable throughout all the world, was consecrated by the coming of the Holy Spirit, Who on the fiftieth day after our Lord's Resurrection flowed into the Apostles and the believing people,[1] even as they had been hoping for Him. And they did hope, because the Lord Jesus had assured them that He would come; not that He should then first begin to be an Indweller[2] in the Saints, but that He should kindle with more fervour, and more abundantly stream into, the bosoms consecrated to Himself; not making an instalment of His gifts, but heaping them yet higher ; and although richer in bounteousness, not on that account new in operation. For never was the majesty of the Holy Spirit separate from the omnipotence of the Father and the Son ; and whatever the Divine government effects in the ordering of all things, comes from the providence of the whole Trinity. In that Trinity, the benignity of mercy is one, the severity of justice is one ; nor is there aught of division in action, where there is nought of diversity in will.[3] What therefore the Father illuminates, that the Son illuminates, that the Holy Spirit illuminates ; and since there is one Person of the Sent, another of the Sender, another of

---

[1] See Note 133.   [2] Comp. Serm. ii. c. 4.
[3] See Serm. x. c. 2.

the Promiser, there is manifested to us at once Unity and Trinity; so that the essence which has equality, and does not admit of solitariness, may be understood to be of the same Substance, and not of the same Person.

2. Whereas, therefore, without prejudice to the cooperation of the inseparable Godhead, some things[1] are wrought by the Father in particular, some by the Son, some by the Holy Spirit, for our redemption is this appointed, for our salvation is this planned. For if man, made after God's image and likeness, had remained in the dignity of his own nature, and had not been deceived by the fraud of the devil into deviating, through appetite, from the law laid down for him, the Creator of the world would not have become a creature,[2] nor would the Everlasting have entered on a temporal condition, nor would God the Son, equal to God the Father, have assumed "the form of a servant" and "the likeness of sinful flesh." But because "by the devil's envy death entered into the world,"[3] and the captivity of man could in no other way be loosened than by His taking up our cause, Who, without losing His own majesty, could become both very Man, and the only Man free from contagion of sin; the merciful Three divided between Themselves the work of our restoration; so that the Father should be propitiated, the Son should propitiate,[4] the Holy Spirit should enkindle. For it was right that those who were to be saved should also do something for themselves,[5] and by conversion of their

---

[1] Comp. Serm. x. c. 2.
[2] See Note 134.
[3] Wisd. ii. 24.
[4] See Note 135.
[5] See Note 136.

hearts to the Redeemer should depart from the dominion of the enemy; for as the Apostle says, "God sent the Spirit of His Son into our hearts, crying, Abba, Father:" "and where the Spirit of the Lord is, there is liberty:" and, "No one can say that Jesus is the Lord, but by the Holy Spirit."[1]

3. If therefore by the guidance of grace, dearly beloved, we faithfully and wisely apprehend what there is in the work of our restoration which is proper to the Father, to the Son, to the Holy Spirit respectively, and what there is which is common to Them all, we shall doubtless receive in such a sense what was done for us in lowly wise and corporeally, as to have no unworthy thoughts about that glory of the Trinity which is one and the same. For although no mind is sufficient to think about God, no tongue to speak about Him, yet[2] whatever be the extent of the conception which by human intelligence we attain to respecting the essence of the Father's Godhead, unless we have one and the same conception when we think either of His Only-begotten Son, or of the Holy Spirit, our minds are not piously informed, but carnally darkened; and we lose even what befitting thoughts we seemed to have respecting the Father; for we depart from the whole Trinity, if we hold not the Unity therein. Now that is in no real sense one which is divided through some inequality.

4. When therefore we bend the gaze of our mind to confess the Father, and the Son, and the Holy Spirit, let us banish far away from our thoughts the forms of visible things, the ages of temporal natures,

[1] Gal. iv. 6; 2 Cor. iii. 17; 1 Cor. xii. 3.
[2] Cf. Serm. xvii. c. 3.

the bodies which exist in places, the places in which bodies exist. Far from our hearts be that which is extended in space, which is enclosed by limit, and whatever is not always everywhere and entire. In the conception which we form respecting the Godhead of the Trinity, let us understand nothing in the way of interval, look for nothing in the way of gradation;[1] and if we have any worthy thoughts about God, let us not dare, in reference to the Trinity, to consider them inapplicable to any one Person, as though we should do more honour to the Father by ascribing to Him what we do not attribute to the Son and the Spirit. It is no piety to prefer the Father to the Only-begotten; to dishonour the Son is to wrong the Father; what is taken away from one is detracted from both. For since They have in common eternity and Godhead, the Father is not esteemed omnipotent, nor immutable, if He either begat One inferior to Himself, or gained somewhat by having One whom (before) He had not.[2]

5. It is true that the Lord Jesus said to His disciples, as has been recited in the Gospel reading, "If ye loved Me, ye would rejoice, because I said, I go to the Father; for My Father is greater than I."[3] But this passage is understood by those ears which have so often heard, "I and the Father are One," and "He that hath seen Me hath seen the Father," as implying no difference of Godhead; nor do they refer it to that essence which they know to be everlasting with the Father, and of the same nature. It is then the advancement of man in the Incarnation of the Word,

---

[1] Comp. Serm. xvii. c. 3. [2] See Serm. ii. c. 2.
[3] Comp. Serm. ii. c. 2. See Note 137.

which is being set forth even to the holy Apostles; and they who were disturbed when the Lord's departure was announced to them, are cheered on towards eternal joys by the increase of their own dignity. "If ye loved Me," saith He, "ye would certainly rejoice, because I go to the Father:" that is, "If ye saw with a perfect knowledge what glory is bestowed on you by the fact, that I, begotten of God the Father, have also been born of a human mother; that I, the Lord of things eternal, have willed to become one of mortals; that I, the Invisible, have presented Myself as visible; that I, Who in the form of God am everlasting, have taken the form of a servant;—then ye would rejoice, because I go to the Father. For it is to you that this Ascension is vouchsafed, and it is your lowliness which in Me is exalted above all heavens to be placed on the Father's right hand.[1] But I, Who with the Father am that which the Father is, remain indivisibly with the Father;[2] and just as in returning to Him I leave you not, so in coming from Him to you I depart not from Him. Rejoice, therefore, because I go to the Father, for the Father is greater than I. For I have united you to Myself, and have become Son of Man that you may be able to be sons of God. Wherefore, although I am One in both (natures), yet whereas I am conformed to you, I am inferior to the Father; but whereas I am not divided from the Father, I am even greater than Myself." Let then the nature which is inferior to the Father go to the Father, that where the Word is always, there the flesh may be; and that the one faith of the Catholic Church may believe Him to be equal

[1] See Serm. xv. c. 4.   [2] See Note 138.

as touching the Godhead, Whom as touching the Manhood she denies not to be inferior.

6. Let us therefore, dearly beloved, contemn the vain and blind craft of heretical impiety, which flatters itself by a perverse interpretation of this sentence, and after the Lord has said, " All things that the Father hath are Mine,"[1] understands not that it is taking away from the Father whatever it dares to deny to the Son, and is so foolish in regard to the things which belong to manhood, as to think that because the Only-begotten assumed what was ours, He lost what was His Father's. Mercy, in God, does not lessen power; nor is the reconciling of a beloved creature[2] a deficiency in everlasting glory. What the Father has, the Son also has; and what the Father and Son have, the Holy Spirit also has; because the whole Trinity together is One God. And this faith is no discovery of earthly wisdom, nor has man's opinion persuaded us to accept it;[3] but the Only-begotten Son Himself has taught it, the Holy Spirit Himself inculcated it—that Spirit of Whom we must think no otherwise than of the Father and the Son. For although He is not the Father nor the Son, yet from the Father and Son He is not divided; and as He has His own personality[4] in the Trinity, so in the Godhead of Father and Son has He one substance, filling all things, containing all things, and with the Father and the Son governing all things; to Whom belong honour and glory for ever and ever. Amen.

[1] S. John xvi. 15.
[2] See Serm. vii. c. 1.
[3] See Serm. viii. c. 2.
[4] " Personam."

THE TWENTY-EIGHTH EPISTLE, OR THE "TOME."

Leo, Bishop, to his dearest brother Flavian, Bishop of Constantinople.

Having read your Affection's letter,[1] the late arrival of which is matter of surprise to us, and having gone through the record of the proceedings of the Bishops,[2] we have now, at last, gained a clear view of the scandal which has risen up among you, against the integrity of the faith; and what at first seemed obscure has now been elucidated and explained. By this means Eutyches, who seemed to be deserving of honour under the title of Presbyter, is now shown to be exceedingly thoughtless and sadly inexperienced,[3] so that to him may apply what the prophet said, "He refused to understand that he might act well: he meditated unrighteousness on his bed."[4] What, indeed, is more unrighteous than to entertain ungodly thoughts, and not to yield to persons wiser and more learned? But into this folly do they fall, who, when hindered by some obscurity from knowing the truth, have recourse, not to the letters

[1] See Note 139.   [2] See Note 140.
[3] See Note 141.   [4] Ps. xxxvi. 4.

of the Apostles, nor to the authority of the Gospels, but to themselves; and become teachers of error, just because they have not been disciples of the truth. For what learning has *he* received from the sacred pages of the New and the Old Testament, who does not so much as understand the very beginning of the Creed? And that which, all the world over, is uttered by the voices of all applicants for regeneration,[1] is still not apprehended by the mind of this aged man.

2. If, then, he knew not what he ought to think about the Incarnation of the Word of God, and was not willing, for the sake of obtaining the light of intelligence, to make laborious search through the whole extent of the Holy Scriptures, he should at least have received with heedful attention that general Confession common to all, whereby the whole body of the faithful profess that they "believe in God the Father Almighty, and in Jesus Christ His only Son our Lord, Who was born of the Holy Spirit and the Virgin Mary."[2] By which three clauses the engines of almost all heretics are shattered. For when God is believed to be both "Almighty" and "Father," it is found that the Son is everlasting together with Himself, differing in nothing from the Father, because He was born as "God from God,"[3] Almighty from Almighty, Co-eternal from Eternal; not later in time, not unlike Him in glory, not divided from Him in essence; and the same Only-begotten and Everlasting Son of an Eternal Parent was "born of the Holy Ghost and the Virgin Mary." This birth in time in no way detracted from, in no way added

[1] See Note 142.   [2] See Note 143.   [3] See Note 144.

to, that divine and everlasting birth; but expended itself wholly in the work of restoring man, who had been deceived, so that it might both overcome death, and by its power "destroy the devil who had the power of death."[1] For we could not have overcome the author of sin and of death, unless He Who could neither be contaminated by sin, nor detained by death, had taken upon Himself our nature, and made it His own. For, in fact, He was "conceived of the Holy Ghost" within the womb of a Virgin Mother, who bare Him, as she had conceived Him, without loss of virginity. But if he (Eutyches) was not able to obtain a true conception from this pure fountain of Christian faith, because by his own blindness he had darkened the brightness of a truth so clear, he should have submitted himself to the Evangelical teaching; and after reading what Matthew says, "The book of the generation of Jesus Christ, the Son of David, the Son of Abraham,"[2] he should also have sought instruction from the Apostolical preaching; and after reading in the Epistle to the Romans, "Paul, a servant of God, called an Apostle, separated unto the gospel of God, which He had promised before by the prophets in the Holy Scriptures, concerning His Son, Who was made unto Him[3] of the seed of David according to the flesh,"[4] he should have bestowed some devout study on the pages of the Prophets; and finding that God's promise said to Abraham, "in thy seed shall all nations be blessed,"[5] in order to avoid all doubt as to the proper meaning of this "seed," he

---

[1] Heb. ii. 14.
[2] S. Matt. i. 1. See Note 145.
[3] Ei. So Vulg.
[4] Rom. i. 1.
[5] Gen. xii. 3.

should have attended to the Apostle's words, "To Abraham and to his seed were the promises made. He saith not, 'and to seeds,' as in the case of many, but, as in the case of one, 'and to thy seed,' which is Christ."[1] He should also have apprehended with his inward ear the declaration of Isaiah, "Behold, a Virgin shall conceive,[2] and bear a Son, and they shall call His name Emmanuel, which is, being interpreted, God with us;" and should have read with faith the words of the same prophet, "Unto us a Child has been born, unto us a Son has been given, whose power is on His shoulder; and they shall call His name, Angel of great counsel, Wonderful, Counsellor, Strong God, Prince of Peace, Father of the age to come."[3] And he should not have spoken idly to the effect that the Word was in such a sense made flesh, that the Christ who was brought forth from the Virgin's womb had the form of a man, but had not a body really derived from His Mother's body.[4] Possibly his reason for thinking that our Lord Jesus Christ was not of our nature was this,—that the Angel who was sent to the blessed and ever-Virgin Mary[5] said, "The Holy Ghost shall come upon thee, and the power of the Highest shall overshadow thee, and therefore also that holy thing which shall be born of thee shall be called Son of God;"[6] as if, because the Virgin's conception was caused by a divine act, therefore the flesh of Him Whom she conceived was not of the nature of her who conceived Him. But we are not to understand that "generation," peerlessly wonderful, and wonderfully

---

[1] Gal. iii. 16.
[2] "In utero accipiet."
[3] Isa. ix. 6. See Note 146.
[4] See Note 147.
[5] See Serm. ii. c. 1.
[6] S. Luke i. 35.

peerless, in such a sense as that the newness of the mode of production did away with the proper character of the kind.¹ For it was the Holy Ghost Who gave fecundity to the Virgin, but it was from a body that a real body was derived; and "when Wisdom was building herself a house,"² "the Word was made flesh, and dwelt among us," that is, in that flesh which He assumed from a human being, and which He animated with the spirit of rational life.

3. Accordingly, while the distinctness of both natures and substances is preserved, and both meet in one Person, lowliness is assumed by majesty, weakness by power, mortality by eternity;³ and, in order to pay the debt of our condition, the inviolable nature has been united to the passible, so that, as the appropriate remedy for our ills, one and the same "Mediator between God and men, the Man Christ Jesus," might from one element be capable of dying, and from the other be incapable. Therefore in the entire and perfect nature of very man was born very God,⁴ whole in what was His, whole in what was ours; for of that which the deceiver brought in, and man, thus deceived, admitted, there was not a trace in the Saviour;⁵ and the fact that He took on Himself a share in our infirmities did not make Him a partaker in our transgressions. He took on Him "the form of a servant" without the defilement of sins, augmenting what was human, not diminishing what was divine;⁶ because that "emptying of Him-

---

[1] "Proprietas . . . generis."   [2] Prov. ix. 1.
[3] See Note 148.   [4] See Note 149.
[5] See Serm. i. c. 1.   [6] See Serm. ii. c. 2.

self," whereby the Invisible made Himself visible, and the Creator and Lord of all things willed to be one among mortals, was a stooping down of compassion, not a failure of power.[1] Accordingly, the Same who, remaining in the form of God, made man,[2] was made Man in the form of a servant. For each of the natures retains its proper character without defect; and as the form of God does not take away the form of a servant, so the form of a servant does not impair the form of God.[3] For since the devil was glorying in the fact that man, deceived by his craft, was bereft of divine gifts, and, being stripped of this endowment of immortality, had come under the grievous sentence of death, and that he himself, amid his miseries, had found a sort of consolation in having a transgressor as his companion,[4] and that God, according to the requirements of the principle of justice, had changed His own resolution in regard to man, whom He had created in so high a position of honour; there was need of a dispensation of secret counsel, in order that the unchangeable God, Whose will could not be deprived of its own benignity, should fulfil by a more secret mystery His original plan of lovingkindness towards us, and that man, who had been led into fault by the wicked subtlety of the devil, should not perish contrary to God's purpose.

4. Accordingly, the Son of God, descending from His seat in heaven, yet not departing from the glory of the Father,[5] enters this lower world, born after a

---

[1] See Note 150. [2] See Note 151.
[3] See Note 152. [4] See Note 153.
[5] See Serm. xviii. c. 5.

new order, by a new mode of birth. After a new order ; because He Who in His own sphere is invisible became visible in ours ; He Who could not be enclosed in space[1] willed to be enclosed ; continuing to be before times, He began to exist in time ; the Lord of the universe allowed His infinite majesty to be overshadowed, and took upon Him the form of a servant: the impassible God did not disdain to become passible, and the immortal One to be subject to the laws of death. And born by a new mode of birth ; because inviolate virginity, while ignorant of concupiscence, supplied the matter of His flesh. What was assumed from the Lord's Mother was nature, not fault ; and the fact that the nativity of our Lord Jesus Christ is wonderful, in that He was born of a Virgin's womb, does not imply that His nature is unlike ours. For the selfsame Who is very God, is also very Man: and there is no illusion in this union, while the lowliness of man and the loftiness of Godhead meet together.[2] For as "God" is not changed by the compassion (exhibited) so "Man" is not consumed by the dignity (bestowed). For each "form" does the acts which belong to it, in communion with the other ; the Word, that is, performing what belongs to the Word, and the flesh carrying out what belongs to the flesh ; the one of these shines out in miracles, the other succumbs to injuries.[3] And as the Word does not withdraw from equality with the Father in glory, so the flesh does not abandon the nature of our kind. For, as we must often be saying, He is one and the same, truly Son of God, and truly Son of Man. God,

[1] See Note 154.   [2] See Note 155.
[3] See Note 156.

inasmuch as "in the beginning was the Word, and the Word was with God, and the Word was God:" Man, inasmuch as "the Word was made flesh, and dwelt among us." God, inasmuch as "all things were made by Him, and without Him nothing was made:" Man, inasmuch as He was "made of a woman, made under the law."[1] The nativity of the flesh is a manifestation of human nature: the Virgin's child-bearing is an indication of Divine power. The infancy of the Babe is exhibited by the humiliation of swaddling clothes: the greatness of the Highest is declared by the voices of angels. He Whom Herod impiously designs to slay is like humanity in its beginnings; but He Whom the Magi rejoice to adore on their knees is Lord of all. Now when He came to the baptism of John His forerunner, lest the fact that the Godhead was covered with a veil of flesh should be concealed, the voice of the Father spake in thunder from heaven, "This is My beloved Son, in Whom I am well pleased."[2] Accordingly, He Who, as man, is tempted by the devil's subtlety, is the same to Whom, as God, angels pay duteous service. To hunger, to thirst, to be weary, and to sleep, is evidently human. But to feed five thousand men with five loaves, and to bestow on the woman of Samaria that living water, to drink of which can secure one from thirsting again; to walk on the surface of the sea with feet that sink not, and by rebuking the storm to bring down the "uplifted waves,"[3] is unquestionably Divine.[4] As then —to pass by many points—it does not belong to the same nature to weep with feelings of pity over a

---

[1] Gal. iv. 4.
[2] See Note 157.
[3] See Ps. xciii. 4.
[4] See Note 158.

dead friend, and, after the mass of stone had been removed from the grave where he had lain four days, by a voice of command to raise him up to life again;[1] or to hang on the wood, and to make all the elements tremble after daylight had been turned into night; or to be transfixed with nails, and to open the gates of paradise to the faith of the robber; so it does not belong to the same nature to say, "I and the Father are one," and to say, "the Father is greater than I."[2] For although in the Lord Jesus Christ there is one Person of God and man, yet that whereby contumely attaches to both is one thing, and that whereby glory attaches to both is another:[3] for from what belongs to us He has that manhood which is inferior to the Father; while from the Father He has equal Godhead with the Father.

5. Accordingly, on account of this unity which is to be understood as existing in both the natures,[4] we read, on the one hand, that "the Son of Man came down from heaven," inasmuch as the Son of God took flesh from that Virgin of whom He was born; and on the other hand, the Son of God is said to have been crucified and buried, inasmuch as He underwent this, not in His actual Godhead, wherein the Only-begotten is coeternal and consubstantial with the Father, but in the weakness of human nature. Wherefore we all, in the very Creed, confess that "the only-begotten Son of God was crucified and buried," according to that saying of the Apostle, "for if they had known it, they would not have crucified the Lord of

[1] See Note 159.
[2] Serm. ii. c. 2.
[3] See Note 160.
[4] See Note 161.

majesty."[1] And when our Lord and Saviour Himself was by His questions instructing the faith of the disciples, He said, "Who do men say that I the Son of Man am?" And when they had mentioned various opinions held by others, He said, "But who say ye that I am?" that is, "I Who am Son of Man, and Whom you see in the form of a servant, and in reality of flesh, who say ye that I am?"[2] Whereupon the blessed Peter, as inspired by God, and about to benefit all nations by his confession, said, "Thou art the Christ, the Son of the living God."[3] Not undeservedly, therefore, was He pronounced blessed by the Lord, and derived from the original[4] Rock that solidity which belonged both to his virtue and to his name, who through revelation from the Father confessed the Selfsame to be both the Son of God and the Christ; because one of these truths, accepted without the other, would not profit unto salvation, and it was equally dangerous to believe the Lord Jesus Christ to be merely God and not man,[5] or merely man and not God. But after the resurrection of the Lord,—which was in truth the resurrection of a real body, for no other person was raised again than He Who had been crucified and had died,—what else was accomplished during that interval of forty days than to make our faith entire and clear of all darkness?[6] For a while He conversed with His disciples, and dwelt with them, and ate with them, and allowed Himself to be handled with careful and inquisitive touch by those who were under the influence of doubt; and *this* was

---

[1] 1 Cor. ii. 8.
[2] See Note 162.
[3] S. Matt. xvi. 13—16.
[4] "Principali."
[5] "Sine homine."
[6] See Serm. xv. c. 2.

His purpose in entering in to them when the doors were shut, and by His breath giving them the Holy Ghost and opening the secrets of Holy Scripture after bestowing on them the light of intelligence, and again in His selfsame Person showing to them the wound in the side, the prints of the nails, and all the fresh tokens of the Passion, saying, " Behold My hands and feet, that it is I Myself; handle Me and see, for a spirit hath not flesh and bones, as ye see Me have;"[1] —that the properties of the divine and the human nature might be acknowledged to remain in Him without causing a division, and that we might in such sort know that the Word is not what the flesh is, as to confess that the one Son of God is both Word and flesh.[2] On which mystery of the faith this Eutyches must be regarded as unhappily having no hold whatever;[3] for he has not acknowledged our nature to exist in the Only-begotten Son of God, either by way of the lowliness of mortality, or of the glory of resurrection. Nor has he been overawed by the declaration of the blessed Apostle and Evangelist John, saying, "Every spirit that confesseth that Jesus Christ has come in the flesh is of God, and every spirit which dissolveth Jesus[4] is not of God, and this is Antichrist." Now what is to dissolve Jesus, but to separate the human nature from Him, and to make void by shameless inventions that mystery[5] by which alone we have been saved ? Moreover, seeing he is blind as to the nature of Christ's body, he must needs be involved in the like senseless blindness

---

[1] S. Luke xxiv. 39.
[3] See Note 164.
[5] "Sacramentum."
[2] See Note 163.
[4] See Note 165.

with regard to His Passion also. For if he does not think the Lord's crucifixion to be unreal, and does not doubt that He really accepted suffering, even unto death,[1] for the sake of the world's salvation; as he believes in His death, let him acknowledge His flesh also, and not doubt that He Whom he recognises as having been capable of suffering is also Man with a body like ours; since to deny His true flesh is also to deny His bodily sufferings. If then he accepts the Christian faith, and does not turn away his ear from the preaching of the Gospel,[2] let him see what nature it was that was transfixed with nails and hung on the wood of the Cross; and let him understand whence it was that, after the side of the Crucified had been pierced by the soldier's spear, blood and water flowed out, that the Church of God might be refreshed[3] both with the Laver and with the Cup. Let him listen also to the blessed Apostle Peter when he declares, that "sanctification by the Spirit" takes place through the "sprinkling of the blood of Christ:" and let him not give a mere cursory reading to the words of the same Apostle, "Knowing that ye were not redeemed with corruptible things, as silver and gold, from your vain way of life received by tradition from your fathers, but with the precious blood of Jesus[4] Christ, as of a Lamb without blemish and without spot."[5] Let him also not resist the testimony of blessed John the Apostle, "And the blood of Jesus the Son of God cleanseth us from all sin."[6] And again, "This is the victory which overcometh the world, even our

---

[1] "Supplicium."
[2] See Note 166.
[3] "Rigaretur." See Note 167.
[4] "Jesu Christi." So Vulg.
[5] 1 S. Pet. i. 2, 18.
[6] 1 S. John i. 7.

faith :" and, "who is he that overcometh the world, but he that believeth that Jesus is the Son of God? This is He that came by water and blood, even Jesus Christ; not by water only, but by water and blood; and it is the Spirit that beareth witness, because the Spirit is truth. For there are three that bear witness, the Spirit, the water, and the blood; and the three are one."[1] That is, the Spirit of sanctification, and the blood of redemption, and the water of baptism; which three things are one, and remain undivided, and not one of them is disjoined from connection with the others: because the Catholic Church lives and advances in this faith, that in Christ Jesus we must believe neither Manhood to exist without true Godhead, nor Godhead without true Manhood.

6. But when Eutyches, on being questioned in your examination of him, answered, "I confess that our Lord was of two natures[2] before the union, but after the union I confess one nature;" I am astonished that so absurd and perverse a profession as this of his was not rebuked by a censure on the part of any of his judges, and that an utterance extremely foolish and extremely blasphemous was passed over, just as if nothing had been heard which could give offence:[3] seeing that it is as impious to say that the Only-begotten Son of God was of two natures before the Incarnation as it is shocking to affirm that, since the Word became flesh, there has been in Him one nature only.[4] But lest Eutyches should think that what he said was correct, or was tolerable, because it was not confuted by any assertion of yours, we ex-

---

[1] 1 S. John v. 4—8. See Note 168. [2] "Ex duabus naturis."
[3] See Note 169. [4] "Singularis."

hort your earnest solicitude, dearly beloved brother, to see that, if by God's merciful inspiration the case should be brought to a satisfactory issue, this inconsiderate and inexperienced man be cleansed also from this pestilent notion of his; seeing that, as the record of the proceedings shows, he had fairly begun to abandon his own opinions,[1] when, on being driven into a corner by authoritative words of yours, he professed himself ready to say what he had not said before, and to give his adhesion to that faith from which he had previously stood aloof. But when he would not consent to anathematise the impious dogma, you understood, brother, that he continued in his own misbelief,[2] and deserved to receive sentence of condemnation. For which if he grieves sincerely and to good purpose, and understands, even though too late, how properly the Episcopal authority has been put in motion, or if, in order to make full satisfaction, he shall condemn *viva voce*, and under his own hand, all that he has held amiss, no compassion, to whatever extent, which can be shown him, will be worthy of blame:[3] for our Lord, the true and good Shepherd, Who laid down His life for His sheep,[4] and Who came to save men's souls and not to destroy them,[5] wills us to imitate His own lovingkindness; so that justice should indeed constrain those who sin, but mercy should not reject those who are converted. For then indeed is the true faith defended with the best results, when a false opinion is condemned even by those who have followed it. But in

---

[1] See Note 170.
[2] "Perfidia."
[3] See Note 171.
[4] S. John x. 15.
[5] S. Luke ix. 56.

order that the whole matter may be piously and faithfully carried out, we have appointed our brethren, Julius, Bishop, and Renatus, Presbyter, and also my son Hilarus, Deacon, to represent us ;[1] and with them we have associated Dulcitius, our Notary, of whose fidelity we have had good proof: trusting that the Divine assistance will be with you, that he who has gone astray may be saved by condemning his own unsound opinion.

May God keep you in good health, dearly beloved brother. Given on the Ides of June, in the Consulate of the illustrious men, Asturius and Protogenes.[2]

---

[1] See Note 172.   [2] I.e. June 13, 449. See Note 173.

NOTES.

1. Here and elsewhere, Leo teaches that our Lord's Nativity was unique, not only in that He had no human father, but in that He was born without any taint of what the Augustinian theology describes as "originale peccatum," a phrase which, if baldly rendered into English, requires some explanatory accompaniments, but which, when thus interpreted, will itself express the gravest convictions of modern thought as to a corrupt tendency *de facto* infecting the moral life of the whole race, and imposing on it a bias towards evil. (Mozley's Lectures, p. 148.)

Of this "taint," or "disorder," or "corruption," which non-Christian thinkers have to account for somehow, and which Christianity traces to a primeval "Fall," Leo speaks frequently, as in Serm. 4 of this volume, c. 3; Serm. 11, c. 1; Serm. 14, c. 2; and also in Nativ. 4, c. 2, "lethali vulnere tabefacta natura;" Nativ. 10, c. 6, "originali . . . præjudicio;" de Jejunio vii. mensis, 5, c. 1, "Habet . . . hoc in se vitium humana natura, non a Creatore insitum, sed a prævaricatore contractum, et in posteros generandi lege transfusum:" and ib. 8, c. 1, "non dubitant in propagine vitiatum esse, quod est in radice corruptum;" Epist. 59, c. 4, "originali peccato transeunte per posteros," &c. From it, he affirms, no one ever born was exempt, except Christ only; see Sermon 4 in this volume, c. 3; Sermon 10, c. 2; Sermon 18, c. 2; and in Nativ. 5, c. 5; "Solus itaque inter filios hominum Dominus Jesus innocens natus est." He does not expressly say, like S. Augustine, that the Blessed Virgin was "ex Adam mortua propter peccatum," (in Ps. xxxiv. Serm. 2, c. 3.) But his language expresses a belief which is simply incompatible with the present Roman doctrine of the Immaculate Conception. The question, of course, was never presented to him: but can any one who answers it affirmatively adopt this great Pope's words in a natural sense?

2. The Blessed Virgin is said to have conceived our Lord in soul or mind, in that she readily believed the Divine promise, and gave herself up to be the instrument of the Divine will. The language is virtually Augustinian. "Illa fide plena, et Christum prius mente quam ventre concipiens, ' Ecce,' inquit, 'ancilla Domini :'" S. Aug. Serm. 215, c. 4. "Beatior ergo Maria percipiendo fidem Christi, quam concipiendo carnem Christi. Nam et dicenti cuidam, ' Beatus venter qui te portavit,' ipse respondit, 'Imo beati qui audiunt verbum Dei et custodiunt.' . . . . Materna propinquitas nihil Mariæ profuisset, nisi felicius Christum corde quam carne gestasset :" de S. Virginitate, c. 3. The same thought is repeated in Tract. 10 in Joan. Ev. c. 3: "Hoc in ea magnificavit Dominus, quia fecit voluntatem Patris, non quia caro genuit carnem. . . . ' Et mater mea quam appellatis felicem, inde felix quia verbum Dei custodit, non quia in illa Verbum caro factum est . . . sed quia custodit ipsum Verbum Dei per quod facta est,'" &c. In the text referred to, S. Luke xi. 28, Jesus does not (of course) deny that Mary heard God's Word, and kept it, (which she did in an eminent degree, S. Luke i. 38, 45, ii. 51 ;) but simply points to holiness as a more blessed thing than any privilege, to grace as far more precious than dignity. Compare S. Luke x. 20; 1 Cor. xii. 31, xiii. 1.

3. "*Dei Genitrix* mox futura." So in the important Epist. 165, to the Emperor Leo, which has been called his "Second Tome," he anathematizes Nestorius for believing the Blessed Virgin to have been "non Dei, sed tantummodo hominis genitricem." *Dei Genitrix* is equivalent to *Deipara*, the Latin rendering of the title *Theotokos*. This latter title, as is well known, was solemnly ascribed to the Blessed Virgin by the Third Œcumenical Council at Ephesus in 431, and again by the Fourth at Chalcedon in 451. It had been applied to her, not only by ordinary Christians in Julian's time, (cf. Cyril,

c. Jul. l. 8, p. 262,) but by many Church writers, from Origen downwards, (Routh, Rell. Sac. ii. 332,) including S. Athanasius, Orat. c. Arian. iii. 14, 29, 33, iv. 32; Eusebius, Vit. Const. iii. 43; and Cyril of Jerusalem, Cat. 10. 9. S. Ignatius, in effect, had said the same; "God in man . . . both from Mary and from God," Eph. 7; "our God Jesus Christ was borne in the womb by Mary," Ib. 18. The theological importance of the title consists in this, that it is a condensed expression of the *personal Divinity* of the Redeemer. The modern license of using theological terms with their legitimate meaning scooped out has extended itself to the phrase " Divinity of Christ," which is sometimes adopted as an imposing or reassuring synonym for " moral supremacy," or " pre-eminent conformity to the Divine mind." Undoubtedly " Theotokos" will not fit in with any such recognition of " divinity." It presupposes that the " ego" or " self" of Jesus Christ is identical with the " ego" or " self" of Him Who " in the beginning was with God, and was God," " the Only-begotten Son, Who was in the bosom of the Father," and " by Whom all things were made:" that this Divine Person did actually assume our humanity by means of an actual birth, without any compromise of His essential, pre-existing, and inalienable Deity. This belief being accepted, it follows that she of whom He was then humanly born may truly be described as " one whose Son is Himself God," that is, of whom was born that body which, from the moment of its origination, He appropriated, so that with it, and in it, He entered our earthly sphere of being, and became Man. This, and neither more nor less, is the purport of " Theotokos." The stronger terms, $\mu\acute{\eta}\tau\eta\rho$ $\Theta\epsilon o\hat{\upsilon}$, used by Eusebius (ad Sanct. Cœt. p. 480,) and " Mater Dei," used implicitly by Tertullian, (de Patientia, 3,) and expressly by S. Ambrose (Hexaem. v. s. 65) as afterwards pointedly by Facundus (pro Def. Trium Capit. i. 1, &c.) do not add to the range of the idea. They do but put into two simple words instead of a single composite one, the most fundamental of those " antitheses of the Incarnation" in which Christian hymnology and Christian oratory have in all ages taken pleasure and to which Christian theology has been felt to give serious warrant. (See Oosterzee, Image of Christ, p. 219.) It is true that a Greek or Latin reader would be more apt than an English one to understand "of God" in this connexion, as meaning, "of the Divine Son considered as under the conditions of Incarnation." The English phrase, "Mother of God," has, indeed, for an English ear, apart from theological training, a certain perplexing abruptness; but when duly explained, or embodied in such a paraphrase as that in our first Reformed Liturgy, "Mother of Jesus Christ our Lord and God," it will be accepted by all who sincerely believe that Jesus Christ is in truth Divine. (Compare Church Quarterly Review, vol. xv. p. 290.) Pearson's note (2) on Art. 3 is worth remembering: "Absit ut quisquam S. Mariam Divinæ gratiæ privilegiis et speciali gloria fraudare conetur." See too Dean Church, Human Life, &c., p. 173.

4. A phrase, perhaps, taken immediately from S. Augustine: "Intelligerent eum assumpsisse quod non erat, et permansisse quod erat," Aug. Serm. 184. 1: compare also Serm. 186. 2, and 213. 2. So S. Cyril of Alexandria says that in taking our flesh "He remained what He was," Ep. ad Nest. 3, and "Quod unus sit Christus" (in Ph. Pusey's edition of Cyril, vol. vii. p. 340.) Newman, in Athan. Treat. ii. 289 (Lib. Fath.) quotes other passages, as S. Greg. Nazianzen's Orat. 29. 19, "What He was, He remained; what He was not, He assumed:" and S. Athanasius c. Apollin. ii. 7, "the Word, remaining God, became man."

5. This sentence, with very slight verbal differences, will be found in the "Tome," c. 3. Leo is here, as in so many other places, affirming the truth of the Hypostatic or Personal Union, i.e., that "God and Man is one Christ," without any confusion of the two natures, Godhead and Manhood. He is carefully excluding errors on either side; the error of Nestorius, who denied the unity of Person, and the error of Eutyches, who denied the duality of Natures. There is one Christ, and not two; the Son of God *is* the Virgin-born. "The selfsame," as S. Proclus expressed it in the early days of the Nestorian controversy, "was in the Father's bosom, and in the Virgin's womb;" for otherwise the gulf between God and mankind would not have been bridged over; there would not have been one "daysman to lay His hand upon both," Job ix. 33; and if Christ differed from other servants of God simply in the degree of His nearness

to God, He would be but the most eminent of the Saints; and no Saint, however eminent, could be our Saviour. On the other hand, this one Christ must be truly God *and* truly Man : neither nature by itself would be sufficient; the higher must not absorb the lower, for this were to destroy the reality of His example, His Sacrifice, His Mediation. "The whole doctrine of our salvation depends on Christ being of one substance with us. He did not merely touch our nature as from the outside . . . He took it all," Gore's Leo the Great, p. 57, where it is added that on this veritable assumption of our humanity depend our re-creation by Christ as the Second Adam, the value of His atoning Sacrifice, the meaning of His Ascension. He must be, as the Council of Chalcedon defined Him to be, " One Christ in Two Natures ;" a single Person, Who, ever since He stooped to "take the form of a servant," has existed in two spheres of being, (see Liddon's Bamp. Lect., p. 261,) which, for the sake of a compendious term, we call "two natures." Leo uses " natura," " substantia," "forma," as equivalents on this subject. A fine passage on this twofold truth is in Nativ. 10, c. 5, " Idem est in forma Dei qui formam suscepit servi . . . Idem Filius Dei atque filius hominis est," &c., which may well be compared with the language of S. Athanasius in Tom. ad Antioch. 7, see Later Treatises of S. Ath. (Lib. Fath.) p. 11. And here we must observe the varied language wherein Holy Scripture enshrines this truth, that the same Person Who from all eternity was very God, has also by the Incarnation become very Man. Because He is "God and Man" in one Person, therefore all His acts and properties are the acts and properties of that one Person, and may be predicated of "God" or of "Man." This proposition was upheld by Cyril of Alexandria in his fourth "anathematism," directed against any who should assign some of the Scriptural expressions concerning Christ to the Word, and others to "a man considered as apart from the Word." (Compare Leo's own description of Nestorianism, as affirming that the Son of Man existed "separatim atque sejunctim" from the Son of God, Ep. 165. 2, with Cyril's ἰδικῶς and ἀνὰ μέρος.) The proposition was admitted by his critic, Andrew of Samosata, (Cyril. Apol. adv. Orient. 4,) and afterwards by Theodoret in his " Dialogues." It supplies the key to the following texts :—

Scripture predicates

What is human of *God;*	What is Divine of *Man;*
"The Word was made flesh," &c., S. John i. 14.	"The Son of Man, Who is in heaven," S. John iii. 13.
"The Church of God, which He purchased with His own blood," Acts xx. 28.	"The Second Man is the Lord from heaven," 1 Cor. xv. 47; (text. rec. Or, "is from heaven.")
"The princes of this world . . . crucified the Lord of glory," 1 Cor. ii. 8.	
"That which was from the beginning, which we have seen . . . and our hands have handled, of the Word of Life." 1 S. John i. 1.	
I.e., not of the Godhead, but in His Manhood.	I.e., not of the Manhood, but in His Godhead.

of Christ's One Person

And this Scriptural language, it will be seen, is our warrant for ascribing to "God," to the Eternal Son, birth from a Mother, and death upon the Cross, in regard to His Manhood. This is that "interchange" of which so much has been said by writers on the Incarnation, modern as well as ancient, and which is technically called Antidosis, or Communicatio Idiomatum. Its propositions, as Dr. Mill says (on Myth. Interpr. p. 17,) are "alone verified by the unity of Person in both natures." So in Serm. 2 in this volume, c. 2; Serm. 8, c. 1. Very pointedly also in Epist. 165, c. 6, "Licet ergo in uno Domino Jesu Christo . . . Verbi et carnis una persona sit, quæ inseparabiliter atque indivise communes habeat actiones, intelligendæ tamen sunt ipsorum operum qualitates," &c. And again, c. 8, "Propter quod sicut Dominus majestatis dicitur crucifixus, ita qui ex sempiternitate æqualis est Deo, dicitur exaltatus," &c. The reader will of course consult the great passages in Hooker, v. 52 and 53; and Pearson, i. 289, Art. 3, "Nor is this union only a scholastic speculation," &c.; i. 324, Art. 4, "For it was no other person," &c. But it is interesting to see how much they were indebted to S. Thomas Aquinas, who says, Sum. Th. iii. 2. 6, that the union is personal; that while some make it unreal by severing the persons, and others reduce it to an absolute singleness of nature, "the Holy Church of God" (here he quotes from the Fifth General Council, A.D. 553, Mansi, ix. 377) "rejects the impiety of either form of unbelief, and confesses the union of God the Word to the flesh to be by way of combination; that is, hypostatic." This means that the Deity and the humanity are combined in one hypostasis or personal self. The term σύνθεσις, used by this Council, is equivalent to Cyril's συνδρομή and σύνοδος, and to Leo's "connexio," (Ep. 28. 5,) or to his similar use of "coire," "convenire." In Sum. iii. 16. 4, Aquinas asks whether the things which belong to the Son of Man can be predicated of the Son of God, and conversely? and gives for answer, that since the two natures belong to one hypostasis, we may use the name of either nature when we mean to speak of that hypostasis, i.e., we may ascribe any of Christ's acts or properties to either "God" or "Man," simply because we mean *Him* Who is both God and Man. Aquinas in his turn, was indebted to John Damascene, de Fide Orthodoxa, iii., c. 4 and 5. "We do not predicate of Godhead the properties of Manhood . . . nor of Manhood those of Godhead . . . But in speaking of the Person in both or either of its elements, we do ascribe to *it* the properties of both natures. Since from one element He is called God, He takes to Him the properties of the co-existing nature, the flesh, being called the crucified Lord of glory, not in that He is God, but in that He, the self-same, is Man. And whereas He is called Man, He receives the properties . . . of the Godhead, not as Man, but in that, being God . . . He became a Child. And this is the mode of the Antidosis"—here begins the sentence quoted by Hooker, v. 53. 4, which Damascene guards by explaining that there is no interchange between the natures themselves, each of which "preserves, unchanged, its own natural property." Such teaching is essentially that of S. Athanasius in a golden passage of his Orat. c. Arian. iii. 31, "Hence the properties of the flesh, as hunger, thirst, suffering, . . . are called *His*, because He was in it; and the peculiar works of the Word, as to raise the dead, . . . He used to do through His own Body; . . . it was *the*

Body of God." And ib. 32, "While the flesh suffered, the Word was not external to it, and therefore the Passion is called the Word's;" and see Cardinal Newman's notes on this passage, Ath. Treat. ii. 443, ff. Of Latin Fathers, Tertullian, in the second century, is here almost verbally like Leo; "Videmus duplicem statum, non confusum, sed conjunctum in una persona Deum et hominem Jesum ... et ... salva est utriusque proprietas substantiæ," adv. Prax. 27. In S. Augustine's Christmas Sermons we find the "birth of God in the flesh" insisted on, while a "confusio naturæ" is excluded, Serm. 191 and 186. And a great passage in Leo's Ep. 28, explaining some of the texts referred to above, as Hooker, Pearson, &c., explain them, is based on a passage in S. Aug. c. Serm. Arian. c. 8 : "Ac per hoc, *propter istam unitatem personæ,* in utraque natura intelligendam, et Filius hominis dicitur descendisse de cœlis ... et Filius Dei dicitur crucifixus," &c., as this, again, appears to be suggested by a passage of S. Ambrose (de Fide, ii. s. 58) which is among those sent by Leo to the Emperor Leo, in proof that the Council of Chalcedon had not broken with the authoritative Doctors of the Church; " Unde illud quod lectum est, ' Dominum majestatis crucifixum esse,' non quasi *in* majestate sua crucifixum putemus, sed quia idem Deus, idem homo, per divinitatem Deus, per conceptionem carnis homo, Christus Jesus Dominus majestatis dicitur crucifixus, quia consors utriusque naturæ, id est humanæ atque divinæ, in natura hominis subiit passionem, ut indiscrete et Dominus majestatis dicatur esse qui passus est, et Filius hominis, sicut scriptum est, qui descendit de cœlo."

6. Here compare Leo's language with that of Athanasius, who in his invaluable treatise, " De Incarnatione Verbi," refers to the doom pronounced on man's disobedience, and proceeds in substance thus :—God could not recall His sentence ; yet neither would it be consonant to His goodness to cast off His reasonable creatures. Repentance could not undo so vast an evil. But if the Word Himself were to interpose, He could be a Deliverer and a Mediator. He could pay the debt due to God ; He, and He only, could make an offering, ἀντὶ πάντων (c. 9); His Body, given up to death, could be a world-redeeming and a life-restoring Sacrifice. (Cp. c. 10, 20; Orat. i. 60, ii. 66.)

There has been needless debate over the questions, whether a redemption, atonement, and propitiation were strictly necessary, and whether they require the agency of a Divine Person. It is vain, and worse than vain, to pronounce on such points irrespectively of Scripture, from *à priori* views of the character of God. Bishop Butler has a well known passage on this point in the fifth chapter of the second part of the "Analogy." See also Wilberforce on Incarnation, p. 160, "If it be asked whether" the Atonement "was a necessary part of the counsels of God, the question is one which we are plainly incompetent to answer." "Revelation," says Dr. Liddon, "does not encourage conjecture" on this subject: but "we may presume, without hardihood, that if God might have saved us in other ways, He has chosen the way which was in itself the best," (Univ. Serm. i. 243,) best for the harmonizing of mercy and truth, of love and righteousness; as Leighton says, (on 1 S. Peter ii. 24,) "that this way wherein our salvation is contrived is most excellent, and suitable to the greatness and goodness of God;" and again (on Psalm cxxxi.), "that nothing can be thought of more worthy of the Divine Majesty, nothing sweeter, nothing more munificent in this respect to unworthy man." Aquinas, who holds that "God's infinite power could have restored mankind by a different act," but that this was the best and fittest mode, in regard to the promotion of faith, hope, love, right action, and to our full communion with God, and the removal of our manifold evils, combines with this passage of S. Leo some words of S. Aug. de Trin. xiii. s. 13, 17, 18, to the effect that, without limiting what was possible with God, "sanandæ nostræ miseriæ convenientiorem modum alium non fuisse, nec esse oportuisse;" and that "it was fitting that the devil should be overcome by the righteousness of the Man Jesus Christ." "Quod factum est," S. Thomas comments, "Christo satisfaciente pro nobis. Homo autem purus" i.e. (a mere man) "satisfacere non poterat pro toto humano genere : Deus autem satisfacere non debebat : unde oportuit Deum et Hominem esse Jesum Christum." Sum. iii. 1. 2. Here we must remember that "satisfaction," like "substitution," is a term which only pretends to illustrate a certain aspect of the mystery, (see Dale on the Atonement, pp. 358, 432; Bp. Barry on Atonement, p. 46.)

The special bearing of Christ's Divinity on the Atonement is sometimes ignored by persons who fully believe in Him as Divine. But surely the fact of His Divinity tends to clear away some difficulties as to the equitableness and the possibility of His Sacrifice. Compare Archbishop Thomson in Aids to Faith, p. 341 : "When we are invited to discuss . . . . . whether vicarious punishment could ever be agreeable to God's justice, we cannot but notice that the Divine nature of Christ is never strongly asserted on that side, nor assumed as an element in the argument. The death of Jesus is discussed as the death of a mere man." See too the excellent preface to Benson's Sermons on Redemption : "All that is said about the injustice of God punishing the innocent to spare the guilty, is really based upon a Socinian view of our Lord's personality . . . . . It is no mere act of morality or compensation that we have to consider. It is a Divine act that we have to adore." It is "the Moral Ruler of our race" Who "asserts the principle" of penal justice "not by inflicting, but by enduring," &c., Dale, p. 392. And, while it might well be asked how any finite being, however pure, could "make agreement unto God" for his fallen brethren, that question is idle in presence of One Who could "steep in the glory of His Divine personality all of human that He wrought," (Trench's Westm. Serm. p. 177,) and impart to His sufferings an infinite value. It is also Christ's Deity which makes it possible for Him to unite all humanity to Himself, and act and suffer for all men. No mere man could thus represent all ; it is because Christ is God that His Manhood has received this vast extension of power. In this way the Incarnation acts on His Manhood in its relation (1) to God, (2) to mankind in general. Generally, as Waterland says, (Works, iv. 508,) "it is the Divinity that stamps the value on the suffering humanity." See S. Thom. Aq. Sum. iii. 48. 2, "Dignitas carnis Christi non est æstimanda solum secundum carnis naturam, sed secundum personam assumentem, in quantum scilicet erat caro Dei, ex quo habebat dignitatem infinitam." Bp. Andrewes, Serm. ii. 152, "That which setteth the high price on this sacrifice, is this; that He which offereth it unto God, is God." Newman, Serm. vi. 71, "There was a virtue in His death which there could be in no other, for He was God." See also Liddon,

Bamp. Lect. p. 480, ff. ed. 11; and Univ. Serm. i. 240, "His Eternal Person gave infinite merit to the" acts and sufferings "of His humanity." The same idea prevailed in the ancient Church: it was a special "motive power" in Cyril's contest with Nestorianism, as when he said that Christ "would not have been equivalent to the whole creation, nor sufficient for purchasing gloriously the life of the whole world, had He been a creature and not truly Son, and God, as from God," (de Trin. Dial. 4, in tom. v. 508.) It was indicated in the famous sermon of S. Proclus, wherein, excluding the possibility of salvation by man or Angel, he spoke of the "one course remaining, that the sinless God should die for sinners;" in the thirteenth Catechetical Lecture of S. Cyril of Jerusalem, "Wonder not if the whole world was redeemed, for He who died on its behalf was not a mere man, but God's Only-begotten Son. . . . . . . One of two things was inevitable, that God should keep His word and destroy all, or show benignity and cancel His sentence; but . . . He preserved both reality for His sentence, and activity for His benignity: Christ took on Him our sins . . . . . . He was God Incarnate: the iniquity of the sinners was not so great as the righteousness of Him Who died for them," c. 2, 33; and in the anonymous Epistle to Diognetus, which belongs to the second century, c. 9, "He gave His own Son a ransom for us, the Holy for the lawless . . . . . the Immortal for the mortals; for what else could cover our sins ἡ ἐκείνου δικαιοσύνη; in whom could we, the wicked and impious, be justified, save in the Son of God alone? O the sweet exchange! O the unsearchable design! O the unexpected benefits! that the wickedness of many should be hidden by a single Righteous One, and the righteousness of One should justify many wicked."

7. Bingham observes (b. xiv. c. 2, s. 1) that Leo here uses, though in a Catholic sense, that form of doxology which had become associated with Arianism. He could well afford to do as S. Athanasius had done, who ascribes glory to the Father, "through the Son," at the conclusion of four treatises, ad Episc. Æg., de Fuga, de Synodis, and ad Afros. See Theodoret, ii. 24, on Leontius' inaudible utterance of the critical words in the doxology.

8. "Sacramentum." This word has had a remarkable history. Originally signifying the pledge or deposit in money, "which in certain suits," according to Roman law, "plaintiff and defendant were alike bound to make" (Trench on Study of Words, p. 70), and which "was in the form of a wager as to the right" (Dict. Antiq. p. 1042); (2) it came to signify the pledge of military fidelity, a voluntary, not an exacted promise; then (3) the exacted oath, which finally took the character of an oath of allegiance; (4) "any solemn oath whatever;" (5) in early Christian use, any sacred and solemn act or event, "and especially any mystery where more was meant than met the eye or ear." (Trench.) Pliny's use of it, in his report as to the Christian religious rites, is well known; he clearly means by it a solemn religious pledge. S. Cyprian uses "Sacramentum" for a sacred bond (de Laps. 7; de Unit. 7), or symbol (de Unit. 7), or meaning (de Orat. 9, 28). S. Augustine regards it as a sign pertaining to Divine things, which may or may not have a gift of grace attached to it; compare Ep. 137. 15. Thus he applies the term to Jewish ordinances, and in reference to the Christian system his employment of it ranges from the salt given to catechumens (de Cat. Rud. s. 50, de Pecc. Mer. ii. s. 42), the Lord's Prayer and the Creed (Serm. 228), the chrism and the imposition of hands (de Bapt. c. Don. v. s. 28), to those "pauca, facillima, augustissima," received from "the Lord Himself and Apostolic discipline, sicuti est baptismi sacramentum, et celebratio Corporis et Sanguinis Domini" (de Doctr. Chr. iii. s. 13), the "sacramenta fontis" and "altaris" (Serm. 228). The Vulgate in two memorable places, Eph. v. 32, 1 Tim. iii. 16, uses it as equivalent to μυστήριον, and Leo appears to have understood "pietatis sacramentum" in the latter passage as the mystery or the sacred work of Divine loving-kindness, *pietas* being an ambiguous word. He himself uses "sacramentum" very frequently (e.g. in Serm. 5 of this volume, Serm. 7, and elsewhere, as in Nativ. 2, 1) in the sense of *mystery, sacred act, fact, rite*, or *meaning;* and in the passage in the text, the idea of solemn observance is implied.

9. He expresses his belief in the Perpetual Virginity of Mary by the words in the Tome (Ep. 28, c. 2), "beatam Mariam sem-

per Virginem." See too his Serm. in Nativ. 2, c. 2, "et Virgo permanserit." In the present passage, he seems to imitate S. Augustine, Serm. 184, "quam virgo ante conceptum, tam virgo post partum;" Serm. 51, s. 18, "Virgo concepit, virgo peperit, virgo permansit" (cp. Serm. 190. 2.); and still more strongly, de Cat. Rud. s. 40, "Virgo concipiens, virgo pariens, virgo moriens." The title "Ever-Virgin" is applied to Mary by S. Athanasius, Or. c. Ar. 2, c. 70 (see Newman, Ath. Treat. ii. 381); and the "Antidicomarians," who denied it to her, were denounced by Epiphanius as depriving her of "honour" due, just as Hooker, E. P. v. 45. 2, speaks of Helvidius as infringing on "the honour of the Blessed Virgin" by "abusing greatly" S. Matt. i. 25. The student will of course consult Pearson, i. 304 (Art. 3), but he will there observe that in the texts quoted, the ordinary inference from "until" is barred by impossibilities, physical or moral, whereas in this case we can only oppose to it a high improbability, as pious reverence has felt; on which see Dr. Mill on the Mythical Interpretation of the Gospels, pp. 269—274. Of course, the title "Ever-Virgin" does not stand on the same footing with the title "Mother of God," nor does Bishop Andrewes, by coupling them together in his Devotions (Engl. Tr. p. 93), mean to represent them as equally momentous; but those who wonder at the repugnance with which the Helvidian theory has been continuously rejected by Church writers, and by devout minds in the Church, can hardly be thought to have taken home in its fulness the fact of the Divine Incarnation. Bishop Lightfoot says that the Fathers "rightly maintained that πρωτότοκον in S. Luke ii. 7 did not necessarily imply that" Mary had other children. (On Colossians, p. 215.)

10. So in Serm. 10, c. 4; 14, c. 2, and Ep. 165, c. 6, "Licet... Verbi et carnis una persona sit.". Strictly speaking, indeed, Christ's Person is Divine; His personality is said to reside originally in the Godhead, for the simple reason that He was God before He became Man. Cp. Sermon 4, c. 3. See Newman, Sermons, vi. 62: "His Person is not human like ours, but Divine. He who was from eternity, continued one and the same, but with an addition." So Wilberforce on Incarnation, p. 132: "In which of His two natures did the personality of Christ our

Lord originally reside? Plainly in His Godhead. For He Himself refers to its actings before His human nature was assumed; 'Before Abraham was, *I* am.'" And Liddon, Bamp. Lect. p. 262: "Our Lord's Godhead is the seat of His personality..... The Person of the Son of Mary is Divine and eternal; it is none other than the Person of the Word..... Christ's Manhood is .... not a seat and centre of personality: it has no conceivable existence apart from the act whereby the Eternal Word, in becoming incarnate, called it into being and made it His own.... In saying that Christ 'took our nature upon Him,' we imply that His Person existed before," &c. See also Later Treatises of S. Athanasius, p. 69. But Leo clearly means that He, the Self-same, was truly God, and became truly Man; not that He gained by the Incarnation a new personal being, but only a new relation of His pre-existing personal being towards human nature, S. Tho. Aq. Sum. iii. 17. 2. So in Sum. iii. 2. 4, it is laid down that although the Person of the Word be simple in itself, yet it is compound as subsisting in two natures. So Damascene, 4, c. 5, that the Person of the Word became composite when it became incarnate. See Hooker, E. P. v. 52. 3, "Christ is .... a Person Divine, because He is personally the Son of God; human, because He hath really the nature of the children of men," &c. See note 34.

11. "Sed ita ut naturæ alteri altera *misceretur.*" This phrase is not to be understood as signifying a confusion of the natures, which was a notion specially abhorrent to Leo. Cp. Serm. de Pass. 14, c. 1, and Ep. 165, c. 6, "nulla permixtione confundimus." The fact is, he is here using language to express the Personal Union which had been employed without scruple, e.g. by Tertullian, "Homo Deo mistus," Apol. 21; S. Cyprian, "Deus cum homine miscetur," de Idol. Van. 6; S. Athanasius, τὴν ἀπαρχὴν ἡμῶν περιθέμενος, καὶ ταύτῃ ἀνακραθείς, Orat. iv. 33; S. Greg. Naz., ἡ καινὴ μίξις, Θεὸς καὶ ἄνθρωπος .... Θεὸς σαρκί .... ἀνεκράθη, Orat. 2. 23; and similarly ib. 38. 13; and S. Hilary, "hujus admixtionis," de Trin. ii. 24, (quoted at end of Leo's Ep. 165.) S. Augustine, in words which show that the idea of fusion was far from his mind, "Sicut in unitate personæ anima unitur corpori, ut homo sit, ita in unitate Personæ Deus

unitur homini, ut Christus sit :" (compare the "Quicunque,") "in illa ergo persona mixtura est animæ et corporis; in hac Persona mixtura est Dei et hominis; *si tamen* recedat auditor a consuetudine corporum, qua solent duo liquores ita commisceri, ut neuter servet integritatem suam," Ep. 137, to Volusianus, s. 11. So Cyril Alex. says that some of the Fathers had used the word κρᾶσις, not with any idea of ἀνάχυσις, as when liquids are blended, but to set forth the perfect ἕνωσις, adv. Nest. 1, c. 3. Gradually this language came to be so much abused by Apollinarians and Eutychians, that it was abandoned by the orthodox, just as other phrases, not strictly accurate, which had been employed by Ante-nicene writers, were abandoned after the rise of Arianism. "Securius locuti sunt," says Quesnel on this passage, "nondum litigantibus Eutychianis; post cujus hæresis ortum cautius . . . locutus est Leo." Already Cyril had found it needful to disclaim all notion of "mixture" properly so called, (σύγκρασις, σύγχυσις, φυρμός,) as in his first letter to Successus; see also the great "second letter to Nestorius," that to John, the Defence against Theodoret (c. 1), the Explanation of Anath. 1, and the first letter to Acacius, in all of which he repudiated the confusion of the natures. On this subject consult Pearson, i. 287, (Art. 3,) ii. 199, with the notes to the Oxford Translation of Tertullian, p. 48, and to S. Athan. Treatises, ii. 551; and the Chalcedonian Definition of Faith, Canons of First Four Councils, p. 34, ed. Oxf.

12. Compare on Arianism, Sermon 4 of this volume, c. 4; 17, c. 4. In one place he alludes to it as an "impia perversitas," in Nativ. 5, c. 3. In Ep. 15. 2, he says that the Priscillianists in part agree with the Arians. Arianism was largely the result of a mental and moral temper fostered by the Greek schools of disputation, and began, as we learn from Socrates (i. 5) with this line of argument;

What is true of human fatherhood is true of the relation between the Father and the Son:
But the father's priority of existence is true of human fatherhood:
Therefore it is true in regard to the Father and the Son:
Therefore, once there was no Son:

Therefore, He was, at some very remote period, created by the Father.

The *petitio principii* in the major premiss is a key to the whole heresy. It was essentially Rationalistic; see Newman's note on Athan. Treatises, i. 256. (Lib. Fath.) The extraordinary versatility, the argumentative subtlety, and the too frequent profanity of Arianism are matters of which a few lines can give no idea. But it is necessary, in even the briefest notice of this long-lived heresy, to remark on the contrast between its changeful inventiveness and the simple steadfastness of Çatholic doctrine. On the one side, some twenty different creeds, (of which several, however, were rather negatively than positively heterodox,) and three main sects,—the Semi-arians with their formula of *Homoiousion*, i.e. "the Son is like in essence to the Father," —the Acacians vaguely calling Him "like," *Homoion*,—the Aetians boldly proclaiming Him "unlike," *Anomoion*, as much as to say, "He is in no sense Divine." On the other side, the Church with the Nicene Creed, confessing Him as *Homoousion*, "of one essence with the Father;" meaning thereby, as her great champion repeatedly bore witness, to secure belief in the reality of His Divine Sonship, and therefore in His real Deity, as distinguished from the titular deity which was so freely conceded to him by the Arians. S. Ath. de Decr. Nic. 20; de Syn. 39, ff.; ad Afros 9. Cp. Liddon, Bamp. Lect. p. 444.

13. S. Leo here, as in other Sermons, e.g. the last in this volume, and in Ep. 28, c. 4, and in Ep. 59, c. 3, "et secundum hominem, Pater major me est," gives that interpretation of S. John xiv. 28 with which we are so familiar through the "Quicunque," "Inferior to the Father as touching His manhood." It is implied in the language of S. Cyprian, Ep. 73. 18 : it is expressly taken in the Sermo Major de Fide (c. 34) which though probably not by S. Athanasius, is a compilation by one of his school; and in Cyril of Alexandria's " Quod unus sit Christus," καταπεφοίτηκε δέ πως ἐπὶ τὸ μὴ ὂν ἐν δόξῃ, καθὰ πέφηνεν ἄνθρωπος, τοιγάρτοι καὶ ἔφασκεν, Ὁ πατὴρ μείζων μού ἐστι. (Vol. vii. 412, Pusey.) Suicer quotes Basil of Seleucia, Leo's contemporary, as similarly referring the words to the οἰκονομία, i.e., to the assumption of humanity (Thesaurus, in v. οἰκονομία.) S. Atha-

nasius, indeed, had seen in our Lord's words a reference to what later writers have called the "Subordinatio Filii," or the "Principatus Patris," that is, to the precedency of the Father as the Fountain of Godhead, cf. Orat. i. 58 ; so S. Chrysostom in loc. But this interpretation was probably felt to be but imperfectly available in controversy with the Arians, who, as we know from Epiphanius (Hær. lxxix. 63) and Gregory Nazianzen (Orat. 29. 71), were wont to insist on this text. Accordingly, the interpretation which refers to the assumption of humanity became the received view in the West : it was adopted at the Council of Paris in 360, (see Hilary, Fragm. xi. 3 ;) and at the Council of Aquileia in 381, when Palladius the Arian adduced this text, S. Ambrose answered, "The Son is inferior as touching the form of a servant, as touching the flesh," (Gest. Conc. Aq. 35 ;) so S. Augustine, in loc. and de Div. Qu. 83, n. 69 ; de Trin. i. s. 14, ii. s. 2 ; Enchir. 35, takes the same interpretation : in de Fid. et Symb. s. 18, he unites it with the Athanasian interpretation, which indeed is actually adopted by Pearson, in Art. 2, "greater in reference to the communication of the Godhead ;" by Newman, Sermons, vi. 60 ; and by Westcott, (on Gospel of S. John, in loc.) Against it is the consideration that our Lord is suggesting an inference. " Because the Father is greater than I, you ought to rejoice that I am going to Him." They might rejoice in that prospect because the Father would be a yet mightier Friend to them than Jesus Himself in His humiliation : but would the mysterious "principatus Patris" be an intelligible reason for such joy ? As to the other text, S. John x. 30, see Ep. 28, c. 4. So Ep. 165, c. 8, " Secundum formam Dei, ipse et Pater unum sunt." Similarly in Ep. 59, c. 5. Our Lord's argument in that place turns not upon unity of will merely, i.e. what has been called a moral union, but upon unity of power, which in this case implies unity of essence. Cf. S. Ath. de Syn. 48. The argument in ver. 36 is à fortiori, and in ver. 38 He virtually repeats the assertion which in ver. 30 had given offence. See Pye Smith's Scripture Testimony to the Messiah, i. 460, that "the kind of union" in question is "a real identity of power ;" that our Lord's words were instantly pronounced to be blasphemous ; that "upon the Unitarian hypothesis, no motive can be imagined why He should not have met" the charge by "protesting that He was merely a man :" that His way of dealing with it was, in fact, to conduct the hearers "to a point" at which they would understand Him again to affirm what had created the offence; that this language, "the Father is in Me, and I in Him," cannot be reduced to an assertion of mere moral union or harmony of wills, because "the case refers not to any moral quality, but to a oneness of power." See also Liddon, Bamp. Lect. p. 185. In regard to the indirectness of our Lord's replies to cavillers, see Archd. Hessey on Moral Difficulties in the Bible, second series, lect. 4.

14. Here and elsewhere—as in the last Sermon in this volume, and de Nativ. 7, c. 2, "Non ... quod in carnem sit Dei natura mutata," and de Pent. 2, c. 3, "Quod enim Pater est, hoc est Filius, hoc est et Spiritus Sanctus, et vera Deitas in nullo esse aut major aut minor potest"—Leo's language reminds us of the "Athanasian Creed," which, whatever be its date, was clearly compiled by some one accustomed to the theological terminology of the Latin Church of the fifth century.

15. Here the impeccability of Christ is affirmed, as by S. Athanasius, c. Apollin. i. 7, 17, ii. 10; and Epiphanius, Hær. lxxvii. 27. There was in His human soul no germ of evil will, no "fomes peccati," no "concupiscentia" for temptation to excite or develope. See Liddon, Bamp. Lect. p. 524, that in "Christian antiquity our Lord's manhood, by the unique conditions of its existence," as personally united to God, "was believed to be wholly exempt from any propensity to, or capacity of, sinful self-will ... however latent and rudimentary." So Mozley on Augustinian Doctrine of Predestination, p. 97 : "Scripture says that our Lord was in all points tempted like as we are : but the Church has not thought it consistent with piety to interpret this text to mean that our Lord had the same direct propension to sin that we have. ... Such direct appetite for what is sinful is the characteristic of our fallen and corrupt nature." But here it is not enough to say that "our Lord did not assume a corrupt, but a sound humanity :" for Adam, as unfallen, was peccable, whereas our Lord's soul was protected by the presence of Godhead from any possibility of contradicting the Divine will;

although it might wish that obedience were "compatible" with a certain object of *per se* innocent desire, it could never "wish to be free from the law of obedience itself." (Liddon, p. 525.) See also an admirable article on "Our Lord's Human Example" in Church Quart. Review, vol. xvi. (July, 1883.) The writer points out that His human nature "had no independent centre of personality in itself :" it never existed except in union with His Divine Person ; and thus, "being one, and personally God, He could not have willed to sin. . . . Evil suggestions were really presented to Him, and He had real human faculties for them to make their appeal to; but . . . ." His "human will could not, in virtue of its essential relation to God, assent to what was not of God." It is added that a Christ Who could have sinned, but actually did not, would be as far removed from "the fellowship of ordinary moral experience" as the Christ of the Church's theology, Whose impeccability does not, in fact, destroy the value of His example, as taken in connection with that re-creating virtue which flows from, and presupposes a Christ personally divine. We may also observe that if, as is sometimes urged, a Christ Who is to be an universal example must have been peccable, then He must have felt and overcome every possible propensity to evil which can be felt by any of our race : and that the two ancient writers who maintained His abstract peccability are Julian, the developer of Pelagianism, and Theodore, the parent of Nestorianism. See more in Hutchings' Mystery of the Temptation, p. 116, ff. ; Trench's Studies in the Gospels, p. 27 ; Later Treatises of S. Athanasius, pp. 109, 128 ; F. W. Robertson, Sermons, i. 116.

16. He means that the Incarnation did but consummate a process which had previously been going on : it effected completely what had before been done imperfectly. As to the religious position of the Old Testament worthies, two truths must be held together. (1.) It is certain that "grace and truth came by Jesus Christ," S. John i. 17 ; that "Moses gave not the true Bread from heaven," vi. 32 ; that "the Holy Spirit was not" plenarily given until Jesus "was glorified," vii. 39 ; that "the ministration of the Spirit is more glorious than that of death," 2 Cor. iii. 7, &c. ; and that the men of faith referred to in Heb.

xi. "obtained not the promise" in their lifetime, and thus were "not made perfect." (2.) It is as certain that the patriarchs have a place in the kingdom, S. Matt. viii. 11 ; that Abraham saw the day of Christ, S. John viii. 56 ; that he and all God's ancient servants were justified by faith, Rom. iv. 1, ff., Heb. xi. 2, ff. Leo held both these truths. While he dwelt on the vast increase of blessing brought by the Incarnation, he was as true to the unity which binds together the two economies, to the revelation of Christ as the End of the law, the Antitype of ancient symbols, the Fulfiller of persevering hopes, the God Whom Judah was to behold ; to that teaching, in short, of the Nunc Dimittis, which Marcionite and Manichean assailants of the Old Testament so rudely flung away, and which our Seventh Article re-affirmed against the Anabaptists. Christ, he knew, was the Christ of the Hebrew Fathers ; the New Testament, as S. Augustine had said, was "the Old unveiled ;" on the hopes which it realized, pure souls had long been living. See Sermon 11 in this volume, c. 2. Not only does he call Christ's birthday "dies præparationis antiquæ," (in Nativ. 2, c. 1,) and affirms that "omnis prorsus antiquitas colentium Deum verum in hac fide vixit," (i.e. faith in the expected Christ, de Pass. 1, c. 1,) but he even says that those who were justified by faith in Christ before His coming, "Christi sunt corpus effecti," (in Nativ. 10, c. 7.) See the Christian Year, Circumcision :

> " Now of Thy love we deem
> As of an ocean vast,
> Mounting in tides against the stream
> Of ages gone and past," &c.

17. Here Leo gives his own answer to a very old objection, "If Christ's Advent was so great a blessing, why were so many generations allowed to pass away without enjoying it ?" The writer of the Epistle to Diognetus (c. 9) says in effect, " In order fully to exhibit man's moral incapacity, and so to prepare him to accept God's grace." Martensen, in his Christian Dogmatics, (E. T. p. 226,) follows this ancient writer : " Because God would show men what by their own power they could accomplish . . . . The kingdom of this world must be revealed in its full range . . . . heathendom must exhaust all its possibilities." A yet

sterner form of this answer is given in Gregory Nyssen's Catechet. c. 29. Justin Martyr glances at the difficulty, and characteristically meets it by claiming as unconscious and anticipative Christians multitudes who before Christ came were taught by the Word to live righteously, (Apol. i. 46.) Origen gives the same answer, c. Cels. iv. 7 ; and, what is more remarkable and interesting, Augustine adopts it in Ep. 102, q. 2. Leo's reply is somewhat fuller; he says that the "delay" is to be looked at in connection with a long process of "fore-announcements :" the more numerous these were, the easier would it be for men to receive the Gospel when it was actually presented to them. But as we have seen, he dwells strongly on the closeness of God's relation to the righteous from the very dawn of human history.

18. "Glorificate *et portate* Deum in corpore vestro," 1 Cor. vi. 20, Vulg. The true Greek text is, δοξάσατε δὴ τὸν Θεὸν ἐν τῷ σώματι ὑμῶν, omitting καὶ ἐν τῷ πνεύματι κ.τ.λ. See Alford in loc. The "et portate" is doubtless a very old gloss (S. Cyprian read it in his text, de Hab. Virg. 2, and Tertullian seems to have read "tollite," adv. Marc. v. 7) suggested by ver. 19. Leo again adopts it, de Pass. 2, c. 3.

19. There was no need for him to say what Sacrifice he meant. All his hearers would at once understand him of the Holy Eucharist, in the oblation of which the faithful were believed to have their part, (so the Roman Canon Missæ, "qui tibi offerunt hoc sacrificium laudis,") in that they brought the elements to the sanctuary, and afterwards supported the Priest, their representative, by the devout energy of their "concordant will." (Carter on the Priesthood, p. 151.) Leo says in Serm. de Jej. vii. mensis, 6, c. 3, "Tunc enim et sacrificii munda est oblatio, et misericordiæ sancta largitio, quando ii qui ista dependunt, quod operantur intelligunt." In Ep. 80, c. 2, "In ecclesia Dei . . . nec rata sunt sacerdotia, nec vera sacrificia, nisi in nostræ proprietate naturæ verus nos Pontifex reconciliet." Ep. 157, c. 5 : "intercepta est sacrificii oblatio." In Serm. de Nat. ips. 5, c. 3, Melchisedech is said to have offered the sacrifice of that Sacrament, &c. ; and Muratori, Lit. Rom.

i. 19, quotes from the "Gemma Animæ," "Leo Papa apposuit (canoni) 'Sanctum sacrificium, immaculatam hostiam,'" the words which conclude the prayer " Supra quæ propitio."

20. "Cum cœlestis militiæ . . . exercitu." Hence probably came the words which occur in some of the Roman Prefaces, e.g., that for Christmas, "Cumque omni militia cœlestis exercitus, hymnum gloriæ tuæ canimus." It is to be observed that Leo's words as to the "Gloria in Excelsis" do not necessarily mean more than that the *original* Angelic Hymn, S. Luke ii. 14, was recited in the Christmas Day service ; and it is to this that Zaccaria (Biblioth. Ritual. ii. 2, p. lx. sq.) in his notes on Maldonatus' Tract. de Cæremoniis (Disput. i. 10) would restrict the statement in the Liber Pontificalis, that Telesphorus, Bishop of Rome in the reign of Hadrian, ordered the "hymnus Angelicus Gloria in Excelsis to be said before the sacrifice" on the Nativity. There is, indeed, no reason for attaching any historic value to this statement; and it may be questioned whether, if Symmachus, the sixth Pope after Leo, is rightly reported to have ordered the "hymn" to be used on all Sundays and Martyrs' days, (Anastasius, Vit. Pontif. i. 89,) this is to be understood of more than the single verse. But as the whole hymn was substantially extant long before Leo's time, it is likely enough that it is referred to in Leo's words, and in the statement about Symmachus. It is "Græcæ absque dubio originis," Gerbert. Vet. Lit. Alemann. i. 299. Compare Daniel, Thesaurus Hymn. ii. 268. It exists in two Greek forms, one in the Alexandrian MS. (see T. Smith's Miscellanea, p. 144, and Palmer's Orig. Lit. ii. 159,) and another in the Apostolical Constitutions, vii. 47, (see Bingham, xiii. 10. 9.) The former brings in the name of the Holy Spirit after "the only-begotten Son Jesus Christ ;" and in this it is followed by old Irish texts of the hymn, and by the text in the Scottish Communion Office as revised in 1764, which, however, has amplified the address to the Holy Spirit, and inserted a new address to the Son, both preceding the words, "O Lord, the only-begotten Son," &c. (See Dowden's Annotated Scottish Communion Office, p. 226.) The latter is a very inferior form, perhaps corrupted by Arianisers ; at any rate "there is no sort of reason to suppose that" it

The "Gloria in Excelsis." 147

"is older or more primitive than that which appears in Codex A." (Church Quart. Review, xxi. 6.) In the East it has always been what it was anciently in Gaul, at Milan, and in Ireland, a part of the Morning Office; see Goar's Euchologion, p. 58. It is called in the East "the Great Doxology." Its Eucharistic use seems to have extended in the West from Rome, until it excluded the more ordinary use; but until the eleventh century no celebrant other than a Bishop might recite the hymn, except on Easter Day. (Muratori, Lit. Rom. ii. 1.) See also Lesley's Preface to the Mozarabic Missal, 70; and note to the Mass "omnium offerentium," Miss. Moz. ed. Migne, 221. The Latin version, as now used in the Roman Mass, and as substantially represented in the English Service, differs from the Eastern by repeating the word "God" twice at the end of the first part; by adding "Thou only art most high;" by altering "to the glory" into "in the glory," and by inserting the mention of the Holy Spirit into that clause, thereby doubly impairing the allusion to Phil. ii. 11. The addition of the clause, "*Thou* that takest away .... have mercy upon us" to our form dates from 1552, and was perhaps due to some oversight. Leo, it will be seen, follows the Latin reading "bonæ voluntatis," from εὐδοκίας, which has been preferred by modern critics on the authority of the older uncials; but Scrivener (Introduct. to Criticism of N. T., p. 590) considers that "solid reason and pure taste revolt against" their "yoke" in this instance, and observes that εὐδοκίας destroys the symmetrical triad, and well nigh defies attempts to "extract some tolerable sense out of it." (Keble's "love towards men of love" is a poetic recasting of the supposed original; see Christian Year, Christmas Day.) Dean Burgon suggests that εὐδοκία became εὐδοκίας after a copyist, with his eyes fixed on the first syllable of ἀνθρώποις, had forgotten the preceding ἐν. (Revision Revised, p. 41.)

21. Baptism, with S. Leo as with the whole ancient Church, was the Sacrament of Regeneration. He even compares the font to the Virgin's womb, in that the same Spirit Who "caused Mary to bear the Saviour causes the water to regenerate the believer," Serm. in Nativ. 5, c. 5; so that, "as in that case the sacred conception made sin to be absent, in this the mystic

washing takes it away," in Nativ. 4, c. 3. See also Serm. 1, c. 3, Serm. 9, c. 6; and de Pass. 18, c. 5, where the regenerating effect of baptism is made to depend on the real assumption of human nature by the Word. In Ep. 16 he calls Baptism a "principal" Sacrament; traces it—as he does in the Tome, and in Epiph. 4, c. 4—to the water from our Lord's side (compare our Baptismal Office, Pearson, Art. 4, and Dr. Pusey on Holy Baptism, pp. 293—301); comments on S. Paul's account of it in Rom. vi. 3; and forbids it to be administered, except in cases of necessity, at any other times than Easter and Pentecost. See de Jej. x. mensis, 7. 1, "natura .... sacro baptismate jam renata," de Pass. 19. 4, "regenerationis ... mysterio."

22. Here, following Phil. iii. 3, Gal. vi. 16, he claims for Christians the character of true Israelites, as in Nativ. 10, c. 7, "veri Israelitæ, et in consortium filiorum Dei veraciter adoptati." In Epiph. 3, c. 3, "Intret in patriarcharum familiam gentium plenitudo," &c. De Pass. 2, c. 3, "Nos, inquam, spiritale semen Abrahæ."

23. Here, alluding to Phil. ii. 13, he puts into the fewest words possible the doctrine of prevenient grace, i.e., that the first movements of the will towards good are the result of a Divine prompting,—the Holy Spirit appealing to the soul, and enabling it to respond to that appeal. Compare the Collect "Prevent us," and those for Easter Day and the Sunday next before Advent. See "Anti-Pelagian Treatises of S. Augustine," p. xiii. Leo often recurs to this thought, e.g., in Epiph. 8, c. 3, "ex Deo ... et effectum operis et initium voluntatis;" de Quadrag. 5, c. 1, "qui ideo dat præceptum ut excitet desiderium;" de Quadrag. 11, c. 4, "cum qui præstitit velle, donet et posse;" de Pass. 16, c. 6, "Juste ... nobis instat præcepto qui præcurrit auxilio;" Ep. 1, c. 3, "Gratia ... principium justitiæ," &c.

24. *Paganus* was originally "a villager." It came to be applied, chiefly in military arrogance, to the whole unwarlike or civilian population. So according to Juvenal, xvi. 33, it was safer to accuse a paganus falsely than a soldier truly; and in

Tac. Hist. iii. 24, at the second battle of Bedriacum, delinquent soldiers are addressed as "pagani." The word became thus associated with the notion of boorishness and ignorance ; comp. Prudentius, Cathem. xi. 86, on the adoration by the shepherds—

"Concurrat ad præsepia
Pagana gens et quadrupes."

And from the middle of the fourth century it became a synonym for one who persisted in idolatry ; partly as a term of reproach, partly because the old superstitions became more and more confined to the rural districts. In this sense we have "paganorum animi" in a law of Valentinian I., Cod. Theod. xvi. 2. 18 ; and in subsequent laws we read, "Qui ex Christianis pagani facti sunt," xvi. 7. 1 ; "vel de hæreticis vel de paganis," xvi. 10, 13 ; "sacerdotales paganæ superstitionis," xvi. 10, 20; "qui profano pagani ritus errore . . . polluuntur, *hoc est Gentiles*," xvi. 10, 21. And see Leo, de Collect. 3, on pagan "superstitions." And so the term is a witness to the Church's successful boldness in first occupying the great towns ("neque civitates *tantum*," &c., says Pliny to Trajan), and also a compendium, as it were, of that strange, sad chapter in European history, the vitality of idolatry, of "heathenism" amid the "heaths" and forests. It calls to our minds the "peasants" refusing the Light, —assembling around the tree, the stone, the fountain, and the Bel-fire (the Scottish Beltane), using divination, scarifying their flesh,—and transmitting the dark tradition of a condemned worship in spite of missionaries, kings and synods. On the history of the term cf. Hooker, v. 80. 2 ; Gibbon, iii. 100 (ed. Smith); Trench on Study of Words, p. 69 ; and on the lingerings of "Paganism," Johnson's Engl. Canons, i. 244, 279, 378 ; Maitland's Dark Ages, p. 151 ; Dean Church's Essays, p. 249 ; Robertson's Hist. Ch., i. 246.

25. He emphasizes the coeternity of the Son in this passage, in Ep. 28, c. 2, and in Nativ. 5, c. 3, "Sempiterne . . . . Filius, Filius est : et sempiterne Pater, Pater est." And de Pentec. 2, c. 1 : "Sempiternum est Patri, coæterni sibi Filii sui esse geni-

torem." This is quite in the Athanasian manner; cf. Orat. c. Ar. i. 14, 18, 20, where S. Athanasius argues, against the Arian ἦν ποτε ὅτε οὐκ ἦν, that God could not begin to be a Father; that a real Divine Sonship implies coeternity; that the Trinity must be eternal; that, given the Father's essence (ὑπόστασις,) πάντως εὐθὺς εἶναι δεῖ τὸν χαρακτῆρα ... ταύτης. So S. Augustine: "Sempiternæ Sapientiæ sua causa est sempiterna; nec tempore prior est quam sua sapientia. Deinde, si Patrem sempiternum esse inest Deo, nec fuit aliquando non Pater,—nunquam sine Filio fuit," de Div. Quæst. 83, n. 16. And cf. Aug. Serm. 140. 5. "Semper Pater, semper Filius."

26. See Note 10. In this passage he teaches that the Manhood of Christ never existed in a *human* personality; He did not unite Himself to *a* man, but He took to Himself Manhood. Comp. this sermon, c. 6; Ep. 28, c. 3; and Serm. in Nativ. 10, c. 5, "Idem est a paterno non divisus throno, et ab impiis crucifixus in ligno;" de Pass. 17, c. 1, "Idem est qui impiorum manibus comprehenditur, et qui nullo fine concluditur." See Hooker, v. 52. 3, "It pleased not the Word or Wisdom of God to take to Itself some one person among men," &c. So Newman, Sermons, vi. 62: "Though man, He was not strictly speaking, in the English sense of the word, *a* man: He was not such as one of us, and one out of a number." And see Liddon, Bamp. Lect. p. 262.

27. Psilanthropism, or the doctrine that Jesus was a mere man, began with Cerinthus, who called Him the son of Joseph and Mary, and distinguished Him from "the Christ," a being emanating from the Deity, which descended on Him at His baptism, and departed from Him before His death. Cerinthus, it is well known, was the great adversary of S. John at Ephesus. See Iren. i. 26; iii. 3; Euseb. iii. 28. Compare Bp. Lightfoot, Apost. Fath., part 2, vol. i. p. 366. Of the Ebionites, who stood, like Cerinthus, between Christianity and Judaism, and appear to have become a sect at the beginning of the second century, some admitted the miraculous conception, but all held our Lord to have been a mere man, eminent for His goodness, Euseb. iii. 27. Burton contends, (Bamp. Lect. Note 84), on the authority

of Epiphanius, (Hær. xxx.) that they agreed with Cerinthus in distinguishing between Jesus—whether regarded as the son of Joseph, or as virginally born—and the "Christ" who descended upon Him: so that it would not be accurate to call them disbelievers in the Divinity of "Christ." But it seems clear from Epiphanius' own words that he was speaking only of one class of Ebionites, those who had affinities with Gnosticism, and whose notion of a pre-existent "Christ" comes out in the Pseudo-Clementine writings. (See Dict. Chr. Biog. art. "Ebionites.") Justin Martyr's reference to an evidently small number of professing Christians, who regarded Christ as a mere man, points clearly to the more simply Judaical Ebionites. (Dial. 48.) He was so regarded by a few of the Gnostics, as Justinus, Carpocrates, and apparently Basilides. But such men, being wholly outside the Church's pale, were not taken account of; and when at the end of the second century, Theodotus, the tanner of Byzantium, being reproached at Rome for having previously fallen away in a persecution, answered, "Why, I did but deny a man!" he was regarded as "the father of the God-denying apostasy," (see the writer quoted by Eusebius, v. 28, and usually identified with Hippolytus, but supposed by Dr. Salmon to be Caius, Introduction to New Testament, p. 66.) This "bad eminence" would be assigned to him as the first "Psilanthropist" among Gentile Christians. Artemas took a similar line; as Neander says, ii. 264, the Artemonites "wanted a Christianity which the understanding could fully comprehend;" and their claim to represent the primitive Gospel was at once repelled on grounds of history and Scripture, Eus. l. c. The writer there quoted, as Dr. Liddon says, refers confidently to "the continuous drift and meaning" of the Church's "belief." (Bamp. Lect. p. 435.) In 269, Paul of Samosata, when forced to avow his opinions, declared Jesus to be a mere man, who so advanced in virtue by aid of the Divine attribute called the Logos, as to attain the honorary title of "Son of God." The Council of Antioch, in condemning him, said, "Let him write letters of communion to Artemas," Euseb. vii. 30. In the middle of the fourth century, Psilanthropism was represented by the clever and pertinacious Photinus, Bishop of Sirmium, who held that the Son of Mary had no pre-existence, but was a mere man in whom the Word, viewed as impersonal, dwelt with special fulness, (see Later Treat. of S. Ath. p. 16.) He was condemned by synods in 345, 347, 348, and 351. Augustine, before his conversion, was for a time a Psilanthropist, Confess. vii. c. 19. Leo mentions this heresy again, in Nativ. 10. 2; "Some believed Him to be merely Son of man."

28. Compare in Nativ. 10, c. 2, "simulatam carnis speciem." "Docetism, or the doctrine that our Lord's Body was an immaterial phantom," (Mansel, Gnostic Heresies, p. 58), originated in the notion, widely spread throughout the farther East, that matter and spirit were in antagonism, and that "evil resulted from the inherent fault of matter," (Dr. Salmon in Dict. Chr. Biogr. art. "Docetism." On its various forms see Bishop Lightfoot, Apostolic Fathers, part ii. vol. i. p. 369, and Salmon l. c.) Its growth and success are facts of great significance : for it never could have sprung up in presence of an originally "Psilanthropist" Christianity. It presupposed our Lord's divine pre-existence, and inferred that He could not have stooped to a real contact with matter. We meet with it first in Simon Magus; Pearson, i. 285, Art. 3; ii. 196, 240. Its effect was, as has been said, to "*unrealize the real, historic, positive basis of the Christian faith;* to attenuate into a mere illusion the history and person of Jesus; and so to make His redemption only ideal and imaginary;" and, as Bp. Alexander remarks, it became, by logical necessity, "anti-sacramental." It shared with Cerinthianism the far-stretching censure of 1 S. John iv. 3; for it "confessed not Jesus Christ come in flesh." His disciple S. Polycarp, Philipp. 7, refers to it as a work of the devil; S. Ignatius denounced it as a deadly plant, an unbelief, a blasphemy, Trall. 11, 10, Smyrn. 2, 5. It was held by Saturninus of Antioch. Tertullian pointed to its results; all Christ's works were "imaginariæ," done "mendacio;" and "thus the whole work of God was overthrown," adv. Marc. iii. 8. In the fourth century S. Cyril of Jerusalem found reason to warn his catechumens, "If the Incarnation is a phantom, so is salvation," Cat. 4, 9, compare Epiphanius, Hær. lxix. 59. In Leo's time Docetism was still potent; it formed part of that many-sided and terrible Manicheism which he called "the devil's fortress" (cf. Serm. in

Nativ. 4, c. 4); as such he alludes to it in Sermon 10 in this volume, c. 1, 2; and he regarded Eutychianism as Docetism in a new form, Serm. in Pass. 14, c. 4; "isti phantasmatici Christiani;" so Ep. 124, c. 2, that Eutyches held." Christum simulatorie omnia egisse," &c. This, be it observed, is not what Eutyches said, but an inference of Leo's from what he said. Docetism mingled itself with the wild misbelief of the Anabaptists: Caspar Schwenckfeld, in Silesia, approached, at any rate, to a Docetic position as early as 1528 (Hardwick, Hist. of Articles, p. 97, 393), and so did some heretics denounced by Henry VIII. in 1540, (Hardwick, Hist. Reform. p. 277.)

29. From a wish to pacify Catholics, the Arian leaders, at an early period of the controversy, adopted a high tone of language about our Lord, speaking of Him as the greatest of creatures, as adorable, and as Divine. See Newman's Arians, p. 216, ff. The Catholic controversialists seized on this inconsistency. "All creatures," they argued, "are, as such, on a level, in comparison of the Uncreate. You who make the Son a creature, so many degrees above the Archangels, and then adore Him as a God, are, *on your own showing*, idolaters. Either disclaim the worship of Christ, or confess His Consubstantiality." We find this argument in S. Athanasius (Orat. iii. 16, &c.), S. Hilary (de Syn. 50), S. Ambrose (de Fide, i. 104), and in the narrative of Peter of Alexandria in Theodoret, iv. 22: and S. Basil, when urged by Modestus to adopt the creed of the Arian emperor, is said to have replied that he "could not endure to worship any creature," (Greg. Naz. Orat. 43. 48:) and Epiphanius taunts Arians with setting up again Nebuchadnezzar's golden image. (Hær. lxix. 31.) In fact, "the Fathers regarded" the Arian conception of a created godhead "with simple detestation;" such a godhead "was a theological monster in their eyes, unlawfully, profanely, and falsely imagined." Mozley on Theory of Development, p. 78. See too Later Treatises of S. Athanasius, p. 63. In the passage before us, Leo seems to be following S. Augustine c. Maximin. ii. 15, to the effect that if the Father (*as* God) is greater and the Son less, then there are two gods. He repeatedly denies that there

can be any "degrees" in Deity. See Sermon 14 in this volume, c. 5, Sermon 18, c. 4, and de Pentec. 2, c. 2, "omnibus existentiæ gradibus exclusis." We thus see that in the Arian controversy the question which was really at stake was not *only* as to the Divine dignity of Christ, not *only* as to the basis and justification of an "absolute devotion" to Him, in recognition of His "eternal supremacy over minds and hearts, (a point excellently brought out by R. W. Dale in "Good Words" for 1878, p. 685, and see Gore, Leo the Great, p. 55, "Not fully God? Then, by an inevitable inference, not able to claim full adoring worship. But that . . . . this He could claim, the whole Christian life involved as its secret, its clue, its inspiration.") This was indeed at stake, but more than this,—namely, the purity and simplicity of the idea of Deity. That idea was impaired and corrupted by Arianism, which was thus, as has often been remarked, a retrograde movement towards Paganism—a fact which goes far to account for its large success in such an age as the fourth century. See Church Quart. Rev. xvi. 376.

30. Compare Ep. 15, 1, where the Priscillianists are said to have derived their notion of a single Person in the Godhead, called at different times Father, Son, and Holy Spirit, from Sabellius, "cujus discipuli etiam 'Patripassiani' merito nuncupantur," &c. The Sabellian heresy, which confounded the Persons in the Godhead, appears to have had two forms; (1) a downright assertion that the Father actually became Incarnate, —that the Son was but the Father under another name; (2) a subtler representation of the Son and the Spirit as emanations from the Father; cf. Newman's Arians, p. 90. Its chief propounders were Praxeas, about A.D. 200; Noetus, of Smyrna; and Sabellius, of Pentapolis, in Africa. But tendencies towards it existed in the time of Justin Martyr, Dial. 128. Its strength lay in its profession of zeal for the Divine Unity; it called the Catholic doctrine Tritheism. "Well, my friends, have we one God, or three?" was a Sabellian sarcasm, (Epiphan. Hær. lxii. 2.) On the other hand, it was doubly weak, in that its more intelligible form might be fairly described as *Patripassianism* ("Patrem crucifixit," was Tertullian's phrase), and that both forms denied the Eternal Sonship, and deprived the Mediation

of all reality. Dionysius of Alexandria, in Euseb. vii. 6, ascribed to Sabellius "unbelief as to the Only-begotten, the Word Incarnate, and insensibility as to the Holy Spirit;" and Beryllus of Bostra was converted from these views by Origen's reasoning from the fact of Christ's human soul, Euseb. vi. 33, Soc. iii. 7. The Arians imputed Sabellianizing to the upholders of the Homoousion, (Newman, Athan. Treat. i. 203;) but S. Athanasius pointed to the Eternal Sonship as a safeguard against Sabellian "impiety," Orat. iii. 36; and S. Chrysostom traced the Church's middle way between Arian "severance" and Sabellian "confusion," de Sacerd. iv. 4. In truth, the Church was safe by not being one-sided: she called our Lord, in Scripture language, not "the Word" only, which would encourage Sabellianism,—not "the Son" only, which would tend to Tritheism,—but "the Word *in* God," so as to preserve the Unity, and "the Son *from* God," so as to preserve the Trinity. See Newman, Arians, p. 174; Liddon, Bamp. Lect. p. 236. In her use of the Latin term *Person*, with regard to the Blessed Three, she excluded alike the original sense of *character* or *aspect*, and, as Olshausen says, (On the Gospels, iii. 334,) "the idea of isolated individuality." So Newman, Ath. Treatises, i. 155, "the original mystery of the Holy Trinity, that Person and Individuum are not equivalent terms." On "the popular tendency of the day to an unconscious Sabellianism," see Wilberforce on the Incarnation, p. 112. Language apparently Trinitarian is sometimes found to refer to an "economic," and not an "ontological" Trinity; whereas the Church professes to "worship one God" as existing "in Trinity," and the Trinity thus acknowledged is called "eternal." The Incarnation, in fact, presupposes that the distinctions which for want of a better term we call personal "have more than a mere relationary existence dependent on external things," that they exist necessarily and absolutely in the Godhead. (Wilberforce, p. 111.)

31. The notion that Christ's Body was ethereal, not human, was a modified Docetism. Leo refers to it, in Nativ. 10, c. 2; "Some thought that His bodily action and form de sublimioris generis prodiisse materia." Valentinus said his "lower Jesus" had such a body, which only "passed through" Mary, and was

not formed from her substance; and this "unclean fancy" (Kingsley's Good News of God, p. 182) was reproduced by some of the early Anabaptists (Hardwick on Articles, p. 92), and punished with death in the person of Joan Bocher; our Christmas Preface, composed at that very time, being a witness against it. Modern as it is, that Preface exactly represents the Fathers' mind; see Cyril. Hier. Cat. iv. 9.

32. This passage, which says that the Apollinarians supposed the "Deity" to supply the place of a rational mind in Christ, is more accurate than that in Nativ. 4, c. 5, which puts "anima" for "mens," in that only some of them went so far as to deny that He had an "animal soul." The history of Apollinaris is peculiarly mournful. (See Newman, Church of the Fathers, p. 156, ff., and Tracts Theol. and Eccl. p. 257, ff.) A learned and able prelate, an old friend of S. Athanasius, intent on opposing Arianism, he fell into error through ill-directed reverence. He appealed to the true and deep-seated Christian conviction of the singleness of Christ's Person, and of His absolute sinlessness. But he gave to these ideas a one-sided and erroneous expression. He assumed that if Christ had all the constituents of humanity, the "two complete" natures thus supposed would make two persons: and that, although Christ might assume an "animal soul" or ψυχή without compromising His Divine sanctity, the intelligent soul or νοῦς, the seat of choice, was necessarily instinct with capacities for evil, and therefore Christ had no such soul, but the Word supplied its place. (See Later Treatises of S. Athanasius, p. 79.) Speaking generally, the Catholic opponents of Apollinaris answered in effect, We agree with you that Christ is one, and that He is sinless: but we reject your inferences from these truths. The Word, we hold, could maintain a human mind, as well as body, in union not with a human individual, but with His own single self: and while appropriating a human mind, He could thereby exempt it from all "subjection to evil," (Epiphanius, Hær. lxxvii. 27.) S. Ambrose has a vigorous passage, in which he seems to say to Apollinarians in regard to their "solicitude" on this point, "Trust God to care for His own honour," (de Incarn. Domin. Sacram. 69.) Damasus, Bishop of Rome, was specially earnest against Apollinaris; he

rightly felt that the Word, if really Incarnate for the restoration of human nature in its entirety, must have assumed "integrum Adam sine peccato," and therefore "a reasonable soul," exempt from sinful tendencies. See his language in Theodoret, H. E. v. 11. Apollinaris was condemned by Councils at Rome in 377, at Alexandria in 378, at Constantinople in 381. Cf. Pearson, i. 286, Art. 3; ii. 197. Some of his adherents, from denying to Christ a human mind, proceeded to deny Him a human body. They revived, in substance, the old Valentinian notion, saying that His body was not formed from the Virgin, but was a portion of the Divine essence clothed with matter. S. Athanasius, S. Basil, and others protested earnestly against this revolting development of a theory which had arisen as if in jealousy for the Majesty of God; and urged that "men could receive no help from the Incarnation, unless a real human body, joined to Godhead, had overcome the power of death," S. Basil Ep. 262. Apollinaris himself, according to his own declarations, did not go beyond asserting that Christ's flesh, while really derived from the Virgin, might be *called* consubstantial with the Word, because of its close union with Him. He could therefore personally disclaim the debasing notions which S. Athanasius combated in his letter to Epictetus, and elsewhere. The Lord's flesh, he owned, was really human; and Godhead had undergone no alteration. Language, indeed, was quoted as his, which went much further: and whether he was disingenuous or inconsistent, or on the other hand was charged with what he had never said, some of his friends and followers, at a very early period, had spoken of the Lord's body not merely as "God's body," and thereby as Hooker says (v. 54. 9), "many ways exalted above the reach of our capacities," but as actually, in its own substance, divine. This was the view of the extreme section of Apollinarians, led by Polemon and Timotheus, as against the moderate section represented by Valentinus; and, as Leo here says, it involved the monstrous consequence of a conversion of part of the Divine essence itself into flesh (compare the "Quicunque") and, in so far, of a destruction of its integrity. Altogether, Apollinarianism, in either or both of its two forms, was a menace to the doctrine of the Incarnation on one side, as Nestorianism was afterwards on the other. Men were being led to think that here, at least, was a decisive barrier against that Arian heresy which persisted in living on, and would not accept defeat,—a complete satisfaction for the felt need of a Redeemer strictly immaculate and personally divine : a whole Apollinarian literature sprang up ; the aged chief of the party, who in earlier life had written book after book in classic style for Christians bereft of Christian schoolteachers, was just as facile in pouring out pamphlets and treatises, and hymns which men and women could sing at their work. (Cf. Sozomen, vi. 25.) The prospect was nothing short of a revival of Oriental mysticism, which would virtually "deny Jesus Christ as come in flesh." How serious it was, we may understand from Gregory Nazianzen's passionate complaints against the "confidence" or "audacity" of Apollinarians: from the fact that, as will presently be explained, this popular heresy was Theodore's stumbling-block: and from the often-recurring disclaimer of "any concern with the opinions of Apollinaris" or the denial of Apollinarian propositions, which the necessities of controversy evoked from Cyril. (Apol. adv. Orient. 3.)

33. On the subtle connection between diverse errors, e.g., Arianism and Sabellianism, which were formally antagonistic to each other, see Newman's note in Athan. Treatises, i. 189. In his "Arians," p. 209, he exhibits the points of agreement and difference between Arianism and four other theologies. Gibbon has observed that "the Sabellian ends where the Ebionite had begun," (iii. 55,) as Paul of Samosata and the Photinians held the Logos to be impersonal and Jesus to be simply human : so Cyril (ad Theodosium, 13) observes that the former of these opinions leads naturally to the latter ; and Wilberforce quotes Blanco White as "truly remarking that Sabellianism is only Socinianism in disguise," (Incarnation, p. 173,) even as F. W. Newman "discerned too plainly that the Sabellian, if consistent, is only a concealed Ebionite," (Phases of Faith, p. 87.) There is an historical affinity between Pelagianism and Nestorianism : those who underestimate the need of redemption will be likely to underestimate the Person of the Redeemer. But Apollinarianism also approached the Pelagian ground by laying stress on the "imitation" of Christ apart from re-creation by Him.

Nestorianism.

In modern times Calvinism has developed a Judaical tendency : and popular Protestantism has unconsciously employed rationalistic arguments against the principle of Sacramental operation. Hooker, in a well known passage, speaks of disparagers of Sacraments as " drawing very near" to Gnosticism, v. 60. 4. Schwenckfeld, already referred to, "was denounced as a Eutychian heretic," (Hardwick, Hist. Ref. p. 291,) and the early Quakers were charged with Sabellianising. And Westcott well observes (Epistles of S. John, p. xxxvi.) that "modern idealism, which aims at securing the pure spiritual conception free from all associations of time and place, is a new Docetism," while " modern realism, by striving to give distinction to the actual outward features of the Lord's life, seems to tend more and more to an Ebionitic" position, and " popular Christology is largely though unconsciously affected by Cerinthian tendencies," separating the Son of God from the Son of Man. (Such tendencies might not less truly be called Nestorian.) Any one who looks at the arguments of a typical Manichean in S. Augustine's "Contra Faustum" will find himself in a strangely modern atmosphere ; and his controversy with those who explained away " grace" anticipates the issue now raised by Naturalism.

34. The history of Nestorianism links on to that of Apollinarianism. The Antiochene school of theology, always averse to mystic extremes, produced an able exponent in Diodore, Bishop of Tarsus, who, in order to secure a full recognition of the humanity of Christ, represented Him as a human individual who had been taken by the Son of God into an exceptional alliance with Himself, so as permanently to abide in that Divine presence into which the prophets had been at times admitted. To Diodore succeeded a much more famous person, Theodore, Bishop of Mopsuestia in Cilicia. He was keen and vehement against Apollinarianism, bent on maintaining the distinction between "the form of God" and "the form of a servant," and, from an ethical standpoint, very anxious about the value of Christ's life as an example. And here it must be allowed that approved writers before his time, as well as after it, had sometimes treated the language of

"humiliation" in the Gospels as "economic," and not representing a true human experience in our Lord. Such language would be a provocation to Theodore: he would say, "This is Docetism." He formulated his Christology somewhat thus: the Divine Son or Word had chosen and dwelt in *a* man, Jesus; the bond between them was best described as a "conjunction;" it might be compared to the conjugal tie. Jesus was the greatest of the saints, the one with whom God was specially "well pleased:" He was the chief of all God's adopted children; His pre-eminence showed itself in the "signal rapidity" with which He discerned good from evil, in His "extraordinary inclination towards good," in the unusual facility with which He practised virtue, and acquired complete control over passion. Such was the Christ of Theodore; not in any real sense an Incarnate Word, but an associate of the Word, Who thus employed him as a specially favoured agent. Theodore's extant language seems sometimes to show a sort of anxiety as to whether such a "conjunction" would seem a sufficient union between God and man, for the purposes of redemption. He stretches it as far as it will go, and makes as much of it as he can. But at its best and utmost, it differs only in degree from the relation between God and a great saint: in effect, it sets Incarnation clean aside, and evacuates of meaning such passages as S. John i. 14 and Phil. ii. 6—8. Theodore had got hold of two truths, as Apollinaris of other two; and like Apollinaris, he distorted truths by exaggerating and isolating them. He did not see that the reality of Christ's manhood could be recognised without lodging it in a human personality; that the moral power of Christ's life could be felt without admitting that it had been possible for Him to rebel against His Father.

If we substantially understand Theodore, we understand Nestorianism; for Nestorius did but popularise, in an unsystematic fashion, the ideas which he had imbibed from Theodore's books, if not from intercourse with him.

It is, then, clear that the question raised by the wide circulation of the discourses of Nestorius as archbishop of Constantinople was not verbal, but vital. Much of his language was irrelevant, and indicated some confusedness of thought: much would, of itself, admit of an orthodox construction; in one of the latest of his sermons, which Garnier dates on Sunday, Dec. 14, 430, he grants that "Theotokos" might be used as signifying that "the temple which was formed in Mary by the Holy Spirit was united to the Godhead:" but it was impossible not to ask whether by "the temple" he meant the body of Jesus, or Jesus Himself regarded as a human individual existing ἰδίᾳ, ἰδικῶς, ἀνὰ μέρος, as Cyril represents his theory,—and whether by "union" he meant more than a close alliance, *ejusdem generis*, in the last analysis, with the relation between God and every saint, or, indeed, every Christian in true moral fellowship with Him,—an alliance which would amount, in Cyril's phrase to no more than a "relative union," and would reduce the Saviour to a "Theophoros,"—the title claimed of old by one of His chief martyrs. And the real identity of Nestorius' view with that of Theodore was but too plainly exhibited by such statements as occur in some of the extracts preserved in Cyril's treatise "Against Nestorius,"—to the effect that Christ was one with the Word by participation in dignity; that "the man" was partaker of Divine power, and in *that* sense not mere man; that He was adored together with the Word; and that "My Lord and my God" was a doxology to the Father;—and, above all, by the words spoken at Ephesus, "I can never allow that a child of three months old was God." If Jesus was not God in His infancy, He was not God in His adult manhood. Leo had in earlier life enlisted the pen of Cassian against Nestorius; and his letters and sermons, as we have seen, are emphatically orthodox on the Hypostatic Union. While contending against Eutychianism, he shows that he has no indulgence for the heresy against which it was a reaction. He is indignant when a Nestorian sense is fraudulently put upon his "Tome." (Ep. 130, c. 3.) In several other places, he "brackets" Nestorianism and Eutychianism together, as equally heretical. See Ep. 30, c. 1; Ep. 102, c. 3; Ep. 123, c. 2. And in Ep. 93, c. 3, he upholds the decisions of the Council of Ephesus, "Ne tunc damnata impietas ideo sibi in aliquo blandiatur quia Eutyches justa exsecratione percellitur." Cp. Ep. 59, c. 5, "Nestorium .... merito ... damnavimus."

35. Eutyches was an old man, the head of a monastery at

Constantinople, very different from Nestorius both in temperament and in theology, yet occupying ground which was equally foreign to the faith. Years before he had been treated by Cyril, and by Cyril's archdeacon, as an important ally in the anti-Nestorian struggle. But afterwards he became a rallying point for that extreme wing of the "Alexandrian" party which was eager to crush Theodoret, as still in heart a Nestorianiser: and Theodoret was thus led to write his famous "Dialogues," in which Eutyches is probably indicated by "Eranistes," the opponent of "Orthodoxus:" while Domnus, patriarch of Antioch, went so far as openly to censure Eutyches for speaking of the Godhead and manhood of Christ as "one nature." (Facundus, Def. Tr. Capit. v. 8.) This points to the "celebrated dictum," as Cardinal Newman calls it, (Athan. Treat. ed. 2, ii. 427,) which Cyril had adopted from a tract believed to be by S. Athanasius: "one $\phi\acute{u}\sigma\iota s$ of God the Word, but *that* a $\phi\acute{u}\sigma\iota s$ incarnate." Cyril used it, as he largely explained (see passages quoted in Later Treatises of S. Athanasius, p. 175) by way of emphasising the singleness of the Lord's Person—of affirming that His divine $\phi\acute{u}\sigma\iota s$, in the sense of "self" or "personality," had assumed a manhood which was "not a second person, for it had never existed till it was His," (Newman, l. c.) In other words, "when the Word became flesh, He continued to be indivisibly Himself." Eutyches, a "dull old monk," whose "intensity and obstinacy of conviction were untempered either by theological insight or by moderation and balance of judgment," (Gore, Leo the Great, pp. 60, 48,) neglected Cyril's explanations of the "dictum;" he had evidently no head for them; he simply clung to his formula, "without note or comment," as if therein lay his whole doctrinal safety. So, when at the close of 448 he was accused before his Bishop, Flavian of Constantinople, the result of a long discussion was this: Eutyches (1) readily admitted that our Lord was "perfect man;" (2) he was reluctantly induced to acknowledge that He was "consubstantial with us in regard to His manhood;" (3) he persisted in saying that after the union of two $\phi\acute{u}\sigma\epsilon\iota s$, i.e. of Godhead with manhood considered in the abstract, had been effected in the Incarnation, there remained "one $\phi\acute{u}\sigma\iota s$ only." There was, he held, no authority for saying "two." It is true that $\phi\acute{u}\sigma\iota s$ had been used with some diversity of meaning; not seldom as equivalent to "person" or "hypostasis," (as in μία φύσις ..... σεσαρκωμένη) but also for "nature;" and Cyril in one remarkable passage, had explained the "hypostatic union" to mean that "the φύσις or ὑπόστασις of the Word, which is the Word Himself, having been really united, without any change or confusion, ἀνθρωπείᾳ φύσει, is considered, and is, one Christ, the selfsame, God and man." (Adv. Theod. 2.) This was not, indeed, an express assertion that the "human φύσις" remained, but it surely implied no less. Athanasius had not only implicitly but explicitly said as much (Orat. ii. 70, a passage relied on by Theodoret; Orat. iii. 43, 58; iv. 36; c. Apollin. ii. 6, 11:) Chrysostom had depicted the exaltation of "our φύσις" by the Ascension: Gregory Nazianzen had repeatedly ascribed two φύσεις to Christ: "nor must it be forgotten," says Card. Newman (Tracts Theol. and Eccles. p. 311), "that Cyril himself accepted the two φύσεις," as appears from passages at the end of Theodoret's second Dialogue. The first of these was adopted into the formulary of Chalcedon; "Not as if the difference of the natures was annulled by the union;" another says that they must be "kept unconfused." Another is still more tersely decisive: "Although it be said that the Only-begotten Word was hypostatically united to flesh, yet we do not mean that any fusion of the natures took place, οὔσης δὲ μᾶλλον ἑκατέρας τοῦθ᾽ ὅπερ ἐστί." This is like saying, "The human nature exists in Christ." It is worth while to observe this, because Cyril has been so often made responsible for Monophysitism. To return to Eutyches: his refusal to admit "two natures" in the Incarnate was fairly interpreted to mean that he did not believe Christ to exist in two spheres of being, and therefore that, like Theodoret's "Eranistes," he held that manhood had been "absorbed" by Godhead. If so, his admission of a "human consubstantiality" was unreal and valueless. But Flavian was not justified in telling Leo that Eutyches refused to make this admission: and it was polemical rhetoric to say that *he* was reviving Apollinarian or Valentinian theories, that *he* supposed Christ's body to have not been derived from Mary, that *he* "made void the truth of Christ's human flesh," that *he* "declared what was visible and palpable in Christ to be of the coeternal substance, as if the Word's Deity had converted itself into flesh and soul." These statements, which we find in Leo's correspondence, are inferences from the formula to which Eutyches had committed himself. That formula might, indeed, lead consistent thinkers to any amount of error in the direction to which it pointed: but where an ancient controversialist would think himself free to load a heretic in person with all the logical contents of his own language, the modern standard of justice towards opponents will bid us lay stress rather on Leo's own description of Eutyches as "multum imprudens et nimis imperitus," (Ep. 28, c. 1, comp. Ep. 29, c. 1, and Ep. 35, c. 1:) while we sympathise with Leo's indignation at the temporary success which Eutychianism achieved through the disastrous issue of the "Robbers' Meeting" at Ephesus in 449, and appreciate his zeal in working for another Council which should vindicate the doctrine of Christ's brotherhood with man, His real human sufferings and exaltation, and His Church's real communion with her Head,—together with the truth of His personal Divinity. This was done at Chalcedon. There, in the first instance, a formulary had been drafted which took special care to meet the expected imputation, "You are in effect Nestorianisers." It also declared Christ to be "*of*" or "*from* two natures." This phrase was ambiguous: Dioscorus, the bold bad prelate who had dominated the recent Council of 449 as a patron of Eutyches, was willing to say as much. It was urged by Leo's legates, and by the imperial commissioners, that something more definite was necessary. Ultimately, under this pressure, the Council adopted the phrase "*in* two natures," which was like saying, "Two natures exist under the Incarnation," or, "He *is*, at this moment, Man as well as God," as Cyril himself had said, that "even *in* our manhood He continued to be that which *He was*," the Only-begotten Word, (Epist. p. 95.) (Compare Serm. 2, c. 2, above, and a Preface for the Ascension in the so-called Leonine Sacramentary, Muratori, Lit. Rom. Vet. i. 314: "dum et in ea gloria quam tecum semper habuit, et in ea natura *est* quam suam fecit ex nobis.") Thus the revised formulary acknowledged "one and the same Christ, perfect in Godhead and in Manhood; truly God and truly Man, consubstantial Divinely with the Father, humanly with us; existing in two natures without confusion, change, division, or severance:"

then partly in Cyril's own words (see his second letter to Nestorius,) "the difference of the natures being nowise annulled by the union, but rather both natures being preserved, and meeting in one person and one hypostasis." One might have thought that such language, while excluding one error, was equally decisive against the opposite; but for years an Eutychianising party continued to charge the Council with Nestorianism; and the Armenians disowned its authority, not from any intelligent objection to what it intended to assert, but because in their own language "two natures" seemed to mean "two persons." (Neale, Introd. to East. Ch. ii. 1080.) Dioscorus and the great majority of the Egyptians rejected the Council, and professed to believe, not that the Manhood was absorbed in the Godhead, but that both together formed one composite nature. (Neale, Hist. Patr. Alex. ii. 8.) This formula still prevails among the Copts. It was largely propagated in the East by the indefatigable exertions of one man, Jacob or James, from whom its adherents have derived the name of "Jacobites:" and who was surnamed "Baradæus" from the "tattered beggar's disguise" in which he traversed Syria and Mesopotamia, animated by the deepest conviction that in preaching the "one nature," he was but contending for the personal oneness of Christ.

36. "Homo" does not here mean "an individual man" or human person, but "manhood." So in Serm. 14, c. 6, below, "hominis" is read antithetically to "deitatis," and in Serm. 16, c. 1, to "divinitatis." See too in Epist. 8, c. 2, where "verum hominem accepit Christus" is followed by "de ipsa naturæ nostræ communione." The passages, de Pass. 1, c. 2, "nec Verbum ibi ab homine disjunctum, nec homo est dissociatus a Verbo," and in Nativ. 2, c. 4, "inseparabilis a suo homine deitatis," and in Ep. 28, c. 4, "homo non consumitur dignitate," are to be similarly explained. The same usage appears in S. Augustine, Enchirid. c. 36, where it is distinctly denied that the "homo" in this case had any personal existence before the union of "Verbum et homo;" and in Civ. Dei, xi. 2, "Deus, Dei Filius, homine assumpto, non Deo consumpto, eamdem constituit . . . fidem, ut ad hominis Deum iter esset homini per Hominem Deum;" and Serm. 80. 5, "Idem enim Deus, idem homo; unus

enim Christus, Deus et homo; homo assumptus, ut in melius mutaremur," &c. Compare the "Leonine Sacramentary," Muratori, Lit. Rom. i. 316, " Dominus noster ..... unitum sibi hominem nostræ substantiæ in gloriæ tuæ dextera collocavit." Similarly S. Athanasius had used ἄνθρωπος for ἀνθρώπινον, see Athan. Treat. ii. 349 : also Newman, Tracts Theol. and Eccles. p. 333.

37. The service of the Epiphany was the last Christian observance attended by Julian before he threw aside the mask of Christian profession (Ammianus Marcellinus, xxi. 2.) It was a very popular festival : Leo corrects as a mistake the opinion of those Sicilians who thought it a more fitting time than Easter itself for solemn baptisms, " because on that day the Lord drew near to the baptism of S. John." (Ep. 16, c. 1, 6.) S. Augustine speaks of its solemn observance as "per universum mundum nota solemnitas," Serm. 202. 1.

38. The Magi were gradually reckoned as three, because of "the threefold gifts which they offered." Trench on Star of Wise Men, p. 15. S. Aug. in his Epiphany Sermons does not call them three; and neither he nor Leo take them to be kings, as Tertullian did, adv. Marc. iii. 13, in connection with Psalm lxxii. 10. In the Middle Ages they were not only called "the Three Kings," and the Epiphany "the Three Kings' Day," or simply "Les Rois," but their names were given as Melchior, Gaspar, and Balthasar. The best information as to the Magi will be found in Trench, l. c. and Mill on Myth. Interpr. p. 302 —10. They were not *such* Magi as Simon or Elymas—cf. Acts viii. 9, and Edersheim, Life and Times of Jesus, i. 203. That the star was a *new* luminary or luminous appearance is maintained by Trench. Edersheim thinks it just probable that it was an "evanescent star" connected with that conjunction of Jupiter and Saturn which appeared two years before, i. 213.

39. Independently of any special revelation, the Magi had expected that a Jewish King was to be born. In a later sermon, in Epiph. 4, c. 2, Leo connects this with Balaam's prophecy of the Star, Numb. xxiv. 17, and in so doing takes part in "the

The Epiphany. 167

general consent of the ancient Church," Mill, 303; Trench, 36—40. Against this see Edersheim, i. 209. Bishop Ellicott, Lect. on Life of our Lord, p. 72, would trace their expectation to "prophecies uttered in their own country, dimly foreshadowing this Divine mystery," e.g. as to Sosioth the raiser and judge of the dead, ib. p. 77. In the often cited words of Suetonius, in Vesp. 4, " Percrebuerat Oriente toto vetus et constans opinio, esse in fatis ut eo tempore Judæa profecti rerum potirentur :" and Tac. Hist. v. 13, " pluribus persuasio inerat, antiquis sacerdotum litteris contineri, eo ipso tempore fore ut valesceret Oriens, profectique Judæa rerum potirentur;" the Roman writers' misuse of this expectation being nothing to our purpose.

40. Compare Serm. in Epiph. 4, c. 2, " Superfluo, Herodes, timore turbaris . . . . . Quem in Judæa regnare non vis, ubique regnat." So in the hymn of Sedulius, which, slightly modernized, occurs in the Roman Breviary for the first Vespers of Epiphany;

> "Hostis Herodes impie,
> Christum venire quid times?
> Non eripit mortalia,
> Qui regna dat cœlestia."

Yet "can we wonder," asks Bishop Ellicott, Lect. p. 74, "that the aged man still on the throne of Judæa was filled with strange trouble and perplexity?" On the "ever-watchful suspicion" which formed part of Herod's character, as an Idumæan whom Roman favour had placed on the throne of David, and on the hideous deeds to which what S. Augustine calls his "cruel fear," (Serm. 199, s. 2,) had led him, see Mill on Myth. Interpr. 282—287, 311, and Edersheim, i. 214.

41. This is the usual symbolism of the Three Gifts, myrrh indicating mortality. S. Leo had probably read in S. Aug. Serm. 202, " Non solum aurum honorandus, et thus adorandus, verum etiam myrrham sepeliendus acceperat." So says S. Irenæus, iii. 9. 2; and S. Ambrose, de Fide, i. s. 31, " Thesaurus regni, sacrificium" (sc. "thus") " Dei, myrrha est sepulturæ." See Prudentius, Cathem. xii. 69;

> "Regem Deumque adnuntiant
> Thesaurus et fragrans odor
> Thuris Sabæi, ac myrrheus
> Pulvis sepulchrum prædocet."

So in the second Vespers of the Sarum and Aberdeen Breviaries. Antiphon at Magnificat; "Obtulerunt aurum sicut Regi magno, thus sicut Deo vero, myrrham sepulturæ ejus, Alleluia." The Sarum Missal has a sequence to the same effect. Yet the frankincense has been otherwise explained; at the end of the same sermon above quoted, S. Augustine makes it a recognition of Christ as the *Priest*. And the Roman Breviary, while prescribing Prudentius' lines for Lauds, has the following in a responsory for Matins on the week days within the octave; "In thure, Sacerdotem magnum considera:" which is also in the Sarum. The symbolism, as ordinarily given, is well drawn out by Archbishop Trench, pp. 66—70. And so Mill, p. 309; "the gifts which, whether consciously on their parts or not, symbolize severally to the faithful of all after ages His sovereignty, His Divinity, and His sufferings." That His superhuman majesty was revealed to them, at least to some extent, seems involved in the whole narrative: it was so far a real Epiphany of "the Only-begotten Son."

42. He means, Christ had a King's power, both as God and as Man. Comp. Pearson, i. 267, Art. 2, on the two Lordships belonging to His Divinity and His Humanity.

·43. On the Martyr-dignity of the Innocents, see Serm. in Epiph. 2, c. 3, "ut disceretur neminem hominum Divini incapacem esse Sacramenti, quando etiam illa ætas gloriæ esset apta martyrii;" and in Epiph. 7, c. 4, "ut .... per communionem ætatis consortes fierent passionis." Similarly S. Augustine, "non frustra illos in honorem martyrum receptos commendat ecclesia," de Lib. Arb. iii. 68. S. Cyprian also recognises them as martyrs, Ep. 58. 6. The lovely stanza of Prudentius,

> "Salvete, flores martyrum,
> Quos lucis ipso in limine
> Christi insecutor sustulit,
> Ceu turbo nascentes rosas,"

The Order of Readers. 169

expresses "the dignity and blessedness of thus suffering, though unconsciously, for Him Who came to redeem mankind," (Mill, 316;) and against the Church's deep consciousness of this, as Trench says, p. 92, "all the *hard-hearted arguments* to the contrary are nothing worth." Our Collect (from the Gelasian Sacramentary) has lost since 1661 the touching antithesis, that they showed forth God's praise "not in speaking, but in dying;" but "infants" is substituted for "innocents."

44. The Ballerini read "Impensa *humanæ salutis* sacramenta venerantes," instead of the old reading, "Impensa *saluti humanæ* gratiæ sacramenta." Surely the latter text, leaving out "gratiæ" as a gloss, is the more probable. We have a similar phrase in Serm. in Nativ. 8, c. 3, "effectum misericordiæ suæ quem restitutio*ni* impendebat humanæ;" de Pass. 15, c. 4, "quæ nostræ impendit salu*ti*;" de Res. 2, c. 1, "salvandis impensa," &c.

45. *Acquirere*, from an old and correct Latin rendering of S. Luke xxi. 19, κτήσασθε, i.e., make your souls your own, get the mastery over them. The A.V. wrongly follows the Vulgate, "possidebitis." See Trench on Auth. Vers. p. 95. The Revised Version has "ye shall win your souls."

46. The "narratio evangelicæ lectionis" refers to the reading of passages of Scripture by the Lector, as a part of the Church service. (Compare Serm. 7, c. 1; 11, c. 1; 14, c. 1.) So in Epiph. 3, c. 1, "secundum consuetudinem evangelicus . . . . . . sermo;" in Epiph. 8, c. 1, "evangelica narratio;" de Pass. 3, c. 5, "qua lectio Dominicæ passionis iterabitur." S. Augustine alludes to this usage in Serm. 17. 1, "Lector ascendit" (i.e., to the "ambon" or desk); Serm. 32. 23, "sonant lectores;" Serm. 67. 1, "ut hoc verbum sonuit in ore lectoris;" in Psal. 138. 1, "psalmum quem mandaveramus cantari a lectore." In Africa boys sometimes discharged this function, S. Aug. Serm. 352. 1; de Cons. Evan. 1, s. 15. So at Milan, S. Ambrose de Excessu Fratris, i. 64. S. Epiphanius of Pavia was a Reader at eight. So in Asia, as in the cases of Julian (Soz. v. 2) and Theodoret (Hist. Relig. 12). The order of Readers is first mentioned by Tertullian (de Præscr. Hæret.

41) and next by S. Cyprian, who took pleasure in commissioning two brave laymen who had confessed Christ in a persecution to read His acts and words in church. (Epistles 38, 39.) S. Chrysostom in early life was Reader under Meletius; he himself, as Bishop, had a faithful Reader named Paul. (See Soc. vi. 15.) Readers were appointed by a solemn form, sometimes with imposition of hands, (Apost. Const. viii. 22,) but more commonly without it, "Conc. Carth. 4," c. 8. The Greek forms vary, Goar's Euchol. p. 234 ff. The African address, "Take this" (roll of Scripture) "and be a reader of God's Word," &c., found its way into the Roman ritual, and thence into the Pontifical of Egbert Archbishop of York.

47. In regard to this Jewish "envy," see Milman, Hist. of Jews, iii. 27; "No doubt the more intemperate members of the Synagogue, when they might do it securely, would revenge themselves by insult or any other means of hostility in their power against the aggressions of the Church," &c.

48. The Pagan remnant in the West had very little power at this time to exhibit "ferocity" against Christians: we must allow for Leo's rhetorical turn, but he may have had in his time some isolated cases in which the deep-seated bitterness of feeling against the new religion which had dethroned Rome's ancient gods, and thereby, as it was often said, had brought calamities on the empire, found opportunities of angry and violent expression. Cp. Salvian, de Gub. Dei, viii. 45.

49. This may remind us of the old proverb, "Sanguis martyrum semen ecclesiæ." Compare Leo's Sermon "in Natali Petri et Pauli," c. 6; "Non minuitur persecutionibus ecclesia, sed augetur; et semper Dominicus ager segete ditiori vestitur, dum grana singula cadunt, multiplicata nascuntur," &c.

50. Christianity had for a long time been the dominant, though occasionally the baffled, power in the Imperial court. Prudentius could write, c. Sym. ii. 766, "Unus nostra regat servetque palatia Christus." S. Augustine, in an Epiphany Sermon, could say that kings now delighted not in slaying like

Need of continual Vigilance. 171

Herod, but in worshipping with the Magi, Serm. 200. Theodosius II., a devout, amiable, and fairly cultured prince, whose weakness once drew him into a murderous plot, (Hodgkin, Italy and her Invaders, ii. 64,) has left a record of his orthodox zeal in Cod. Th. xvi. 5. 63, " Omnes Catholicæ legis inimicos insectamur errores ;" but it was not always easy to make him see which side was orthodox. His sister Pulcheria is worthily reckoned among royal Saints ; she gave extreme satisfaction to Leo by "her love for the Catholic Faith" as to the Two Natures, Ep. 60. Valentinian III., in matters ecclesiastical, submitted his conscience to Leo, lent his authority to the aggrandisement of the Roman see, and supported Leo's views in a letter to Theodosius, Ep. 55 ; but Leo could not keep him from the degrading vices which contributed to bring him, in 455, to a terrible end, cp. Gibbon, c. 35 (vol. iv. p. 251.)

51. Leo repeatedly insists on the need of moral vigilance, as not diminished by the cessation of one particular form of trial, that which was embodied in persecution. So in de Jej. x. mensis, 7, c. 1, "Sciendum tamen est . . . retuso aculeo timoris, causam manere certaminis, quod . . . terribiliter quidem furore persecutionis movetur, sed nocentius specie pacis infertur . . . Adversarius cruentas inimicitias ad quietas convertit insidias," &c. De Quadrag. 2, c. 2 : " Semper quidem tibi, O anima Christiana, vigilandum contra salutis tuæ adversarium fuit, sed modo tibi major cautio . . . est adhibenda . . . Fremit . . . exspoliati hostis impius furor, et novum quærit lucrum, quia jus perdidit antiquum. Captat . . . si quas reperiat oves a sacris gregibus negligentius evagantes . . . inflammat iras, nutrit odia, acuit cupiditates," &c. De Quadrag. 9, c. 1 : " Unum nomen est persecutionis, sed non una est causa certaminis, et plus plerumque periculi est in insidiatore occulto quam in hoste manifesto . . . Omnis hæc vita tentatio est," &c.

52. The common identification of the Pagan deities with evil spirits was an overstrained inference from 1 Cor. x. 19, the sense of which is, " The idol in itself is a nullity ; but the strings of the puppet are pulled by an unseen diabolical power. The evil spirits energise through the worship ; it may be considered as,

in effect, passing on to them. If Christians advisedly join in it, they stain their souls, they compromise their religious loyalty, they contradict in act their Sacramental relations to their true Lord ; and thereby they serve the cause of the great enemy."

53. That probation ends with life, that there is no repentance beyond the grave, is affirmed by Leo again, in Epiph. 5, c. 4 : "In inferno nulla est correctio ; nec datur remedium satisfactionis, ubi jam non superest actio voluntatis."

54. The idea of "reconciliation of the guilty" involves the idea of a "reconciliation of God to man," which some have called "unscriptural," opposed to S. Paul's teaching, and theologically erroneous. It is found, however, in S. Clement's genuine Epistle, c. 48, "that He, being made propitious, may be reconciled to us ;" and it has been expressly defended by Pearson against the Socinians, (see vol. i. 614, Art. 10,) and before him by S. Thomas Aquinas, who in Sum. iii. 49. 4 discusses this point, meeting the objection, "God always loved us," with the answer, "He always does love us in regard to our nature, but not in regard to our sins ;" they are an "odii causa," which the Passion of Christ removed. S. Chrysostom, who felt God's love as strongly as any man since S. John's death, distinctly affirms a reconciliation of God as well as of man, Hom. de Ascens. c. 2. Tertullian sees in the word "grace" the indication of an offence forgiven, adv. Marc. v. 5 ; as Olshausen (who once thought otherwise) observes that a "ministry of reconciliation" implies a reconciliation *ex parte Dei*, Comm. on Rom. iii. 24, and Bishop Browne points to what is involved in "not imputing," on Articles, i. 101. See Archb. Trench on Parab. p. 355 (on the Barren Fig-tree;) and in Westminster Sermons, p. 178, "The Atonement is a reconciling not merely of man to God, but of God to man . . . . Christ *made* the peace which He announced . . . . Through the sacrifice of His death, the disturbed, and in part suspended relations between God and His sinful creatures were constituted anew." The radical question is, Were those relations at all suspended on *God's* side? The answer must be, that sin as such is necessarily an objective

barrier between God and His creatures; and that "reconciliation" is primarily associated by S. Paul with forgiveness of sins and deliverance from "wrath," and only secondarily with man's change of heart, (see Dale on the Atonement, pp. 239, 242, 262.)

55. Pagans would still on occasion repeat the old sneers at "a crucified god," or, in Lucian's phrase, (de Morte Peregrini,) "that impaled sophist" of the Christians,—the ignorant rustic teacher, according to Julian, whose cures wrought on a few sick people in Galilee had been so greatly overrated. (See Rendall, The Emperor Julian, p. 235.) As long as Paganism lingered among old noble families in Rome, this contempt would be the more intense in private because public expression of it was not safe. It must be remembered that even after Leo's death, a Pagan remnant could point to a Roman general, Marcellinus, as a worshipper of the ancient gods: and the Lupercalia might still give occasion for much license of Pagan talk, although professedly the festival had been stripped of Pagan associations.

56. When he denies a "conflict of feelings" in Christ, he does not mean (as the context shows) to deny the reality of the Agony, although here and in de Pass. 7, c. 5, he may seem to dwell too much on the instructive or exemplary character of Christ's words, too little on the actual feeling which they indicated; yet elsewhere he speaks absolutely of fear as having been, equally with compassion, within the range of our Lord's human experience, Ep. 139, c. 2. It is indeed true that "hæc vox Capitis salus est corporis .... Hæc vox omnes fideles instruxit, omnes confessores accendit, omnes martyres coronavit," de Pass. 7, c. 5. In the context Leo affirms the existence of two wills in Christ, a higher and a lower. Athanasius, indeed, had said, "The will belongs to the Godhead only," c. Apollin. ii. 10: but this was said in support of the statement that our Lord's "flesh" was devoid of "carnal desires," and is followed by the statement that He had "the whole of the first Adam." In the "de Incarn. et c. Arianos," c. 21, there is an express assertion of "two wills:" but that treatise is probably not by Athanasius himself. S. Ambrose plainly says, "Suscepit voluntatem meam, suscepit tristitiam meam," de Fide, ii.

s. 53. Early in the seventh century there grew out of the controversy on Christ's Natures a controversy as to whether He had one or two Wills, it being hoped by the Eastern court that the Monophysite schism might be healed if the Church would grant that Christ had but one will and one activity. (Robertson, Hist. Ch. iii. 422.) The "one will" was asserted by some, as Sergius and Cyrus, on quasi-Monophysite grounds; by others, as Pope Honorius, from the mistaken notion that "two wills" implied a conflict. The co-existence, without conflict, of two wills, as a consequence of the two natures, was insisted on by the first Council of Lateran in 649, and ultimately by the Sixth General Council at Constantinople in 680, and which was thus a kind of supplement to the Fourth Council, as the Fifth had been to the Third; and which, besides condemning *Monothelites*, living and dead, (Honorius being among the latter,) pronounced that our Lord had "two natural wills and two natural operations," each nature willing and "working what belonged to it, in communion with the other." At first sight, the exceeding earnestness of the orthodox in this matter may appear overstrained; but if we consider that Christ's true Manhood was once again the point at issue, we shall not wonder that Sophronius of Jerusalem, placing one of his suffragans "on the holy Golgotha," adjured him to maintain the truth against Monothelites, as he should answer to that Lord Who "in this holy place was *voluntarily* crucified:" nor that Pope Martin I.—the story of whose noble confessorship is among the most touching in Church history—serenely endured, under the tyrant Constans II., the extremities of brutal treatment and hopeless exile in the cause of a *real* Incarnation. The question, says Trench, (Huls. Lect. p. 214,) "was one for life and death; the denial of a human will in Christ was in fact a denial of His Sacrifice." See Hooker, v. 48. 9; Pearson, i. 285, Art. 3. Compare Aquinas, Sum. iii. 18, 1, 6: "ad perfectionem humanæ naturæ pertinet voluntas, quæ est naturalis ejus potentia . . . . Unde necesse est dicere quod Filius Dei humanam voluntatem assumpserit cum humana natura;" but he adds that the "voluntas naturalis," or instinctive wish to avoid suffering, obeyed "the voluntas rationalis" and the Divine will, so that there was no "contrariety of wills." See also Liddon's Bamp. Lect. p. 265, where an analogy is suggested between the two principles of volition observable "within the precincts of a single human soul," (as in Rom. vii. 17, ff.) and the coexistence of a real human will with a Divine will in the incarnate Christ: but it is added, by way of *caveat*, that the human will "corresponded to the eternal will with unvarying accuracy ... from the first was controlled by the Divine will." See note 15, on the impeccability of Christ.

57. The subject of God's merciful refusals was one which Leo might have repeatedly seen discussed by S. Augustine; e.g. Enarr. 2 in Ps. xxvi., "et propitius Deus, cum male amamus, negat quod amamus;" and in Jo. Ev. Tr. 73, 3, 4. "Quod videt peti contra salutem, non faciendo potius se exhibet Salvatorem .... Petamus, quando bene petimus, ut non faciat quod non bene petimus." Comp. Christian Year, 17th Sunday after Trinity:

". . . . In very love refuse
Whate'er Thou know'st our weakness would abuse."

58. On Wednesday before Easter it is probable that Leo was wont to offer a Collect, which the "Gelasian Sacramentary" provides for that day, Muratori, i. 548, and which occurs in the "Leonine Sacramentary" as a Preface for one of the Masses in the "fast of the seventh month," ib. 421. "(Omnipotens sempiterne Deus) Qui Christi tui beata Passione nos reparas, conserva in nobis opera misericordiæ tuæ; ut in hujus celebritate mysterii perpetua devotione vivamus, per," &c. The next Gelasian prayer resembles in tone these sermons of S. Leo, in that it speaks of the "piaculum perfidorum" becoming the "salus omnium." The Leonine Sacramentary, so called, exists only as a fragment, and its Passiontide portion is lost; but we can form some idea of the Leonine ritual for this day by turning to the Ordo Romanus I. at the end of Murat. vol. ii., which Mabillon ascribes to the age of Gregory the Great, and which probably embodies many older liturgical traditions. This Ordo, for "feria IV. quæ est pridie In Cœna Domini," prescribes that the "Pontifex" is to come at 9 a.m. to the altar "in ecclesia majore," and say the solemn prayers of intercession, (as on Good Friday; the third of them being now our second Good

Friday Collect,) omitting only the prayer for himself. At 2 p.m. 'they come in to Mass;" there is an Introit, Collect, a Lection, probably "Who is this that cometh from Edom," a Gradual from Ps. lxix., another Lection, probably "Who hath believed our report," a "Canticle" (or "Tract") from Ps. cii., and "the Passion according to S. Luke;" after which, "expletur Missa ordine suo." The *afternoon* Celebration on this day of solemn fasting is no precedent for Sunday "Evening Communions."

59. The "festival of the Passion" may seem a strange phrase, (yet compare G. Herbert's "dear feast of Lent,") but Leo expresses by it exactly what is meant by our phrase "*Good* Friday." So Bp. Andrewes, Serm. ii. 153, that in one sense it is "a day of joy and jubilee." Archbishop Mepeham, in his constitutions of 1328, orders Good Friday to be observed "festive," simply in the sense of "as a holy day."

60. This passage is the fourth Lesson, as others in the same sermon are the fifth and sixth, at Matins in the Roman Office for Palm Sunday. Compare what Leo says of Christmas, de Nativ. 9, c. 1. "Inde oritur difficultas fandi, unde adest ratio non tacendi . . . . Ideo nunquam materia deficit laudis, quia nunquam sufficit copia laudatoris. Gaudeamus igitur quod ad eloquendum tantum misericordiæ sacramentum impares sumus; et cum salutis nostræ altitudinem non valemus explicare, sentiamus nobis bonum esse quod vincimur." See Nehem. ix. 5; and compare Ecclus. xliii. 27—31, which suggested to Aquinas the rapturous words, in his "Lauda Sion,"

> "Quantum potes, tantum aude,
> Quia major omni laude,
>   Nec laudare sufficis!"

S. Augustine says to the same effect, Conf. i. c. 4, "Quid dicit aliquis cum de te dicit? Et væ tacentibus de te! quoniam loquaces muti sunt."

61. Here he treats the ordinary Roman Creed as handed down from the Apostles. So in the "tractatus against Eutychianism," which is reckoned as his ninety-sixth sermon:

Various Readings in the Creed. 177

"instituto a sacris apostolis symbolo." And in a letter to Pulcheria, Epist. 31. 4 : " Catholici symboli brevis et perfecta confessio, quæ duodecim apostolorum totidem est signata sententiis." Here we find the long popular notion that each Apostle contributed a sentence, Peter beginning, " I believe in God," &c., as in the Sermons reckoned as 240 and 241 in the appendix to S. Augustine's genuine Sermons.

62. There are six forms of this article in the various types of the old Western Creed. (1) That in the text, "*de* Spiritu Sancto natum *ex* Maria Virgine." This is found in the Creed of Aquileia as given by Rufinus, of Ravenna as given by Peter Chrysologus, of Turin as given by Maximus of Turin, of Gaul as given by Venantius Fortunatus (see Heurtley, Harmonia Symbolica, pp. 26—50): compare a pseudo-Augustinian Sermon, 238th in the appendix. See Leo, Serm. 2, c. 1, for "ex . . . Maria" simply. (2) Again, by a slight change, which produces some uncertainty as to reading, (e.g. in the Tome, c. 2,) "*de* Spiritu Sancto *et* Virgine Maria." This is found in S. Augustine's Enchiridion, c. 38, in his de Symbolo ad Catechumenos, s. 6, and Sermons 212 and 214. Both *ex* and *et* occur in his Serm. 215, (see Heurtley, pp. 42, 49). *De* . . . *et* occurs in the Laudian Codex. It seems to have been the reading of the Roman Creed when Marcellus of Ancyra presented a confession to Pope Julius, which was evidently the Roman Creed rendered into Greek (Heurtley, p. 23), and which contained the words γεννηθέντα ἐκ Πνεύματος ἁγίου καὶ Μαρίας τῆς παρθένου (Epiphanius, Hær. lxxii. 3; compare the "Constantinopolitan" recension of the Nicene, σαρκωθέντα ἐκ Πνεύματος ἁγίου καὶ Μαρίας τῆς παρθένου, the reading followed in the Gelasian version of that Creed, "de Spiritu Sancto et Maria Virgine," Murat. i. 540, and in two old English versions, Heurtley, p. 162; but altered in the present Roman and English versions into nearer conformity with the received text of the Apostles' Creed, as the Armenian Church has altered it into ἐκ Μαρίας . . . διὰ Πνεύματος ἁγίου, Hort, Two Dissertations, p. 146). Leo uses "de Maria Virgine" simply, in Nativ. 4, c. 4. (3) Again, Facundus, about a century after Leo, reads "natum *ex* Spiritu Sancto *et* Maria Virgine," in the "epistle" at the end of his "Pro Defensione

Trium Capitulorum." (4) We have "*per* Spiritum Sanctum *ex* Virgine Maria" in S. Augustine de Fide et Symbolo, s. 8. (5) A Gallic form, "*de* Maria . . . *per* Spiritum Sanctum." (Heurtley, p. 67.) (6) The present full form "conceptus est *de* Spiritu Sancto, natus *ex* Virgine Maria," occurs in S. Augustine's Serm. 213; in a Creed gathered from two expository homilies ascribed to various authors, but apparently by a Gallic bishop of the province of Arles (Heurtley, p. 57;) and in the Creeds of the seventh and eighth centuries, &c., (ib. p. 68.)

63. The passage is not very clear; but he appears to be combining the two thoughts, "alike in glory and in humiliation He is one and the same," and "this personal unity is compatible with the distinct functions of Godhead and Manhood." Most intimate, indeed, is the combination of the two elements; but it does not produce an interchange of properties, whereby the Almighty essence itself could suffer, or the weakness of humanity be annulled. Compare the celebrated passage in the Tome, "Agit enim utraque forma, cum alterius communione, quod proprium est:" which probably was in Hooker's mind when he wrote, "Of both natures there is a co-operation often, an association always, but never any mutual participation whereby the properties of the one are infused into the other," (v. 53. 3.) "The only true communication of properties," as Pearson says, is the ascription of Divine and human acts or qualities to the one Person of Christ, whether under the title of "God" or of "Man," see above, note 5. This does not satisfy Dorner, who criticises the Chalcedonian Christology from the Lutheran point of view, which apparently requires such a communication as amounts to the "mutual participation" between the natures as such.

64. It is undeniable (1) that Leo differed from the general line of Patristic teaching by ascribing to S. Peter, not merely a primacy in the sense of a precedency and representative character, but also a certain superiority of power, as in Sermon 15 of this volume, c. 2, and more plainly in Ep. 14. 11, "inter beatissimos Apostolos in similitudine honoris fuit *quædam* discretio potestatis;" and both in Serm. de Nat. ipsius, 4, c. 2, 3, and Ep. 10. 1, he makes the daring assertion that the powers of the other

Apostles were transmitted to them *through* Peter : (2) that, as the "heir" of S. Peter, he put forth high pretensions (for which he procured Valentinian's sanction) to a general authority over the whole Church. The Easterns, in the Council of Chalcedon, allowed him the first place and great influence, but steadily ignored his theories of supremacy ; declining to accept as final his decision in favour of Theodoret, approving his "Tome" on the ground of its ascertained conformity to received standards, and passing a canon which placed the pre-eminence of Rome on a civil basis. But we are now concerned only with his view of S. Peter and of S. Peter's Confession,—the parent of Christian Creeds. He seems to have taken "this rock" to mean S. Peter, considered as confessing the Divinity of our Lord, the "original Rock" or "cornerstone" (Serm. l. c.; Ep. 28. 5) *and* as appointed to "proclaim this faith," and to perpetuate it in his own see. Three elements combine in the idea : (1) Christ Himself, (2) the faith in Christ, and (3) Peter, considered as the chief of the Apostles, and, under Christ, the head of the Church. Hence we have Christ spoken of as *the* "petra :" then in the same sermon, that against which the "portæ inferi" are not to prevail is called Peter's confession, and to that faith "soliditas" is attributed in de Nat. ips. 3, c. 3. So Ep. 119. 2, "Catholicæ fidei petra." Again, Peter is called absolutely the "petra" in de Pass. 9, c. 4 ; "soliditas" is attributed to him in Ep. 10, c. 1 ; and in de Nat. ips. 4, c. 2, we read, "Tu quoque petra es, quia mea virtute solidaris." Leo's way of looking at the passage was most practically illustrated by his continuous unhesitating assertion of "Petrine" powers for himself as the "heir of Peter," see de Nat. ips. 5. 4. The name of "Peter" is made to serve as warrant for any claim of power that Leo thinks well to assert. Hilary of Arles stands up, firmly but respectfully, for his own metropolitical authority : this, according to Leo, is "not to endure to be subject to the blessed Apostle Peter," "to diminish by somewhat arrogant words the reverence due to the most blessed Peter." (Ep. 10, c. 2; see Gore, Leo the Great, p. 108.) It is rather a long step from S. Ambrose's observation that Peter, in making his great confession, "primatum egit, confessionis utique, non honoris . . . . . fidei, non ordinis," (de Incarn. Dom. Sacram. s. 32,) to Leo's assertion that in reward of his faith Christ granted to him "apostolicæ dignitatis primatum" in such sense as to fix the Church's basis in "fundamenti ipsius soliditate," and to invest all his successors with an universal "solicitude," Ep. 5. 2, or to say that he has "never quitted that guidance of the Church which he received," a proposition explained in the words which presently follow, "cujus in sede sua vivit potestas et excellit auctoritas," in Nat. ips. 3, c. 3. Cp. in Nat. ips. 5, c. 4.

65. The concealment of Christ's Divinity from Satan was a favourite idea of the Fathers, from S. Ignatius (Eph. 19) downwards. But on this supposition, combined with Scriptural imagery of "redemption" and the Scriptural language on the dominion of Satan over "this world," was built up a mode of speaking which unless we can treat it as a "rhetorical playing with words," (Aids to Faith, p. 341), must needs be deemed a strange and repulsive theory. It was presumed that he had acquired a real right of property in man as fallen, which right he could not lose except by fair purchase; that the price offered to him was the life of Jesus: but that he would not have accepted the equivalent if he had not been misled by the purely human surroundings of that life, so as to slay One who, being Divine and sinless, was in no sense subject to his claim. See Oxenham on Cath. Doctr. of Atonement, p. 121, ff.; and Dale on the Atonement, p. 273, ff., who pertinently observes that "the more intolerable . . . . this hypothesis is, the more conclusively it proves the depth and strength of the faith of the Church in the reality of the *objective* element in the Atonement. In the earliest ages, Christian men were quite sure that Christ died to deliver them from some great objective evil, and . . . they were willing to accept even this preposterous explanation of the manner in which His death delivered us, if no better could be found. But nothing can be more certain than that the idea of an objective Atonement was not invented to satisfy such a theory as this: the theory was a most irreligious method of satisfying the idea." It was also not very coherent: in one aspect, it spoke of a bargain and purchase, of a claim surrendered in view of compensation: in the other, of a deceit practised upon Satan whereby he was led to seize one over whom he had no right, and thus to forfeit his right over others. (Oxen-

What "Redemption" involves.

ham, p. 137.) And yet, although Athanasius entertained far worthier views of the efficacy of Christ's death, and Gregory Nazianzen, while still permitting himself to speak of Satan as "ensnared" by it, (Orat. 39. 13,) denounced as "outrageous" the notion of a ransom paid to Satan instead of to the Father (Orat. 45. 22), the theory, in one or other of its parts, was popular until the days of S. Anselm : and the words of Venantius Fortunatus, still sung in the course of the Roman Office for Good Friday, "Multiformis proditoris ars ut artem falleret," are but an echo of the distressing language in Gregory Nyssen's "Catechetical Oration," as to the justice of that ἀπάτη whereby the old deceiver was deceived. Leo himself says, in Nativ. 2, c. 4, " Illusa est securi hostis astutia :" in the text, and de Pass. 9, c. 3, he does not go so far. Of course, there is a truth represented by such terms as "ransom," and another truth represented by such texts as S. John xii. 31 ; and in Archb. Trench's words, "it was part of the great scheme of redemption that the victory over evil should be a moral triumph, not a triumph obtained by the mere putting forth of superior strength ; we can see how important it was for this end that man, who lost the battle, should also win it, 1 Cor. xv. 21," (on Parables, p. 94 ;) as Cardinal Newman has so grandly expressed it,

> "O wisest love ! that flesh and blood,
>   Which did in Adam fail,
> Should strive afresh against their foe,
> Should strive and should prevail :"

but this is no warrant for condensing one part only of the Scriptural imagery on the Atonement into a theory, and letting the fancy play around it in disregard alike of moral considerations and of other representations of a many-sided mystery. In the context before us, Leo shows that he could not conceive of the price as really paid to Satan, but to the Divine justice which had punished man by leaving him, to a great extent, under the evil master whom he had chosen by his sin. Repeatedly, also, he speaks of Christ's death as a "sacrifice," of course to the Father : see below, note 84 ; as in Serm. 2, c. 3, 10, c. 3, and 11, c. 3. So Dr. Mill, who insists on the truth underlying the old patristic language, and cites S. Bernard as maintaining it, adds "that in his view the selfsame Divine justice that left fallen man in the power of Satan at first, is that which accepted the satisfaction," and also considers that this was, in fact, the belief of the Fathers in question. (Sermons on our Lord's Temptation, p. 148.) So Aquinas, Sum. iii. 48. 4, that the captivity of man under Satan was by God's permission and just appointment; therefore redemption had reference to God; and to Him, *not* to Satan, the price was to be paid. See above, note 6.

66. "Et pretium et poculum." This combination of the redemptive efficacy and the Eucharistic reception of Christ's blood was perhaps suggested by S. Augustine's language, "Cogito pretium meum, et manduco, et bibo." Confess. x. s. 70; and "gentibus .... pia humilitate bibentibus pretium suum," de Trin. iv. s. 18. Leo again refers to the Eucharistic cup in the Tome, c. 5. See note 81.

67. That Christ died for all, is affirmed in 2 Cor. v. 14. S. Augustine had been led by his Predestinarian opinions to explain away (see de Corrept. et Grat. 44) the parallel statement of 1 Tim. ii. 4. But S. Leo asserts the largeness of the Divine benignity without reserve, in the text, and in Serm. 11. 3. As to the general view of the Fathers, see S. Athan. de Incarn. 20, "It was on behalf of all that He offered the Sacrifice, giving up His own temple to death ἀντὶ πάντων," (ἀντὶ has plainly a vicarious sense, for he had just said, "That which was due from all had to be paid," &c.) S. Chrys. in Heb. Hom. 17, c. 2. "So far as He was concerned, He died for all, to save all; for that death was an equivalent for the perdition of all. But He did not take away the sins of all, because they were not willing." And S. Ambrose, in Ps. 118, Serm. 15. 10: "Passio Salvatoris omnes redemit." The proposition that He did *not* die for all, was maintained by Gottschalk in the ninth century; and Hincmar, Archbishop of Rheims, who took a strong line against extreme predestinarianism, caused Gottschalk's theology to be condemned by the Council of Quiercy in 853, which declared, "As there never was, nor will be, nor is, any man whose nature Christ did not assume, so there neither is, was, nor will be any

Judas.

man for whom He did not suffer..... The cup of man's salvation, composed of our weakness and Divine power, has the capacity of benefiting all, *but it does not heal if it is not drunk.*" One of the five propositions imputed to Jansenius, and condemned by Innocent X. in 1653, was "Semi-pelagianum est dicere, Christum pro omnibus omnino hominibus mortuum esse aut sanguinem fudisse." Möhler says that the Roman Church and the Lutheran formularies agree in the truth of Christ's having died for all: Symbolism, i. 137, E. Tr.

68. Of Judas he says again in de Pass. 1, c. 5, that had he but repented in earnest, he would have been forgiven; and so, de Pass. 3, c. 3, that despair drew him to the halter: that he ought to have waited until (obs. this use of *donec*, as of ἕως) Christ had died for sinners. See de Pass. 7, c. 3, on the forbearance indicated in "One of you shall betray Me." Like most of the Fathers, he considers that Jesus "repelled him not from the Communion of His Body and Blood," ib. and see de Pass. 7, c. 3, "ne ab hoc quidem mysterio traditore submoto .... Non sacramentorum tibi communio denegatur." Comp. S. Chrys. de Prod. Judæ, i. 6, with our Exhortation, "Lest after the taking," &c. The exception to the general Patristic consent on this point is S. Hilary; "sine quo," he says, referring to Judas, "Pascha accepto calice et fracto pane conficitur, dignus enim æternorum sacramentorum communione non fuerat," Comm. in Matt. c. 30. 2. If S. Luke xxii. 21 is in the actual order of time, Judas must have been a communicant; but if, as Bp. Ellicott thinks, (Lectures, p. 325,) S. Matt. xxvi. 25 corresponds to S. John xiii. 26, a Harmony should read, "He went out, and it was night," ib. 30, *before* the Consecration.

69. Leo is thus one of those Fathers who recognise the "Pericope Adulteræ." S. Chrysostom's and S. Cyril's Commentaries ignore it. S. Aug. de Conj. Adult. ii. s. 6, thought it had been erased as dangerous. S. Jerome, adv. Pelag. ii. 17, says that it was in *many* Greek and Latin copies. See Scrivener's Introduction to Criticism of N. T. p. 610; he thinks the passage may have been added by S. John in a "second edition" of his Gospel. Bp. Ellicott inclines to ascribe it to S. Luke, Lect. p. 253.

70. See on Pilate, de Pass. 3, c. 5, "lotis manibus et ore polluto;" and de Pass. 8, c. 2, "Non purgant contaminatum animum manus lotæ .... Excessit quidem Pilati culpam facinus Judæorum .... Sed nec ipse evasit reatum, qui cooperatus seditiosis, reliquit judicium proprium, et in crimen transivit alienum."

71. "Nostra augendo, non propria;" compare Dean Milman's "Martyr of Antioch;"

> "Thou, that couldst nothing win
> By saving worlds from sin,
> Nor aught of glory add to Thy all-glorious Name."

72. Although Leo lays stress on the Lord's manhood in connection with His title of "first-born of all creation," we need not suppose that, like S. Athanasius, he imported into that passage of S. Paul, Col. i. 15, the idea of His Headship as the Incarnate Founder of a new order of spiritual existence, a reference which Estius thinks "forced and irrelevant," and which, in Bishop Lightfoot's opinion, "shatters the context." Leo's words here, if they stood alone, might at first sight seem capable of Nestorian perversion, as if the difference between Jesus and the Saints were merely in degree: but it is plain that he means, not in any sense to deny the Personal Union—on which, indeed, he is more than sufficiently explicit—but to emphasise the intimate presence of the Divine Redeemer with His "body mystical." See Newman's Arians, p. 233; "It is a known peculiarity of the message of mercy, that it views the Church of Christ as if clothed with, or hidden within, the glory of Him Who ransomed it," &c. So Pusey, Serm. i. p. ix. ff.

73. Leo may here again be illustrated from S. Athanasius c. Ar. iii. 32, 34; "It was meet for the Lord, when putting on human flesh, to put it on entire with the feelings belonging to it; that as we say that the body was His own, so too the feelings of the body may be called simply His own, though they did not touch Him as to His Godhead .... When He is said to hunger and thirst, and to be weary, and *not to know*" (i.e.

S. Mark xiii. 32) "and to sleep, and weep, and ask, and flee, and be born, and deprecate the cup,—and generally all that belongs to the flesh; it should in all fitness be said in each case, —'Christ hungering and thirsting for our sake in *flesh.*'" Or take Cyril of Jerusalem, Cat. iv. 9; "really eating as Man, just as we do, for He had the same bodily feelings that we have, but feeding the five thousand with five loaves, as God; . . . . really sleeping in the ship as Man, and walking on the waters as God." In the text, and in de Pass. 14, c. 2, Leo brings together, (1) the reality of our Lord's human feelings, and (2) their exemplary value; making the latter depend upon the former. In de Pass. 7, c. 4, Leo warns his hearers not to infer, from the spiritual significances of Christ's life, that the tears shed by Him were unreal, or His hungering fictitious; "Veros et corporis sensus et animi suscepit affectus." The weariness and the sleep, he urges, de Quadr. 8, c. 2, belong to true Manhood; and so in the Tome, c. 4, he sets human properties over against Divine. In a very touching passage, Ep. 139. 2, he bids Juvenal of Jerusalem enforce the true doctrine by referring to the very places where the Child was born and the Man lived, and dwells also on the supposed identification, not only of the sepulchre, but of the actual cross. It may be added that extreme Monophysitism showed itself in the theory of Julian of Halicarnassus, to the effect that the physical infirmities, needs, and sufferings, to which our Lord submitted Himself in His earthly life and at His death, were not properly incident to His body, which of itself was, in this large sense, "incorruptible." Ath. Treat. ii. 375. Justinian scandalised orthodoxy by adopting and dying in this belief: Evagrius, iv. 39; Gibbon, vi. 41.

74. Here "exemplum" is used in the sense in which "forma" occurs at the end of Serm. 8. The antithesis of "sacramentum" and "exemplum" occurs again in Serm. 14, c. 1; also in Nativ. 5, c. 6, "Hæc Domini nostri opera . . . non solum sacramento nobis utilia sunt, sed etiam imitationis exemplo, si in disciplinam ipsa remedia transferantur, quodque impensum est mysteriis prosit et moribus." So in Epiph. 5, c. 3, we have the "sacramentum" with its saving efficacy, and the "exemplum" with its spur to exertion: and compare Serm. 4, c. 3. This is a

cardinal point, as the "imitation" of Adam by actual sin is but an outflowing from the mystery of "original sin," (Article 9,) so the imitation of Christ is to be accounted for by a supernatural union with Him. His acts *are* "the greatest moral acts ever done in the world;" but they are so because of their mysterious, redemptive, Divine virtue. Compare the Collect for the Second Sunday after Easter. See Gore, "A Word for Peace on Justification," p. 4, that an example which, by itself, would be too high for us to follow, is made effective by the infusion into us of a divine life from Him Whose character presents it; so as "to mould us inwardly into conformity with what He has shown us and requires of us outwardly," &c. See note 15.

75. "Judicanti se *in*juste." The Vulgate reading of 1 S. Peter ii. 23, where the true text is τῷ κρίνοντι δικαίως, i.e. to God. Estius ascribes the erroneous Latin rendering to some copyists who did not understand this text. He refers to S. Aug. in Joan. Tr. 21, 12, where the passage is cited rightly, "commendabat illi qui *juste* judicat."

76. So de Jej. vii. mens. 7, 1 : "Quamvis enim varietates hostiarum, differentiæ baptismatum, et otia sabbatorum cum ipsa carnis circumcisione cessaverunt, manent tamen ex ipsis voluminibus etiam apud nos plurima præcepta moralia." Compare our Seventh Article. On the types of the Old Law, see Serm. 11, c. 2; also de Pass. 7, c. 1, "Oportebat ut manifesto implerentur effectu quæ diu fuerant figurato promissa mysterio : ut ovem significativam ovis vera removeret," &c.

77. "Dantia salutem .... promittentia Salvatorem :" the Augustinian contrast between Christian and Jewish ordinances ; Enarr. in Ps. lxxiii. 2. " Sacramenta Novi Testamenti dant salutem ; sacramenta Veteris Testamenti promiserunt Salvatorem." The same thought is worked out in c. Faust. xix. 8—14. For S. Augustine clearly recognised a difference in *kind* between the two classes of ordinances (see note 16), in that the old prefigured what the new effected ; the old were shadowy, the new had " the very image ;" the Law gave tokens of a coming fulness of grace, the Gospel provided channels through which its streams should ac-

Baptismal Renunciations. 187

tually flow in. This "high view of Sacraments" was simply a consequence of high thoughts about the Incarnation, as the source of new and special gifts ; (Liddon, Bampt. Lect. p. 489 ; Sadler, Church Doctr. Bible Truth, p. 396 ;) and when in the Calvinistic theology, (e.g. in the Scottish Confession of 1560) the difference here referred to was denied, the Jewish rites were not raised to a Christian dignity, but the Christian lowered to the Jewish level ; all alike were "seals" and "assurances" of Divine favours which were common to both covenants. Cf. Bp. Bethell on Regeneration, pp. 53—56 : Pusey, Scriptural Views of Holy Baptism, p. 323 ; Hardwick, Hist. of Articles, p. 94.

78. Baptismal Renunciations, in the Roman church of Leo's time, seem to have run thus, Gelas. Sacr. in Murat. Lit. Rom. i. 563 : "Dost thou renounce Satan? I renounce him. And all his works? I renounce. And all his pomps? I renounce." At Milan the form included a renunciation of the world, its lust, its pleasures ; S. Ambrose de Myst. s. 5 ; so in Gaul, "the pomps of the world and its pleasures," Muratori, Lit. Rom. ii. 741. Salvian cites a Gallic form, "diabolo, pompis, spectaculis, et operibus ejus," de Gub. Dei, vi. 6. At Jerusalem, "I renounce thee, Satan, and all thy works, and all thy pomp, and all thy worship." S. Cyril. Cat. Myst. 1. At Antioch, more simply, "and thy pomp and thy worship," S. Chrys. ad Illuminand. ii. 4. The form referred to by Tertullian, de Cor. Mil. 3, renounces "the devil, and his pomp, and his angels." His "pomp" meant all the Vanity-fair of Heathenism, with its alluring splendour and stateliness, which was primarily in S. John's mind when he wrote, "The world is passing away." S. Ambrose quotes a peculiar form, "Abrenuntio tibi, diabole, et angelis tuis, et operibus tuis, et imperiis tuis;" Hexaem. ii. 14. S. Augustine more than once alludes to the renunciation as made by infants through sponsors, e.g., "Prius exorcizatur in eis . . . potestas contraria, cui etiam verbis eorum a quibus portantur se renuntiare respondent," de Pecc. Orig. s. 45 ; cp. Op. imperf. c. Jul. ii. 224. Compare the old Sarum form: "Abrenuntias Sathanæ? *Respondeant compatrini et commatrinæ*, Abrenuntio. *Item Sacerdos:* Et omnibus operibus ejus? Ry. Abrenuntio. Et omnibus pompis ejus? Ry. Abrenuntio." Maskell,

Monum. Rit. i. 23. The renunciations were followed, as Leo here intimates, by a profession of faith; on which see below, note 142, and Heurtley, Harm. Symb. p. 103. Comp. Hooker, v. 63. 3, where, after referring to the engagements to renounce and to believe, he quotes Justin Martyr as showing "how such as the Church in those days did baptise made profession of Christian belief, and undertook to live accordingly. Neither do I think it an easy matter for any man to prove that ever baptism did use to be administered without interrogatories of these *two* kinds." But the special interrogatory, "Wilt thou then obediently keep," &c., was added to our Office in 1661.

79. This strong expression is quoted by Hooker, v. 60. 2 as descriptive of baptismal "incorporation into Christ." It is obvious that Leo is specially thinking of the obligation laid "on a baptised person, in the language of the Prayer Book, to die from sin, and rise again unto righteousness." It need hardly be said that Leo does not mean that Christ is "received" in Baptism in the same sense as in the Holy Eucharist; see Wilberforce on the Holy Eucharist, p. 228, ff. on the points which "discriminate" the Fathers' language on the relation of Baptism to Christ's blood from their language on the Eucharistic gift. S. Cyril, he says, "sums up the contrast in a few words, observing that in Baptism men are made members of Christ through the gift of His Spirit, but that His presence in the Holy Eucharist is brought about through the presence of His Body. " Baptism is truly Christ's and from Christ, and the force of the mystical Eucharist arises to us from His sacred Flesh." (Cyr. in Joan. l. xii. vol. v. p. 103, ed. Pusey.)

80. "Meritum." He appears to mean any good deed which God approves: as in de Collect. 1. where he uses it as equivalent to "virtus." The idea of acceptableness, of desert *in a certain sense*, goes along with the term, e.g. de Collect. 6, c. 2, de Jej. x. mens. 4, c. 2; and he applies the Augustinian phrase, "nullis præcedentibus meritis,"[4] to his people's choice of him as bishop, de Nat. ips. 1. But his use of the elastic word *mereri* is illustrated by Serm. in Quadr. 1, c. 6, where he exhorts to almsgiving, "ut *misericordiam* in judicio mereamur invenire;" he

repeatedly testifies against self-reliance, in Epiph. 8, c. 3, de Quadr. 6, c. 1; he speaks of God as a "benignus æstimator operum nostrorum, Who will reward even a cup of cold water," de Jej. x. mens. 3, c. 2. Naturally enough, he uses "merito" in a stricter sense, when he means desert for *evil*, in Epiph. 7, c. 3; and equally so in Serm. 4 of this volume, c. 3, where Christ is said to profit us "et exemplo et merito." He agrees with the Augustinian teaching that the "merita" of Christians must really be resolved into "munera" of God, S. Aug. Ep. 194. 19; and whether or not he drew up the Articles on Grace which have been wrongly annexed to a letter of Pope Celestine in 431, he would have heartily accepted their teaching, that man's "merits" are the gift of God, Who works in man "both to will and to do," and enables man to co-operate with His grace; see note 136.

81. On the Holy Communion see his Sermon de Jej. vii. mens. 6, c. 3 : "Nam dicente Domino, ' Nisi manducaveritis carnem Filii hominis, et biberitis ejus sanguinem, non habebitis vitam in vobis,'—sic sacræ mensæ communicare debetis, ut nihil prorsus de veritate corporis Christi et sanguinis ambigatis. Hoc enim ore sumitur, quod fide creditur; et frustra ab illis 'Amen' respondetur" (the usual response of communicants,) "a quibus contra id quod accipitur disputatur." And Ep. 59. 2; "Ut nec ab infantium linguis veritas corporis et sanguinis Christi inter communionis sacramenta taceatur; quia in illa mystica distributione spiritalis alimoniæ hoc impartitur, hoc sumitur, ut accipientes virtutem cœlestis cibi, in carnem ipsius, qui caro nostra factus est, transeamus." On which see Wilberforce on the Holy Euch. p. 353. As Cyril had argued against the Nestorians, "We should not eat Christ's Flesh in the Eucharist, unless we believed it to be the Flesh of God, and therefore life-giving," so Leo against the Eutychians, "We should not communicate, unless we believed Christ's Flesh, thus received, to be most true and real." In Serm. de Quadr. 4, c. 5, he says of the crypto-Manicheans at Rome, "Ita in sacramentorum communione se temperant, ut interdum, ne penitus latere non possint, ore indigno Christi corpus accipiunt, sanguinem autem redemptionis nostræ haurire omnino declinent."

82. See S. Augustine, Serm. 311, c. 2: "Viderant quod dicebant; nam quando pro ea re morerentur quam non viderant?" So Butler, Anal. part ii. c. 7; "If the Apostles and their contemporaries 'did believe the facts in attestation of which they exposed themselves to sufferings and death, this their belief, or rather knowledge, must be a proof of those facts; for they were such that came under the observation of their senses." Against the "Vision-theory," see Milligan on the Resurrection, p. 92.

83. That "the acts of the Trinity are in common" means "that by reason of the unity of the Divine substance, there is the most perfect intercommunion" (technically called *Perichoresis* or Coinherence, Newman, Arians, p. 178) "between the Father, Son, and Holy Spirit, in Their existence, revelations, and works. . . . The Father created, the Son created, and the Holy Ghost created. And yet there is this difference that . . . it is to the Second Person . . . . that the agency in creation is ascribed;" Archdeacon Hannah, Discourses on the Fall, p. 67. Cf. Hooker, v. 56. 5. See S. Aug. c. Serm. Arian. 4, "Inseparabilia quippe sunt opera Trinitatis." S. Leo explains his meaning more fully in the last two sermons of this volume; in de Pass. 7, c. 4, "In salvandis omnibus per crucem Christi, communis erat voluntas Patris et Filii," &c.; and de Pass. 1, c. 5, "Una est enim Patris et Filii voluntas, ut est una Divinitas;" a thought which disposes of that shallowest of cavils, that the received doctrine of the Atonement represents the Father as reluctantly induced, by the value of so much pain and blood, to abandon a vindictive purpose. The doctrine supposes the Father and the Son to have the same essence, and therefore the same love, the same justice, the same counsel. No thoughtful believer in the doctrine forgets that "God loved the world," and *how* He showed His love for it, S. John iii. 16; 1 S. John iv. 10. Cf. Benson on Redemption, p. xii.: "We often find this matter stated . . . as if justice were the special attribute of God the Father, injured by the sins of man, and love the special attribute of God the Son, Who came on earth to satisfy the requirements of the Father's wrath. Now, the justice of the Father and of the Son is one justice. . . . And further . . . their love towards man is one love." So Dale on the Atonement, p. 167; "The

84. This passage is repeated in Ep. 124, c. 4, and Ep. 165, c. 5. Leo speaks of Christ's death as a Sacrifice in Serm. 2, c. 3; and in Pass. 4, c. 3, "Crux ergo Christi sacramentum veri et prænuntiati habet altaris" (i.e., the mysterious character of an altar, see note 8) "ubi per hostiam salutarem, naturæ humanæ celebraretur oblatio. Ibi sanguis immaculati Agni antiquæ prævaricationis pacta delebat." De Pass. 7, c. 1: "Ut ergo umbræ cederent corpori, ... hostia in hostiam transit." De Pass. 8, c. 5 : "Ut ... nova hostia novo imponeretur altari," &c. De Pass. 17, c. 3: "Offerebatur enim Deo pro salute mundi hostia singularis."

85. On this great text, S. John xii. 32, see Serm. de Pass. 6, c. 4, "Id est, totam causam humani generis agam," &c., and de Pass. 8, c. 7 : "O admirabilis potentia Crucis ! O ineffabilis gloria Passionis ! in qua et tribunal Domini, et judicium mundi, et potestas est Crucifixi. Traxisti enim, Domine, omnia ad te ; et cum expandisses tota die manus tuas ad populum non credentem et contradicentem tibi, confitendæ majestatis tuæ sensum totus mundus accepit. .... Traxisti, Domine, omnia ad te ; quoniam scisso templi velo, sancta sanctorum ab indignis pontificibus recesserunt, ... Traxisti, Domine, omnia ad te ; ut quod in uno Judææ templo obumbratis significationibus agebatur, pleno apertoque sacramento universarum ubique nationum devotio celebraret. Nunc etenim et ordo clarior Levitarum, et dignitas amplior seniorum, et sacratior est unctio sacerdotum ; quia crux tua omnium fons benedictionum, omnium est causa gratiarum ; per quam credentibus datur virtus de infirmitate, gloria de opprobrio, vita de morte. Nunc etiam, carnalium sacrificiorum varietate cessante, omnes differentias hostiarum una corporis et sanguinis tui implet oblatio : quoniam tu es verus Agnus Dei, qui tollis peccata mundi, et ita in te universa perficis mysteria, ut sicut unum est pro omni victima sacrificium, ita unum de omni gente sit regnum."

86. The passage in the text is inserted by Leo into Ep. 124,

c. 5, Ep. 165, c. 6. Compare the antitheses in the Tome, c. 4; also de Quadrag. 8, c. 2; "Formam servi obvolutam pannis, jacentem in præsepio cognosce : sed annuntiatam ab angelis, declaratam ab elementis, adoratam a magis, formam Domini confitere." In Nativ. 10, c. 5, "In Salvatore nostro manifesta cognoscimus geminæ signa naturæ," &c.

87. "Catholica fides" recurs in the same connection in Ep. 89 to the Emperor Marcian. Compare Ep. 161, c. 1. "Catholica fides, quæ vera et una est, nulla se patitur diversitate violari :" and in Nativ. 4, c. 6, "Magnum præsidium est fides integra, fides vera, in qua nec augeri ab ullo quidquam nec minui potest ; quia nisi una est, fides non est." So Ep. 29, "Catholicam veritatem ;" Ep. 30, c. 2, "Catholica prædicatio ;" Ep. 31, c. 1, "a catholico tramite ;" Ep. 102, c. 2, "hanc esse vere apostolicam et catholicam fidem."

88. Compare S. Augustine, on the supernatural inspiration of Scripture, Ep. 82. 3 : " Ego fateor caritati tuæ, solis eis Scripturarum libris qui jam Canonici appellantur didici hunc timorem honoremque deferre, ut nullum eorum auctorem scribendo aliquid errasse firmissime credam. Ac si aliquid in eis offendero litteris, quod videtur contrarium veritati ; nihil aliud, quam vel mendosum esse codicem, vel interpretem non assecutum esse quod dictum est, vel me minime intellexisse, non ambigam."

89. So in Nativ. 4, c. 2, " Qui cum origini humanæ multum dederit, quod nos ad imaginem suam fecit, reparationi nostræ longe amplius tribuit, cum servili formæ ipse se Dominus coaptavit."

90. So in Ep. 156 he tells the Emperor Leo, that the savage murder of Bishop Proterius, at Alexandria, has interrupted the sacrifice, and caused the "hallowing of chrism" to cease. This chrism was that which, from the second century, had been administered in connection with Confirmation. The idea, doubtless, was, to symbolise the unction from the Holy One (1 S. John ii. 20 ; 2 Cor. i. 21), which made the regenerate people "a royal priesthood ;" as Leo says in Serm. de Nat. ips. 4, c. 1, "Omnes

in Christo regeneratos . . . Sancti Spiritus unctio consecrat sacerdotes," &c. So Tertullian explains it, de Bapt. 7, where he mentions that the oil was blessed. S. Cyprian, in a difficult passage, Ep. 70. 3, speaks of the oil as sanctified on the altar. S. Cyril, in his third Mystagogic Lecture, tells us that this "holy chrism" was applied to the forehead, ears, nostrils, and breast. The Council of Laodicea alludes to the "heavenly chrism." S. Ambrose does not speak of Chrism when he describes "Christ's" act of "Confirmation"—(the earliest passage in which the laying-on of hands is so named is this, in de Myst. 42)—but he mentions a previous unction just after Baptism. Some controversy has arisen as to these unctions; but it would seem that, as Confirmation became more and more regarded as a distinct rite, (instead of being, as in the earliest times, a "part of" the Baptismal rite, Pusey on Baptism, p. 153,) the anointing act was, as it were, parted into two. The priest, after administering Baptism, was allowed to pour oil, episcopally hallowed, on the top of the head; but, as Pope Innocent wrote in 416, the Bishops alone were privileged to anoint the forehead, when they "imparted the Holy Spirit." This was the chrismation of Confirmation, which had practically the effect of effacing the "laying on of hands." Leo, however, in Ep. 159. 7, says, simply, "per impositionem manuum confirmandi sunt." The Gelasian ritual for Easter-eve and Whitsun-eve provides that the presbyter shall anoint the newly-baptised "in cerebro;" after which the Bishop, placing his hand on the heads of the persons so anointed, offers up a prayer, substantially the same with our Confirmation-collect, and then "signs them on the forehead with chrism, saying, 'The Sign of Christ unto life eternal, Amen.'" Murat. i. 570, 596. There is a Gelasian Missa Chrismalis, for the benediction of the Chrism, on Maundy Thursday. An unction was also given *before* Baptism, Bingh. xi. 9. 1; and Pope Innocent mentions the anointing of the sick, Epist. i. 8, to Decentius.

91. See Serm. de Pass. 2, c. 1, to the effect that the robber's great act of faith was produced by a special grace from our Lord: and that the "Hodie mecum eris" was spoken rather "from a throne" than from a cross. Cyril of Jerusalem has a

glowing passage, Cat. xiii. 31 : "What power enlightened thee, O robber? Who taught thee to worship thy despised fellow-sufferer? .... To-day shalt thou be with Me ... because to-day thou hast heard My voice. .... Fear not the fiery sword; it sinks in awe before the Sovereign," &c. S. Chrys. de Cruce et Latrone, ii. 2, 3, (a Good Friday sermon,) magnifies the robber's faith, but observes that confession of sins had preceded it. " He confessed, and found boldness βασιλείαν αἰτῆσαι."

92. Here he emphatically makes the presence of a common nature with Christ depend on supernatural conditions. Men have it "if" they receive Him, i.e., if they are regenerated by His Spirit in Baptism. This "if" is momentous : and modern tendencies to naturalism make it now more significant than ever. According to a mode of speech which was largely current some years ago, in one school of religious thought, all men, simply *as* men, and irrespectively of any "event" in their religious history, (see Maurice's Kingdom of Christ, i. 428, where the germs of the theory are observable,) from their natural birth upwards, are to be regarded as members of Christ and children of God; and baptism is not the means whereby they become so, but a witness that they have always been so. By an ingenious extension of Calvinistic language, it becomes a token, on God's part, of sonship *already* granted, not indeed to an "elect" class, but to every human being, baptised or unbaptised. In three ways, apparently, this theory gratifies certain minds. They are glad to explain away the text, Eph. ii. 3, which pronounces all men, "by nature, children of wrath ;" to believe in acceptance as independent of any Sacramental medium; above all, to ignore all special Gospel-privileges, and represent the Church as co-extensive with the world, or at least with civilised society. Thus the tendency of the language in question is downwards ; and the sacred terms, when extended to all men apart from sacred conditions, are evacuated of their meaning ; instead of the conception of humanity at large being spiritualised, the conception of Christian privileges is secularised; "the tide of Divine economy is sucked back again into the earthly vortex," (Mozley's Essays, ii. 30, as to the German theory which absorbs the Church into the State.) The Pelagianism of

this view is not concealed by language about Christ being the Root of humanity; in fact, it tends to substitute a "Divine immanence in all souls" for the "miracle" of a Divine Incarnation; and it is hardly too much to say, that it would require large portions of the New Testament to be re-written. Not by nature, but by grace,—not by birth, but by regeneration,—by the act of "the One Spirit" in Baptism, does man, in the Apostolic theology, gain his interest in the Second Adam, and his right to say, "Our Father." The Incarnation is the source of a transcendent life, which "by nature we cannot have;" if "the last Adam was" indeed to be "a quickening Spirit," His nature, as a principle of life, must be imparted by means supernatural; and the Church is a mysterious organisation pervaded by that life as so imparted,—a new creation, diverse from the old in its basis and its agencies,—a "body of Christ," with "joints and bands" of its own, conveying to its members their portion of the fulness of the Head. Cp. Hooker, v. 56. 7, "It is too cold an interpretation," &c., i.e., the view that we are "in Christ" inasmuch as our "nature is in Him." So Wilberforce on the Incarnation, p. 203, that our union with Christ "does not merely mean the union which He has with our nature, but the union which *we* have with His:" and ib. p. 232, "It is Christ's manhood which binds men through Sacraments to His mystic body:" and compare Sadler on the Second Adam, p. 12, "If Jesus Christ . . . . . . is to be an Adam at all, if His undefiled human náture is to be . . . . . . a principle of life, counteracting the death received from the human nature of the first Adam, this cannot be in the way of nature : it must be effected supernaturally." So Hardwick's Christ and other Masters, i. 53; "The only 'higher unity' connecting men together is the spiritual nature they derive in common by regeneration into Christ, the New Head of humanity; but this birth is most expressly said to be 'not of blood,' ($αἱμάτων$.) S. John i. 13."

93. He alludes to the result of the Council of Chalcedon. So in Ep. 120, he calls the condemnation of Eutychianism a victory of Christ; "Vicit per nos et pro nobis ille," &c.

94. He probably used, on Good Friday, the eighth interces-

sion for that day in the Gelasian rites, Murat. i. 562; its words, at least, resemble his own: "Qui etiam Judaicam perfidiam a tua misericordia non repellis." Compare in Epiph. 5, c. 3, "Optandum nobis et studendum ut et hic populus, qui ab illa spiritali patrum nobilitate defecit, ramis suæ arboris inseratur." The martyr Paulus, in Euseb. Mart. Pal. 8, prays first for the Church, then "for the conversion of the Jews to God, through Christ." Compare the Apostolic Constitutions, v. 19.

95. "Inconsequens et irrationabile." S. Augustine more than once refers to dogmatism of this kind. Sometimes it implied grave mistakes as to what the Church really taught. In the Confessions he repeatedly tells us that he had once imputed to her anthropomorphic views of God's nature; in de Mor. Eccl. Cath., having alluded to the Manicheans' persistent demand of "rational" proof, i. 3, he says of these misconceptions, "Talem fidem qua Deo inconveniens aliquid creditur, nos vehementius et uberius accusamus," i. 17. So Volusianus tells S. Augustine that he had heard, in a debating society, the question propounded, How could the Lord of all things confine Himself within an infant body? And S. Augustine answers, Ep. 137. 4, that He did not abandon the government of the world. Again, Volusianus had heard it said (as Julian had said before) that Christ's miracles were but poor evidences: why should not God Incarnate have done more? Augustine answers, Besides what are commonly called His works, what think you of "nasci de Virgine, a mortuis resurgere, in cœlum ascendere?" Ep. 137. 13. The Pagans repeated the old scoff, "Qualem Deum colitis qui natus est?" Enarr. in Ps. xciii. 15; (so too Chrys. says, in Diem Natal. 7, c. 6;) and "In nulla re tam vehementer, tam pertinaciter, tam obnixe et contentiose contradicitur fidei Christianæ, sicut de carnis resurrectione . . . . . ut dicant *fieri non posse*," &c., in Ps. lxxxviii. 2, 5. Ancient theologians were thus familiar with the question, "whether Christian belief was reasonable." See too Origen c. Cels. iii. 75.

96. Here, and in Serm. 13, c. 2, he asserts, as a consequence of the Personal Union, that our Lord's Godhead was not separated from His Manhood during the short interval between His death

The Personal and Vital Unions.

and His Resurrection. S. Athanasius says as much, c. Apollin. i. 18, and still more explicitly, ii. 14, "The Godhead did not desert the body in the sepulchre, nor was the soul separated from it in Hades." Some words of S. Irenæus, (iii. 19, 3,) S. Hilary (in Matt. c. 33. s. 6,) and S. Ambrose (in Luc. l. 10. s. 127,) which have been supposed to bear a different sense, may be understood with reference to the mysterious "forsaking," and to the withdrawal of such Divine presence as would have kept off death. Fulgentius, de Fide ad Petrum, 11, is very emphatic; "In sepulchro idem Deus homo factus, jacuit, et ab inferis idem Deus homo factus . . . . . resurrexit." So S. Thomas rules, Sum. iii. q. 50, that the Godhead was never, even in death, separated from Christ's body, much less from His soul. So Hooker, v. 52. 4 : "Even when His soul forsook the tabernacle of His body, His Deity forsook neither body nor soul," &c.; and Bishop Forbes on Nicene Creed, p. 224, "In His death the vital union between His body and soul was dissolved . . . . but the personal union was never severed," &c. See too Newman's Sermons, ii. 34.

97. On the trine immersion see Tertullian, c. Praxeam, 26: "Nec semel, sed ter ad singula nomina, in Personas singulas tingimur." Cyril of Jerusalem, Cat. Myst. 2. 4 : "Each of you was asked, whether he believed in the Name of the Father, and of the Son, and of the Holy Spirit. And you made that saving confession, and you were dipped thrice into the water, and emerged again ; symbolically representing also, in this circumstance, the three days' sepulture of Christ," &c. In S. Ambrose, de Mysteriis, 21, 28, the three confessions are mentioned, and the three immersions implied. Bingham, xi. 11. 6, gives other references, and speaks of the double symbolism as to the Holy Trinity and the three days' burial. The latter, however, was clearly an after-thought. In the days of Gregory the Great (Ep. i. 43) the Spanish Arians appealed to trine immersion as a witness to their own doctrine of different Essences. Gregory, being consulted by Leander of Seville, advised the Spanish Catholics, under these circumstances, to use *single* immersion, as a protest against the denial of the Consubstantiality. The Roman ritual, however, retained the old usage : and it was prescribed in the Prayer Book of 1549.

98. The voice of the ancient Church, on the duty of earnest living after Baptism, was as emphatic as that of our own Church in the exhortations which close her Baptismal Offices. Leo says elsewhere, de Jej. x. mens. 7, c. 1, " Natura quippe mutabilis . . . . . . licet jam redempta, et in sacro baptismate renata, in quantum est passibilis, in tantum est ad deteriora proclivis . . . Sciendum . . . est, formidinem sublatam esse, non pugnam." So, de Quadr. 3, c. 2, Satan is said to be all the fiercer against men "ex quo ei in baptismo renuntiavimus." S. Augustine is great on this subject; e.g., de Pecc. Meritis, i. s. 25, " Baptizatus parvulus, si ad rationales annos veniens non crediderit, nec se ab illicitis concupiscentiis abstinuerit, nihil ei proderit quod parvus accepit ;" and ib. s. 70, " Si post baptismum vixerit, . . . habet cum qua pugnet" (i.e., concupiscence) " eamque adjuvante Deo superet, si non in vacuum gratiam ejus susceperit, si reprobatus esse noluerit." S. Chrys. in Joan. Hom. 10. 2 : " Much earnestness is needful, in order to preserve the image of adoption, impressed on us in baptism, unsullied." Cyril. Hier. Cat. xviii. 33 : " How you ought for the time to come to walk worthily of this grace, both in acts and words." The address to candidates in Gelas. Sacr., Mur. i. 543, says much the same : " Diabolus, qui hominem tentare non desinit, munitos vos hoc Symbolo semper inveniat, ut . . . . gratiam Domini incorruptam et immaculatam, (ipso, confitemini, protegente,) servetis." See also Collects in Mur. i. 577.

99. The idea is, of course, taken from S. Matt. xxv. 40. In de Collect. 1, Leo says, that Christ "tantum nobis pauperes commendavit, ut se in ipsis vestiri ac suscipi testaretur."

100. A bishop named Boniface asked S. Augustine, " Utrum parentes baptizatis parvulis suis noceant, cum eos dæmoniorum sacrificiis sanare conantur," Aug. Ep. 98. 1. So Aug. in Jo. Evan. Tr. 7. 7 : " Non, quando nobis dolet caput, curramus ad præcantatores." So in a sermon (supposed to be by S. Cæsarius of Arles) in the appendix to S. Augustine, (No. 278,) Christians are warned against consulting diviners, "de qualibet causa aut infirmitate." So S. Eligius, in what

Maitland (Dark Ages, p. 150) calls his "well known, or at least much talked of, sermon," (App. to Aug. tom. vi.): "Quoties aliqua infirmitas evenerit, non quærantur præcantatores . . . . . neque . . . . . diabolica phylacteria exerceantur." S. Chrysostom condemns the use of amulets in illness, in Col. Hom. 8. 5.

101. The word *Pascha*, as applied to a Christian solemnity, is of course connected with 1 Cor. v. 7, and so testifies to Christ as the Peace-offering of the New Covenant, and to "the blood of sprinkling which speaketh better things than that of Abel," Heb. xii. 24. "The general idea of propitiation underlay the Paschal offering; yet the offering itself was not for the sake of removing sin, but of claiming the privilege of a promise already given. It therefore was *in itself* rather a Peace-offering . . . . a type of Christ's oblation as the Advocate of His Church:" Benson on Redemption, pp. 312—315. Such were the thoughts which S. Paul's words would suggest to a Christian accustomed to meditate on the Legal ritual. And this twofold idea of propitiation and pleading—first the Sin-offering, to expiate, and then the Peace-offering, to preserve in grace—corresponds to the twofold aspect which the Paschal solemnity possessed in earliest times. It was a commemoration of the Crucifixion,— *Pascha Staurosimon;* but as Passion-tide leads on to Easter, the joyful celebration of the Resurrection, *Pascha Anastasimon*, followed hard upon the former, and gradually appropriated to itself the Paschal name. It is striking to see, in the old Easter-day services, the intensest realization of the Atonement, and of the privilege of pleading it sacramentally to the Father. Take that sublime Gelasian Preface, which enriches our own Liturgy: or see, in the Gelasian book, the oft-recurring association of "the Paschal sacramentum, the Paschal mystery," with the blotting out of the "chirographum" and the pardon of sin. Or take the venerable hymn, "Ad cœnam Agni providi," which in one or other form occurs in most of our Hymnals. The most splendid, perhaps, of all ritual passages on "the Pasch" is that in the Greek office translated by Dr. Neale, (Introd. East. Ch. ii. 886,) in which the solemnity itself, "the Lord's Pasch of delight," is merged as it were in His own Person, "the

Pasch which *is* Christ the Redeemer;" as in the Latin lines which many know in their English rendering—

> "O Jesu blest, to every breast
> Unceasing Paschal gladness be!"

102. This Sabbath, of course, is "the Great Sabbath," Holy Saturday, or Easter Eve. Its observance, as a solemn vigil and as a day of baptisms, was extremely ancient. Narcissus, Bishop of Jerusalem, A.D. 196, was believed to have miraculously obtained oil for the church lamps "at the great night-long Paschal vigil," Euseb. vi. 9: (cp. ib. ii. 17, vi. 34;) so Tertullian speaks of the vigil lasting all night, ad Ux. ii. 4. Constantine provided many lights for it, Euseb. Vit. C. iv. 22. S. Aug. says of it, that its "tam clara celebritas" compelled even unbelievers "vigilare carne;" that this night was "as clear as the day;" (so also S. Cyril, Procat. 15) that it was spent in prayer, and in meditation "on that life which He began for us in His own flesh, which He raised from the dead to die no more," Serm. 219, 221. Compare Prudentius, Cathem. hymn. 5, "Inventor rutili Dux bone luminis," which dwells on the fire being lit from a flint, and after dilating on the Exodus, speaks of the long vigil in the churches brilliantly lighted up with "lumina quæ suffixa micant per laquearia." The Mozarabic Missal calls it "a night glorious throughout the world." The Gelasian services for the day began with the recitation of the Creed by the "infantes," who were to be baptised in the evening. Then came exorcism,—the symbolic touching of ears and nostrils with spittle,—the renunciations, and the candidates' prayer and dismissal. A little before 3 p.m. the clergy entered the church with a Litany; and the Archdeacon, lighting the great Paschal candle, the symbol of Easter glory and joy, (which, says Prudentius, is "dedicated roscidæ noctis principio,") chanted the "benedictio cerei;" of which, however, the Gregorian book supplies a far more majestic form, "Exultet jam angelica turba." The whole heart of the Church seems to overflow into some of these rapturous thanksgivings; they speak of the earth as "illuminated by the splendour of the eternal King," Whose Paschal "victory was the exultation of Angels;" they dwell on "this holy night" as "freeing

the captives, gladdening the mourners, washing away faults, purifying the fallen." Then came twelve Lections ("consuetis lectionibus nocte sancta decursis," Leon. Ep. 3. 3,) with appropriate prayers: then a procession, with Litany, to the font, which was solemnly blessed to be "a regenerating water:—I bless thee, creature of water, by the living God, by the holy God, by the God Who in the beginning separated thee from the dry land .... and I bless thee by Jesus Christ His only Son our Lord, Who .... turned thee into wine, walked upon thee, was baptised by John in thee, brought thee forth from His side with blood, and commanded His disciples that believers should be baptised in thee, saying, 'Go, teach,'" &c. (Compare our Collect for the "sanctification" of the water.) Then followed the interrogative creed, the three immersions, the anointing on the crown of the head, the Episcopal imposition of hands, the unction on the brow. Soon afterwards, a third Litany was chanted; "and they enter the church for the Vigil-Mass, as soon as a star has appeared in the sky." This nocturnal Eucharist was specially for the new-baptised; it contained the Preface above referred to. It is worth while to dwell on these details, because the Easter-eve observances were perhaps the most characteristic of any in the ancient Church, the most expressive of her loving devotion to a present and everlasting Lord.

103. See his exhortations in Lent Sermons; de Quadr. 9, c. 1, "ut per commune consortium crucis Christi, etiam nos aliquid in eo quod propter nos gessit ageremus, sicut Apostolus ait, 'Si compatimur, et conglorificamur'"(combining Rom. viii. 17, 2 Tim. ii. 12:) de Quadr. 12, c. 1, "nos ... præparare" (i.e. by fasting) "ut in cujus sumus resurrectione conresuscitati, in ipsius inveniamur passione commortui." As to the duration of Lent, there was anciently much diversity. (S. Irenæus ap. Euseb. v. 24.) Originally, as it would seem, (although the point is disputed) a fast of forty *hours* in commemoration of the Passion, it gradually included more and more of the days and weeks preceding. Although it was not until the time of Gregory II. that it became strictly a forty *days'* fast, there is no doubt that in the fourth century, if not earlier, a period was generally observed which might be called "forty days." Leo claims for "forty days" Apostolical

institution; but he would be prone to make that claim for any institute of his own church, (see Bingham, xxi. 1. 8.) What Socrates, v. 22, says of the Romans observing a three weeks' fast must apply, if true, to the Novatians of Rome.

104. The Latins, says Estius on 1 Cor. xv. 47, "constanter legunt id quod habet nostra Vulgata versio," i.e. "secundus homo de cœlo cœlestis;" as Leo, in the text, quotes the passage. S. Chrysostom's commentary assumes the received Greek text; the Revised text reads simply, "is from heaven." In verse 49 the Vulgate, like Leo, has *portemus;* so has Tertullian, adv. Marc. v. 10. The true Greek text is φορέσομεν, the other reading φορέσωμεν (which Chrysostom had before him, and on which his gloss is, "Let us do what is best") is supposed to be an *itacism*, or confusion by a copyist between two similar letters. (Scrivener, Introd. to Criticism of N. T., p. 627.)

105. S. Augustine says, "Moli autem corporis ubi divinitas erat, ostia clausa non obstiterunt," in Jo. Evan. Tr. 121. 4. It is usual to see in this twice recorded incident (S. John xx. 19, 26) an instance of the unique powers of Christ's risen body. See Macpherson on the Resurrection, pp. 310, 313.

106. Compare the two adverbs which respectively exclude Nestorianism and Eutychianism, ἀδιαιρέτως, ἀσυγχύτως, Hooker, v. 54. 10. See below, note 163.

107. In this passage he assumes that 2 Cor. v. 16 refers to our Lord's "flesh" in its non-glorified condition. This is surely a mistake; S. Paul is using κατὰ σάρκα as in Rom. viii. 1, 2 Cor. x. 2, for "as men of the world do, whose point of view is secular and not religious;" he means to say, "Before the love of Christ began to constrain me, before I was *in* Christ, I thought in one way; now, I think in another. I now look on no man in a mere worldly light; even as to Christ, *I once thought as other men did;* but now, such unworthy thoughts have passed away, and all my feelings, as to Him and every one else, are the feelings of one new-created." To infer that he no longer laid stress on the "historical" life of Jesus is to make the text contradict

Rom. i. 3; ix. 5; 1 Cor. xv. 3; Gal. iv. 4; 2 Tim. ii. 8. The student must be on his guard against tendencies to use "carnal" *ad invidiam*, in disparagement of the bodily reality of the Incarnation or the Resurrection. As to the glorified condition of Christ's body, see Milligan on the Resurrection, p. 11, that while "in various important respects" it was "similar to what it had been," retaining a "material structure closely corresponding to that which our Lord possessed before His crucifixion," yet it was not "subject to the same conditions of ponderable matter as before," &c.; and Liddon, Easter in S. Paul's, i. 107, ff., that it "was literally the very body which had been crucified, and yet . . . while retaining physical substance and unimpaired identity, was yet endowed and interpenetrated with some of the properties of spirit," &c.

108. "Mens intenta mansuris." Compare a Collect in the Leonine Sacram., Mur. i. 313; "Da nobis, Domine, non terrena sapere, sed amare cœlestia; et inter prætereuntia constitutos jam nunc inhærere *mansuris*."

109. The idea of retaining throughout the year the blessings of the Easter festival occurs in several old Collects. As in the Gelasian, "ut Paschalis perceptio sacramenti continuata in nostris mentibus perseveret," Murat. i. 573: "ut quod Paschalibus exsequimur institutis, fructiferum nobis omni tempore sentiamus," ib. i. 581; and still more in the Gregorian for the First Sunday after Easter, "ut qui Paschalia festa peregimus, hæc, te largiente, moribus et vita teneamus," ib. ii. 75. See "Ancient Collects," p. 56, ff.

110. Here and elsewhere Leo uses "sacerdos" specifically of himself as a bishop; as he speaks of bishops under the name of "sacerdos" in Ep. 4. 1; 14. 6; 10. 2, &c., and of his own episcopal office as "sacerdotii mei," de Nat. ipsius, 1. Cp. Ep. 4. 1. He speaks also of the "secundi ordinis sacerdotes," in de Quadr. 10, c. 1, (cp. Ep. 9. 1, "sacerdotalis ordinatio,") and would assuredly have recognised no antagonism between that designation and the name of "presbyter," which he commonly adopts, (e.g. Ep. 1. 1, ff., 9. 3, and 24. 1, " Eutychem presbyterum,") any

more than between the ascription of a specific sacerdotal character to this or that order of the ministry and that "royal priesthood" belonging to all "spiritales et rationabiles Christiani," of which he says, de Nat. ipsius, 4. 1, "Quid tam sacerdotale quam . . . immaculatas pietatis hostias de altari cordis offerre?" Doubtless, if he had been told that the ideas of a ministerial and of a general priesthood excluded each other, he would have answered, in effect, that the former was the appointed organ of the corporate exercise of the latter, and in no way interfered with its individual exercise. See Gore, The Church and the Ministry, p. 27 : Carter on the Priesthood, p. 146.

111. He refers again to this text, S. John xiv. 6, in de Pass. 18, c. 3, where he explains "Veritas" somewhat differently, "in expectatione rei certæ."

112. Christ is here regarded as the Creator. So in the Tome, c. 3, and in Serm. 18, c. 2.

113. Comp. Ep. 80, c. 2. "Qui licet in Patris sit dextera constitutus, in eadem tamen carne quam sumpsit ex Virgine sacramentum propitiationis exsequitur." There the Intercession in Heaven is the thought before us, here it is rather the Presence with the Church ; both being aspects of the truth, "We are not forsaken by our Lord." So in the Leonine Sacramentary, Murat. Lit. Rom. i. 313, "ut sicut . . . Salvatorem consedere tecum . . . confidimus, ita usque ad consummationem sæculi manere nobiscum . . . sentiamus."

114. There is some doubt as to the genuineness of the words, "veritatis sinceritate," as also of words above in c. 2, "quæ se in quas voluerit mensuras benignitatis inflectit," &c.

115. "Nulla varietate mutabilis." The Nicene Creed, as framed at Nicæa, had certain anathemas against Arians, condemning, among other of their statements, the notion that the Son was "changeable," Soc. i. 8. See S. Athanasius, Orat. c. Arian. i. 35. Leo, in Nativ. 5, c. 3, argues that on Arian principles, "mutability" must belong to the Father ; for He must be supposed to

No "degrees" in Godhead.

have begun to be a Father, if "once the Son was not." But Leo was specially concerned to insist on the immutability of the Son in order to guard against any return, by the way of Eutychianism, to the Apollinarian theory described in the " Quicunque" as that of a "conversion of the Godhead" into manhood. For if the Incarnate were deemed to exist in "only one nature," i.e. His Godhead, then, unless actual Docetism were adopted, the Godhead itself would be supposed to have in some sense become materialised. Hence Leo says in the Tome, c. 4, "Deus non mutatur miseratione:" Ep. 35. 2, "Nec enim Verbum aut in carnem aut in animam aliquā sui parte conversum est, cum simplex et incommutabilis natura Deitatis tota in sua sit semper essentia, nec damnum sui recipiens, nec augmentum." So de Quadr. 8. 1, "impassibilem Dei Verbi atque incommutabilem deitatem." He is in effect following Tertullian, who (as if condemning Monophysitism beforehand) argues that the Word was not "transformed" into flesh, because "Deus neque desinit esse, neque aliud potest esse," and the Word must remain in His own "form," adv. Prax. 27. Observe this as against modern exaggerations of the κένωσις. See below, note 150.

116. See above, note 29. The term "gradus," in reference to the Holy Trinity, might be used in two senses. Tertullian, writing against "Patripassians," and contending that in order to hold the Unity, it was not necessary to explain away the Trinity, might say that the Father, Son, and Spirit were "tres non statu, sed gradu," meaning thereby, (as the context shows—for he adds, "unius autem substantiæ," &c.) not that one was more or less truly God than another, but that beside the First Person there was a Second and also a Third, adv. Prax. 3, 8, 12, 19, 30. See Bp. Bull, Defence of Nicene Faith, b. 2, c. 7, s. 6. On the other hand, post-Nicene writers might, for fear of seeming to Arianise, deny, as Pelagius did in his confession of faith, that there was any "gradus" in the Trinity, explaining, "There is nothing which can be called inferior or superior, but the whole Godhead is equal in Its own perfection;" compare the Athanasian Creed, "And in this Trinity none is greater or less," &c. So S. Ambrose de Fide, v. s. 202, to the Arians, "gradus quosdam facitis." So S. Aug. Serm. 264

7, "non gradibus sibi adjecti, sed majestate adunati." So Leo, here and in Sermons 17 and 18 of this volume, denies any "gradus," which would, in his sense of the word, be a division of the essential unity; again de Pent. 2, c. 2, "Omnibus existentiæ gradibus exclusis." Compare S. Greg. Naz. Ep. 101, condemning the idea of a κλίμαξ θεότητος.

117. Compare our Collect for S. Thomas' Day; and R. H. Hutton, Essays Theol. and Literary, i. 124, on the evidential value of the fact "that the assertion of the Resurrection was at first received with disbelief and doubt, which were certainly turned within a few days into a sort of confidence and even of enthusiastic assurance, very much exceeding, as far as we can judge, anything which had existed among the Apostles before." See also Christlieb, Modern Doubt, &c. p. 498, E. T. Leo considers that the whole period of the "Great Forty Days" was characterised by a gradual confirmation of their faith and by a communication of sacred truths. See Bishop Moberly, Sayings of the Great Forty Days, p. 16; "Spoken .... in His royalty and glory, spoken to convey, and in the very form of expression obviously conveying direct, immediate, actual commissions and powers, they form the charter of the Kingdom," (referring to Acts i. 3.) So the "Leonine Sacramentary," Murat. i. 314, that Christ was seen by His disciples "usque ad quadragesimum diem ...... in id proficientibus per has moras ecclesiæ primitivis, ut et certius fieret quod credidissent, et plenius discerent quod docerent."

118. This noble passage is read in the Roman Matins of Ascension Day. The sentence beginning, "Quia igitur Christi ascensio nostra provectio est," is adduced by Hooker as the best possible comment on the sentence in the "Te Deum" as to the opening of the kingdom of heaven to all believers, v. 45, 2. Compare the "Leonine Sacramentary," Muratori, i. 314, 315, "per hæc sacrosancta mysteria in totius Ecclesiæ confidimus corpore faciendum, quod ejus præcessit in Capite;" and i. 315, "illuc subsequi tuorum membra fidelium, quo Caput nostrum Principiumque præcessit." As to the exaltation of Christ's Manhood, S. Leo, in this sermon, comes near S. Chrysostom, Hom.

in Asc.: "He offered the first-fruits of our nature to the Father, ... ascended above Angels, passed by Archangels, transcended the Cherubim, soared above the Seraphim, passed beyond the Powers, stayed not till He attained the throne of sovereignty. ... To-day Archangels saw what they had long desired to see,—our own nature flashing light from the Kingly throne, resplendent with immortal glory and beauty." Compare the hymn, "Regnat Deus Dei caro." "Carnem Christi sedentem ad dexteram Patris adorant Angeli," S. Aug. Serm. 225; as Hooker, v. 54. 9, "all the Angels of heaven adore" Christ's body. See Pusey's Parochial Sermons, ii. 216—239, on "the Ascension our glory and joy;" and Liddon's University Sermons, i. 283—305. Pearson's words glow, as with devout exultation, as he speaks of Christ's entrance within the inmost Presence; his account of the results of the Ascension is simplified from that of Aquinas, Sum. iii. 57. 6, who calls it a cause of our salvation—(1) on our part, in that it gives scope to faith, hope, love, and reverence; (2) on His part, in that the Head prepares a place for the members, the High Priest intercedes for us in the heavenly sanctuary, ("for the very presentation of Himself, from the human nature which He introduced into heaven, is a kind of intercession for us," Heb. ix. 24,) and the Divine Lord, enthroned on high, sends down His gifts to man. Both Aquinas and Pearson quote Micah ii. 13, "The breaker is come up," &c. On the necessity of a literal belief in this exaltation of our Head, as the ground of that hope which can alone support His members—a belief which "is, in itself, belief in the whole mystery of" the Incarnation, but which has been deadened in so many by "the falsely spiritualising tendencies of the age,"—see Bp. Ellicott's Lectures, pp. 414—417. "We can only," says Dean Vaughan, (Four Sermons at Cambridge, p. 2,) "pass to the Ascension through the Resurrection and through the Divinity of Christ." That the "heaven" of the Ascension was not "the mere physical firmament," but the inmost sanctuary of the Divine presence, whatever it might be, see Wace, "Gospel and its Witnesses," p. 167.

119. It is plain from the context, that the presence of our Lord's Humanity which Leo is excluding is a presence palpable

or "natural," which would be an object to sense, not to faith. He uses exactly the same phrase, "corporal presence," which the note at the end of the English Communion Office uses for such a presence as is not to be looked for in the Holy Eucharist.

120. He speaks of "innumera martyrum millia," de Pentec. 2, c. 6, of their affinity to our Lord in love and in sufferings, and of the vast moral benefit of their example, in that "plus est opere docere quam voce," in Nat. S. Laurentii, c. 1. In the passage before us he is probably thinking, among others, of such "boys" and "maidens" as S. Pancras and S. Agnes, whom the Roman church specially honoured.

121. Leo here understands "Touch Me not," as pointing to the spiritual intercourse which the believing soul would hold with our Lord when removed from "the sphere of sense," (compare Liddon, Univ. Serm. i. 295.) Other expositors of the passage have seen in it a gentle warning as to the deeper reverence demanded by the glorification of the Lord's body. S. Augustine thinks that the Magdalene is admonished to recognise in Jesus more than a mere human teacher, Sermon 245. 2. But, although high authorities concur in treating this saying mysteriously as indicative of some high truth, or some deep law of Divine manifestation, it may be, after all, that the words simply mean, "Do not spend time in taking hold of Me :" (cp. S. Matt. xxviii. 9;) "I am not, as you imagine, on the point of leaving the world : the matter now in hand is to inform My brethren." See Macpherson on the Resurrection, p. 160.

122. "*Sursum* vocatos animos," &c. It is evident that he is alluding to those glorious words with which the Church from the very earliest times, as we may believe, has entered into the most inmost sanctuary of her worship ; the "Lift up your hearts," with its response, "We lift them up unto the Lord," at the opening of the Anaphora, or most solemn portion of all Liturgies. See the vivid description in Pater's "Marius the Epicurean," ii. 154. Compare S. Cyprian, de Orat. Dom. c. 31 : " Sacerdos, ante orationem præfatione præmissa, parat fratrum

mentes dicendo, 'Sursum corda,' ut dum respondet plebs, ' Habemus ad Dominum,' admoneatur nihil aliud se quam Dominum cogitare debere." Cyril of Jerusalem, Cat. Myst. v. 4 : "The Priest exclaims, ' Lift up your hearts.' For indeed, at that most awful hour, one ought to have one's heart lifted up to God..... Virtually, the Priest bids us at that hour to lay aside all worldly cares," &c. S. Aug. de Vera Relig. s. 5 : " Ut quotidie per universum orbem humanum genus una pæne voce respondeat, ' sursum corda se habere ad Dominum.' " The Latin form was always " Sursum corda," " Up with hearts !" The Greek Liturgies differ; some have the form lengthened, and so far weakened; e.g., S. James's, " Let us lift up our mind and hearts." S. Chrysostom's : " Let us lift up our hearts." On the other hand the Clementine has simply "Up with the mind." It was usual to prefix a salutation, or blessing, with its response, " And with thy spirit."

123. So de Jej. vii. mens. 5. 3 ; " Ut peregrinantibus nobis, et ad patriam redire properantibus, quidquid de prosperitatibus mundi hujus occurrerit, viaticum sit itineris, non illecebra mansionis." A favourite thought of S. Augustine's: as in Psal. xxxiv. Serm. 1, c. 6, " Consolatur (Deus) tanquam in via, sed si nos intelligamus viam : quia tota ista vita, et omnia quibus uteris in hac vita, sic tibi debent esse tanquam stabulum viatori, non tanquam domus habitatori: memento peregisse te aliquid, restare aliquid ; divertisse te ad refectionem, non ad defectionem." And in Ps. xl. c. 5, " Ne viator, tendens ad patriam, stabulum amet pro domo sua." The words in the text, " so pass through these temporal things," may be the basis of the " sic transeamus per bona temporalia," in the original of our Collect for the Fourth Sunday after Trinity.

124. "Dispertitæ linguæ," Vulg. Acts ii. 2. Διαμεριζόμεναι is not "cloven," but "parted" or "divided," the fiery radiance broken into separate streams. See Christian Year, Fourth Sunday after Easter :

> " The floods of glory earthward pour,
> They part like shower-drops in mid air."

And in Lyra Innocentium, p. 342 :

> " In many a living line they sped
> To rest on each anointed head."

Compare 1 Cor. xii. 7—11.

125. Compare S. Aug. Serm. 267, c. 2 ; "Omnes qui aderant unam linguam didicerant. Venit Spiritus Sanctus ; impleti sunt, cœperunt loqui linguis variis omnium gentium, quas non noverant nec didicerant." See Bishop Chr. Wordsworth in loc. Döllinger identifies this "gift of divers languages" with the gift of tongues, First Age of the Church, p. 314, E. T.

126. See this passage quoted in Swete's Hist. of Doctr. of Procession, p. 157. It is not so explicit an assertion of the Double Procession as repeatedly occurs in S. Augustine, or as is found in Leo's Ep. 15. 1, " de utroque processit."

127. He insists more than once on the ineffableness of God. In Nativ. 9, c. 1 ; " Nemo enim ad cognitionem veritatis magis propinquat, quam qui intelligit in rebus divinis, etiamsi multum proficiat, semper sibi superesse quod quærat. Nam qui se ad id, in quod tendit, pervenisse præsumit, non quæsita reperit, sed in inquisitione defecit." And see Sermon 18 of this volume, de Pent. 3, c. 3, " Quamvis nulla mens ad cogitandum de Deo, nulla ad loquendum lingua sufficiat." So S. Augustine repeatedly declares that no human words can measure infinite truths,—that God's mysteries transcend expression. "Cum quæritur quid Tres, magna prorsus inopia humanum laborat eloquium. Dictum est tamen, tres ' Personæ,' non ut illud diceretur, sed ne taceretur," de Trinitate, v. s. 10. "Verius enim cogitatur Deus quam dicitur, et verius *est* quam cogitatur," ib. vii. s. 7. " Quid restat, nisi ut fateamur loquendi necessitate parta hæc vocabula, cum opus esset copiosa disputatione adversum insidias vel errores hæreticorum ?" ib. vii. s. 9. " Quid facimus nos? Silebimus? Utinam liceret ! Forsitan enim silendo, aliquid dignum de ineffabili cogitaretur. Nam quidquid potest fari, non est ineffabile. Ineffabilis est autem Deus ;" Serm. 117, s. 7. So Hilary de Trin. iv. 2, " Non ignoramus autem, ad res

divinas explicandas, neque hominum elocutionem neque naturæ humanæ comparationem posse sufficere." See too ib. iii. 1. Novatian de Trin. ii., "Sentire enim illum aliquatenus possumus : *ut* autem ipse est, sermone explicare non possumus." Similarly the great representatives of Eastern theology ; S. Athanasius, Orat. ii. 32, " Since human nature is incapable of comprehending God, Scripture has propounded examples and images, that by means of these we may be able, in some very poor and faint way, to have such thoughts as we can attain to ;" and S. Basil, Ep. 234, " It is from His acts that we say we know our God, but we do not profess to draw near to His very essence." And S. Cyril ; "μείων δέ που τῆς ἀληθείας ὁ λόγος," Schol. 8 : "ἀσθενεῖ μὲν πᾶσα παραδειγμάτων δύναμις," Quod unus sit Christus, (Op. vii. 420, Pusey.) And again, " The mode of the Incarnation (τῆς ἐνανθρωπήσεως) is . . . . not within the compass of our understandings," ad Theodosium (ib. vii. 70.) Thoroughly did the Fathers feel that, as Bp. Bull says of one great mystery, "no similitude could in every respect illustrate" the things of God, no " language could set them forth worthily;" that " in this darkness we both conceive and speak, or rather lisp, like children," Def. F. N. b. 4, c. 4, s. 14. We could not more utterly mistake their aim and view than by supposing that their doctrinal formulas " pretend to grasp the whole matter revealed, and to bring its unfathomable depths within the cognizance of the understanding ; they profess only to methodize . . . . the great outlines of the faith," or to deny " some heretical proposition by which it had been proposed to explain, and so evacuate the revealed mystery ;" Mill on the Temptation, p. 17. Compare Newman, Grammar of Assent, p. 123, " No human words indeed are worthy of the Supreme Being, none are adequate, but we have no words to use but human." S. Athanasius knew that some misconceived the term Homoousion : Cyril was well aware that φύσις had several shades of meaning : no modern divine pretends that the use of " Person" or " Persons" in regard to God is intellectually unobjectionable, or more than, so to speak, an οἰκονομία. There were, indeed, persons in the fourth century who declared that human language could explain the whole essence of God. But they were the extremest of Arians, Eunomius and his school, Soc.

212   *Coequality and Subordination.*

iv. 7, who taunted the Catholics with worshipping a God whom they "knew not :" to which Basil replied, that "knowledge" had various senses, Epist. 236. That our knowledge of God, though inadequate, is real, see Church's Gifts of Civilisation, &c., p. 439; Shairp, Culture and Religion, p. 121.

128. This passage probably suggested the Gelasian Preface for "Sunday in Octave of Pentecost," Murat. i. 606, which is now, in a shorter form, our Preface for "the Feast of Trinity." "Qui cum unigenito Filio tuo et Sancto Spiritu unus es Deus, unus es Dominus, non in unius singularitate personæ, sed in unius Trinitate substantiæ. Quod enim de tua gloria, revelante te, credimus, hoc de Filio tuo, hoc de Spiritu Sancto, sine differentia discretionis sentimus. Ut in confessione veræ sempiternæque Deitatis, et in personis proprietas, et in essentia unitas, et in majestate adoretur æqualitas. Quem laudant Angeli." Compare Leo, de Pentec. 2. 3, "et vera Deitas in nullo esse aut major aut minor potest, quæ sic in tribus est confitenda personis, ut et solitudinem non recipiat Trinitas, et unitatem servet æqualitas." It was one of Coleridge's *dicta* (Table Talk, p. 42) that the Athanasian Creed implicitly denied the doctrine of the Nicene, as to "the Filial Subordination." The fact is that, the essence of Godhead admitting of no degrees, the Nicene Creed never meant, by its Θεὸν ἐκ Θεοῦ, to admit the slightest inferiority in the Son *as* God, but simply to affirm the fact of His eternal generation from the Father as the Fountain of Godhead. On the other hand, the Athanasian Creed was emphatic in excluding the idea of inferiority, but admitted the fact of Sonship, and therewith the "subordination" in its true sense, i.e., that the Father is named first, as being "of none," the Son being the second Person, as "from the Father." (Cp. Newman, Arians, pp. 168, 180; Liddon, Bamp. Lect., p. 202.) In his Tracts Theol. and Eccl. p. 128, Newman "would rather avoid the term subordination," as "in its effect misleading," and prefers "Principatus Patris," i.e. that the Father is, as such, "principium Filii." There was a theologian, indeed, to whom Coleridge's words would apply; one who "presumptuously undervalued the terminology of the ancient Creeds," and "disparaged the words Trinity and Person" (Hardwick's Hist. of Re-

form. p. 126,) who "called the Nicene Creed *frigida cantilena*, treated the doctrine expressed in the words, 'God *of* God,' as a mere dream of Platonizing Greeks, and pressed," in opposition to that formula, "for the use of the word αὐτόθεος, in relation to the Son," (Keble's Pref. to Hooker, p. lxxxi. Cp. Bull, Def. Fid. Nic b. 4, c. 1, s. 8.) Contrast Calvin with Hooker, who glories in defending "the Creed of Athanasius," v. 42, 11, and who also offended Calvinists by speaking of the Father as the origin of Deity, v. 54, 2. That the "subordination" was not so much dwelt upon, at least by Westerns, after the growth of Arianism as before it, is true, and easily to be accounted for; cf. Mozley on Theory of Development, p. 186. But such a typical theologian as Pearson asserts that "in that perfect and absolute equality there is, notwithstanding, this disparity, that . . . the Son hath the Godhead from the Father," (i. 243.) In Serm. xviii. of this volume, c. 4, Leo insists on the Son's coeternity in a passage which, while it reminds us of the Athanasian argument that if the Father ever *began* to be a Father, His Divine immutability was compromised, may connect itself with a thought on which modern theologians have reasonably insisted, that the doctrine of an absolute or essential Trinity, of a Son and Spirit coeternal with the Father, can alone secure in its full significance the assertion that "God is love." See Bishop Alexander's comment on 1 S. John iv. 8; and the excellent remarks in Medd's Bampton Lectures, p. 14, "To assert the personal singularity of God is to assert the *loneliness* of God. Such an assertion presents us with" an "essentially cold and sterile conception . . . Our God is love; and love . . . implies necessarily an object of love, and that object a Person . . . . Wherefore, by an eternal generation from the depths of the Divine fecundity, which is the source of all life, there is eternally begotten an Only Son, who is the forth-flashing brightness of the Father's glory, the adequate expression of the invisible God, and so a satisfying object of His love," &c. Further on the Son is described as "equal in being and essence to God's own infinity," p. 27.

129. The Semi-arian party in the fourth century attempted to steer a middle course between calling the Son Consubstan-

tial and calling Him a creature. Their position, indeed, was untenable, but several persisted in clinging to it; and it was adopted by Macedonius, who occupied the see of Constantinople. It was through their adoption of a more reverential language about the Son than had been used by the old Arians, that what is called the Macedonian heresy showed itself. Arianism had spoken both of the Son and the Holy Spirit as creatures. The Macedonians, rising up out of Semi-arianism, gradually reached the Church's belief as to the uncreated majesty of the Son, even if they retained their objection to the Homoousion as a formula. But having, in their previously Semi-arian position, refused to extend their own "Homoiousion" to the Holy Spirit, they afterwards persisted in regarding Him as "external to the one indivisible Godhead," Newman's Arians, p. 226; or as Tillemont says, (Mem. vi. 527,) "the denial of the divinity of the Holy Spirit was at last their capital or only error." S. Athanasius, while in exile under Constantius for the second time, "heard with pain," as he says, (Ep. i. ad Serap. 1,) that "some who had left the Arians from disgust at their blasphemy against the Son of God, yet called the Spirit a creature, and one of the ministering spirits, differing only in degree from the Angels:" and soon afterwards, in 362, the Council of Alexandria condemned the notion that the Spirit was a creature, as being "no true avoidance of the detestable Arian heresy." See "Later Treatises of S. Athanasius," p. 5. Athanasius insisted that the Nicene Fathers, although silent on the nature of the Holy Spirit, had by implication ranked Him with the Father and the Son as an object of belief, (ad Afros, 11.) After the death of S. Athanasius, the new heresy was rejected on behalf of the West by Pope Damasus, who declared the Spirit to be truly and properly from the Father (as the Son from the Divine substance) and very God, "omnia posse et omnia nosse, et ubique esse," coequal and adorable, (Mansi, iii. 483.) The Illyrian bishops also, in 374, wrote to the bishops of Asia Minor, affirming the consubstantiality of the Three Divine Persons, (Theodoret, iv. 9:) S. Basil wrote his *De Spiritu Sancto* in the same sense, (see Swete, Early History of the Doctrine of the Holy Spirit, pp. 58, 67:) and in order to vindicate this truth against the *Pneumatomachi*, as the Macedonians were called by the Catholics, the "Constantinopolitan" recension of the Nicene Creed added the words, "the Lord and the Life-giver, proceeding from the Father, with the Father and the Son worshipped and glorified," &c., which had already formed part of local Creeds in the East. S. Leo says, in Nativ. 4, c. 5, "Macedonius . . . . Divinitatem S. Spiritus non recepit, sed in Patre et Filio . . . . . eamdem confessus est esse naturam." See Pearson, i. 529, Art. 8, in proof of the Spirit's *Divine* Personality, and his note (b), ii. 424. Of all the ancient heresies, Macedonianism has been the most short-lived. Too often is the Holy Spirit regarded as an attribute; but hardly any would now regard Him as a creature. His Personality and His Divinity are both set forth in that magnificent Invocation which adorns the Alexandrian Liturgy called S. Mark's, and was probably drawn up about the time of the Council of Constantinople; "Send forth from Thy holy height, from Thy prepared abode, from Thine uncircumscribed bosom,—the Paraclete Himself, the Spirit of truth, the Holy, the Lord, the Life-giver, Who spoke in the Law, and Prophets, and Apostles; Who is everywhere present, and filleth all things, and by His own right, and not as a servant, worketh sanctification in whom He willeth, according to Thy pleasure; Who is simple in nature, manifold in working; the Fountain of Divine graces; One in essence with Thee, proceeding from Thee, sharing the throne of the kingdom with Thee and Thine Only-begotten Son, our Lord God and Saviour Jesus Christ. Yea, send down Thy Holy Spirit upon us, and upon these loaves, and upon these cups, that He may sanctify and consecrate them as God Almighty, and make the bread the Body, and the cup the Blood," &c.

130. S. Augustine treats this awful subject much more thoughtfully. He says that those who reject Christianity, or who are Arians, or Macedonians, &c., have sinned against the Holy Spirit, but have not necessarily committed the unpardonable sin, which he defines clearly as "duritia cordis usque ad finem hujus vitæ." Epist. 185, c. 11. In Serm. 71, said to be the "libellus" on the subject referred to in Enchirid. c. 83, Augustine says that the difficulty which he felt had kept him from

preaching about it, until on that very day he was strongly moved to do so: that not every sin or blasphemy against the Holy Spirit (e.g., on the part of Pagans, Jews, or heretics) is unpardonable, but only one kind of such sin, a "perseverans duritia cordis impœnitentis." So in his "Inchoata Expositio" of the Epistle to the Romans, c. 22, 23, "perseverantia in nequitia et malignitate cum desperatione indulgentiæ Dei." To "speak," in the sense of S. Matt. xii. 32, against the Holy Spirit, is, he says, to "persevere in sins, desperata atque impia mentis obstinatione." Comp. Döllinger, First Age of the Church, p. 202.

131. The twofold office of the Paraclete, as kindling and illuminating, has often been set forth in prayers and hymns. In the Gelasian prayers for Vespers during Whitsun-week, Mur. i. 602, we find one Collect which dwells upon the fervour of Divine love, and another which begs for illumination of mind. The adoption of *red* as the ecclesiastical colour of this festival was doubtless intended to symbolise spiritual "fire." Compare the " Veni Creator ;"

> "Fons vivus, ignis, caritas . . . .
> Accende lumen sensibus."

So Adam of S. Victor, (see Trench's Sacred Latin Poetry, p. 170,)

> "Fac ferventes in te mentes
> Flamma tua divite . . .
> Lumen clarum, lumen carum,
> Internarum tenebrarum
> Effugas caliginem."

So Archbishop Langton, if he, and not King Robert the Pious, be the author of the Golden Sequence (see Notes and Queries, 2nd series, vol. i.,)

> "Veni, lumen cordium . . . .
> Fove quod est frigidum."

The enkindling power has seldom been more exquisitely described than in the Christian Year, Fourth Sunday after Easter,

> "Where'er the Lord is, there are they;
>   In every heart that gives them room,
> They light His altar every day,
>   Zeal to inflame, and vice consume."

132. In his first Sermon on the Pentecostal Fast, he says that it was meant to guard against any negligence which might follow on the joy of Easter-tide. So Athanasius speaks of his people as "having observed the fast in the week after the holy Pentecost," Apol. de Fuga, 6; using "Pentecost" (as the Nicene Council, can. 20, had done,) for the whole Paschal season which closed at Whitsuntide. See Bingham, xx. 6. 3. Leo names three other fasts, the spring fast of Lent, the autumn fast in September, the winter fast in December, Serm. de Jej. x. mens. 8, c. 2. But he does not recognize the Lent Ember fast as a distinct season; it is with him not distinguished from "Quadragesima." His sermons for the other Ember seasons generally announce a fast for the Saturday. A Collect for the Pentecostal fast, in the Leonine Sacramentary, Mur. i. 319, prays that the fast may produce in the soul a greater aptitude for the Holy Spirit's gifts. The connection of Ordination with the Ember weeks is due to Pope Gelasius; see Maskell, Mon. Ritual. iii. p. cxxii.

133. Leo here follows S. Augustine in interpreting "all" in Acts ii. 1 of the hundred and twenty, not merely of the Apostolic College; "Venit enim die Pentecostes Spiritus Sanctus in centum viginti homines congregatos, in quibus et Apostoli omnes erant;" Aug. in Joan. Ev. Tr. 92, c. 1; and in a Pentecostal sermon, "Duodecim enim elegit, et in centum viginti Spiritum misit," Serm. 267, 1. See Bishop Wordsworth in loc.

134. The question, Whether Christ would have been Incarnate if man had not sinned, which Leo here summarily decides in the negative, is discussed in Sum. iii. 1. 3, where Aquinas recognises a diversity of opinions, but thinks the negative answer best. "For things which happen simply by God's will, above all that is due to the creature, cannot be known to us except so far as they are delivered in Holy Scripture, whereby the Divine will is known to us. Wherefore, since in Holy

Scripture the cause of the Incarnation is everywhere assigned as flowing from the first man's sin, it is more befittingly said that the work of the Incarnation was planned by God as a remedy for sin ; so that, had there been no sin, there would have been no Incarnation." S. Athanasius sanctions the Thomist view in Orat. i. 49, ii. 54; compare Newman, Athan. Treat. ii. 356, and Liddon, Univ. Serm. i. 241, referring to certain texts. The other view is taken by Abp. Trench, Five Sermons at Cambridge, p. 10, on the ground that all things, and man above all, were created "not merely by the Son, but in Him, and for Him, and to Him ;" and Westcott, on Epistles of S. John, p. 274, ff. Attractive as such speculations may be, they would seem to be precarious, and in some hands they might be perilous. S. Thomas has here, at least, the advantage of not even seeming to be wise above that which is written. Man *has* fallen, and God *has* become Incarnate ; that may well suffice "until the shadows flee away." The argument from Col. ii. 15, ff., proves too much, for the passage refers primarily not to men, but to Angels, and compare Heb. ii. 16.

135. Here the idea of propitiation is pointedly exhibited as in harmony with the fact of God's "original" essential love, (Döllinger, First Age of the Church, p. 173, E. T. ;) it is by the "misericordia Trinitatis" that a propitiation is preordained. Leo, perhaps, was thinking of 1 S. John iv. 10, where the supreme proof of the Father's love is that "He sent His Son as a propitiation for our sins." On ἱλασμός see Liddon, Bamp. Lect. p. 486 ; Lias, Doctrinal System of S. John, p. 137 ; and Dale on the Atonement, p. 163, ff., where, in reply to an American writer, it is pointedly observed that "the poetic genius of religious language" cannot "be pleaded as a reason for alleging that when Christ is described as a propitiation for our sins, it may mean that He inclines *us* to forsake them ;" and it is added that propitiation in the Old Testament had always presupposed, not (as in Paganism) any capricious anger to be soothed, but a just displeasure against sin, which indeed, as Döllinger says, is merely " His holiness in its relation to men." See note 54.

136. On Leo's assertion of the doctrine of grace, see above,

note 23. He here recognises very clearly the part which man has in co-operating with the grace of God. The truth has never been more exactly stated than in the admirable propositions of the Second Council of Orange in 529, which condemned Semi-pelagianism, without falling into errors of an opposite kind. They are explicit on the Fall, original sin, the necessity of real inward grace for a single good thought,—in other words, of "grace preventing us, that we may have a good will;" but they also affirm the reality of the acts whereby man, under grace, chooses good, so that grace "works with him when he has that good will," as our Tenth Article words it. They pronounce that all the baptised, having received grace through Baptism, *can* by Christ's assistance accomplish their salvation, and are therefore bound to do so. The great passage in the Epistles on this twofold truth, of grace and free-will, is Phil. ii. 12, 13 : see Bp. Bull's Harm. Apost. i. 218 (Lib. A. C. Th.), deprecating any attempt to define precisely the manner of their combined agency, but enforcing the truth of the fact. See Mill's Univ. Sermons, p. 361, on this same text; Trench on S. Augustine, p. 149; Wilberforce on Baptism, p. 173, citing the words of S. Bernard (de Grat. et Lib. Arbitrio, c. 1) : "Tolle liberum arbitrium, et non erit quod salvetur; tolle gratiam, non erit unde salvetur." S. Bernard, it may be added, goes on to say, "Opus hoc sine duobus effici non potest ; uno, *a quo* fit—altero, *cui* vel *in quo* fit." The first act of God, in His "preventing" grace, has been called His operating act ; it is *His* act only. The second, in His "subsequent" grace, has been called His co-operating act. Cf. Aquin. $1^a\,2^{ae}$, 111. 2. In Bernard's way of representing it, de Grat. et Lib. Arbitr. c. 14, the first grace is that which infuses the thought of goodness *sine nobis;* the second, that which unites us to itself by assent, when it changes our evil will to a desire of goodness,—this is done *nobiscum;* the third, that which aids us in doing good,—this works *per nos*. We may accept the sober statements of Möhler, Symbolism, i. 122, E. Tr., as to man's part in allowing himself to be excited, vivified, raised up by grace; that grace being, on the one hand, absolutely necessary for the first motions of good in man (the truth denied by Semi-pelagians); and on the other hand, not such an exertion of omnipotent power as would *compel* man to accept salvation, and so destroy "that moral order which the Divine Wisdom has founded on liberty." See Introduction to "Anti-Pelagian Treatises of S. Augustine," pp. xiii. lxv.

137. S. John xiv. 28. It is interesting to observe that we still read on Whit-Sunday the same Gospel which was read at Rome under S. Leo. The old Roman Lectionary or *Comes* (see Pamelius, Liturg. Lat. ii. 32) prescribes as the Gospel for Whit-Sunday the latter part of this chapter from verse 23, as we now find it in the Roman Missal. In the First Prayer Book of Edward VI., the Gospel began, as now with us, at verse 15, but ended at ver. 21.

138. It was usual with S. Augustine to express the Son's unity of essence with the Father by saying that when He came in the flesh upon earth, He still continued with the Father: not meaning to deny that He did, in a true sense, "empty Himself" of His glory, and "when He was rich, became for our sakes poor,"—but in order to exclude any such notions as that He had ever for a moment ceased to be very God, or that His Godhead had been "converted into flesh." See S. Aug. Serm. 184, "in homine ad nos venisse, et a Patre non recessisse :" Serm. 186, "*fieri* potuit, manens quod erat." See note 95. S. Leo adopts the same phraseology ; see also Serm. 18, c. 5, and in Nativ. 2, c. 2, "de cœlesti sede descendens, et a paterna gloria non recedens ;" in Nativ. 10, c. 5, "a paterno non divisus throno ;" and the Homily on the Transfiguration, c. 6, "Filius Meus.... manens in forma gloriæ meæ." See S. John iii. 13. Aquinas, in a Sacramental hymn, has the same thought ;

> "Verbum supernum prodiens,
> Nec Patris linquens dexteram."

---

139. In order to understand the situation, we must observe that Eutyches in the early part of 448, had apprised Leo of "a revival of Nestorianism," and had received a brief but sympa-

thetic reply (Ep. 20).[1] Five months later, he had been condemned for heresy by a local synod at Constantinople, under the presidency of Flavian as archbishop, on the 22nd of November, 448. Thereupon he wrote again to Leo. The letter is extant in a Latin version, and forms the 21st letter in the Leonine series. It is to this effect: "I have been falsely accused by Eusebius, Bishop of Dorylæum. Flavian summoned me to appear; in spite of my age, and of illness, I came, not knowing that an intrigue had been got up against me. I put in a document, signed, and containing my profession of faith. Flavian would not receive it. I declared, orally, my adhesion to the Nicene Creed, reaffirmed at Ephesus. I was called upon to confess 'two natures,' and to anathematise those who denied this. I feared to transgress the Ephesine prohibition by adding anything to the Nicene Creed: I knew that Julius and Felix (of Rome), Athanasius and Gregory, had rejected the phrase 'two natures,' and as I did not dare to discuss the nature of God the Word, who became incarnate without change and was made man in reality, not in 'phantasm,' I asked that the case might be laid before you for judgment.[2] This was refused, and a sentence of deposition, which had been drawn up before my trial, was published. The hostile feeling against me was such, that I was indebted to military protection for security. Other abbots were commanded to sign my deposition,—a step not taken against Nestorius himself. I was prevented from stating my belief openly for the satisfaction of the people. Under these circumstances, I invoke your help. Although I anathematise Apollinaris, Valentinus, Manes, and Nestorius, and those who say that our Lord's flesh came from heaven, and not from the Holy Spirit and the Virgin Mary, and all heresies up to Simon Magus, still I am in peril of death on the ground of heresy. I pray you, let not the recent proceedings prejudice my claim to a hearing: do not suffer me, after seventy years, to

---

[1] Leo doubtless did not know that Domnus, patriarch of Antioch, had already denounced Eutyches as heretical: Facundus, viii. 5.

[2] This was disingenuous; he had said in a low voice to the patrician Florentius, that he appealed to the Synods of Rome, Egypt, and Jerusalem: Mansi, vi. 817.

be cast out of the number of the orthodox, and shipwrecked at the very end of life." To this letter Eutyches appended the document which, as he asserted, the synod had declined to receive. It began in the words of S. Paul, 1 Tim. vi. 13; it referred to the Nicene faith as at Ephesus pronounced unalterable, professed entire adherence to the doctrinal decisions of Ephesus, and entire accordance of belief with approved Fathers, including Proclus of Constantinople, who had taken a strong part against Nestorius at the opening of the Nestorian controversy, and who afterwards, in his excellent 'Tome' to the Armenians, which Cyril described as "full of good thoughts and right doctrines," had substituted "one $\dot{\upsilon}\pi\dot{o}\sigma\tau\alpha\sigma\iota\varsigma$ incarnate" for "one $\phi\dot{\upsilon}\sigma\iota\varsigma$ incarnate," and emphasised the existence of a human $\phi\dot{\upsilon}\sigma\iota\varsigma$ or "nature" in our Lord. After referring to such authorities, Eutyches proceeded to anathematise all heretics, and to express belief in the Incarnation as having taken place "without change and without conversion" (of Godhead into flesh) "even as He knows and willed. And He Who is always, before the ages, perfect God, became Himself perfect man at the end of days, for us and for our salvation. Let your Holinesses accept this my explicit profession. I, Eutyches, presbyter and archimandrite" (abbot) "sign this 'libellus' with my own hand." He subjoined a passage attributed by the Eutychian party to Julius of Rome, absolutely denying "two natures," and asserting one, on the authority of S. John i. 14, 1 Cor. viii. 6, with a reference to the long-current analogy, "as the reasonable soul and flesh is one man," or, as it is here expressed, one "nature,"—and with the argument that if there were two natures, then He Who came from heaven could not be called Son of Man, nor He Who was born of a woman Son of God, that one nature would be adorable, the other not, and men would be baptised into one, not into the other; in short, that to say two natures was to say two persons, whereas the Lord's personality was indivisibly one. But it was afterwards shown that this passage was by Apollinaris himself. (See Leontius of Byzantium, de Sectis, viii. 4, ap. Galland. Biblioth. Patr. xii. 651.) Soon after this missive came from Eutyches, Leo received a letter from Theodosius II., which apparently gave him the impression that Eutyches had been badly treated. So he afterwards wrote to Julian of Cos,

"Diu apud nos incertum fuit quid in ipso (sc. Eutyche) catholicis displiceret; et cum .... Flaviani nullas litteras sumeremus, ipse autem scriptis suis Nestorianam hæresim repullulare quereretur," &c. Ep. 34. Nothing on the other side had as yet reached him when on the 18th of February, 449, he wrote to Flavian, expressing surprise at not having heard from him, requesting information as to the merits of the case, and suggesting that all care should be taken to maintain charity while defending the truth : Ep. 23. To Theodosius he wrote in a similar strain, implying that Flavian ought to have written to him, and that now at any rate, it was to be hoped that he would do so. Already, we observe, he is assuming the position of an arbiter, whereas Flavian had not yet solicited his intervention. This letter apparently crossed one from Flavian, which was somewhat unaccountably delayed in its transit to Rome. It forms the 22nd Leonine, and is extant in the original Greek and in two Latin versions, (the older and less correct beginning " Nulla res," the later and more accurate beginning " Nihil est.") It may be thus summarised : "I have had to grieve over the spiritual ruin of one of my own clergy. I could not rescue him from 'the wolf:' he was carried away, indeed he leapt forth, disregarding all remonstrances." Then, by a sudden change of imagery, he describes Eutyches as himself a wolf in sheep's clothing. " This presbyter and abbot was long deemed orthodox, a hearty anti-Nestorian : but now he has attempted to subvert the Nicene Creed, and the letter of Cyril of holy memory to Nestorius" (i.e. the second letter, not the third to which the twelve anathemas were appended) "and his letter to the Easterns" (i.e. the letter to John of Antioch) " to which all gave assent, and to renew the old heterodoxy of Valentinus and Apollinaris. He said expressly before a synod that our Lord was not to be acknowledged as of two natures" ($\dot{\epsilon}\kappa$ δύο φύσεων, rendered in the earlier version *de*, in the later *ex* duabus naturis) "after the Incarnation, in one hypostasis and in one person," (this, of course, is put in to guard against all appearance of Nestorianising,) "nor was His flesh consubstantial with us, as being assumed from us, and hypostatically" ("secundum subsistentiam :" the first version incorrectly reads, "secundum substantiam") " united to God the Word ; but he said that although His Virgin Mother was consubstantial with us, yet He had not taken flesh consubstantial with us from her, and that His body, that which was from the Virgin, was not the body of a man, yet was a human body;—in opposition to all the statements of the Fathers." Flavian concludes by saying that he sends a copy of the proceedings (πρᾶξιν—Latin, "gesta," or "quidquid egimus," phrases equivalent to "acts") including the sentence of deposition from priesthood and from abbacy, and of excommunication: and then, without a single word which might warrant the assumption that he recognised in his Roman brother a right to re-hear the case, he simply requests Leo to inform his suffragans as to its true merits. This letter, we should observe, is not quite consistent with the account given in the "Acts," where Eutyches appears as consenting, under pressure of authority, to call Christ "consubstantial with us as man;"—his reluctance to own this being a proof that he had not really acquiesced in the formulary of reunion between Cyril and John of Antioch, wherein our Lord's twofold 'consubstantiality' was expressly asserted. (Cyr. Ep. to John.) Flavian's letter, on its arrival, was acknowledged in a brief note, which Leo dates on the 21st of May, and in which, while expressing his sympathy with Flavian, he promises to write "more fully," and quietly assumes, after his fashion, that Flavian will need to be instructed, "quid de tota causa constitui debeat." (Ep. 27.) This promise he now fulfils in the Tome. We must think of him as writing with the older Latin version of Flavian's letter before him; and it is especially necessary, in reading the Tome, which ranks as "Ep. 28," to take no account of Flavian's second letter, or "Ep. 26," which did not reach him until later, and which he acknowledges in Ep. 36, dated a week after the date of the Tome. (See the Ballerini, Admonit. in Ep. 22.) The Tome was written in order to influence the deliberations of the Council which had been summoned by the Emperor Theodosius, against the wish of Flavian and of Leo himself, to meet in Ephesus, and which Leo afterwards—in one of those scathing phrases which become historic appellations—described as characterised by "latrocinium" or brigandage (Ep. 95. 2) under the tyrannous presidency of Dioscorus, who took care that the Tome should not be read in its hearing.

The Baptismal Creed.

140. That is, of Flavian's synod at Constantinople. It was what was called the σύνοδος ἐνδημοῦσα, composed of the bishops who might be, for the time, staying at Constantinople on account of their own church business. See "Notes on Canons of First Four Councils," p. 159 (on Chalc. c. 9.) On this occasion it had assembled for the purpose of adjusting a dispute between the Metropolitan of Sardis and two suffragans : and after this had been done, Eusebius of Dorylæum took advantage of the synod to accuse Eutyches. See Mansi, vi. 652 ; Hefele, Hist. of Councils, b. x. c. 2, s. 172.

141. See above, note 35. Compare also Tillemont, xv. 487, "Saint Léon a cru qu'Eutyche s'etait jetté dans ce malheur plus par ignorance que par malice : il l'appelle quelquefois un vieillard également imprudent et ignorant." Leo says in Ep. 30, that formerly Eutyches had seemed laudable "humilitatis proposito," but that his error had sprung "de imperitia magis quam de versutia ;" in Ep. 34. 2, he calls him "indoctus ;" in Ep. 29 and 33, he says that he was "sadly in the dark," and "that he did not adorn the grey hairs of old age with ripeness of mind."

142. Here, and in Ep. 124. 8, "symboli salutaris, et confessionis quam pronuntiantes coram multis testibus sacramentum baptismi suscepistis," and more briefly in de Nativ. 4. 6, "fide quam confessi estis . . . . . et in qua renati," he refers to the solemn profession of faith exacted as a preliminary to baptism. Reference may be here made to the "Traditio Symboli," or delivery of the Creed to catechumens to be learnt : it was afterwards repeated by the candidates, according to Eastern usage, on Maundy Thursday (Conc. Laodic. c. 46 ;) at Rome, on the morning of Holy Saturday, the actual day of baptism, as the Gelasian rubric for that day says, "Mane infantes reddunt symbolum," Murat. i. 563. Finally, just before entering the "font," the candidate, or in the case of an infant, the sponsor as his representative, was interrogated,—according to the form which Leo, doubtless, was wont to use,—"Credis in Deum Patrem omnipotentem ? *Resp.* Credo. Credis et in Jesum Christum, Filium ejus unicum, Dominum nostrum, natum et passum ? Credo. Credis et in Spiri-

tum Sanctum, Sanctam Ecclesiam, Remissionem peccatorum, Carnis resurrectionem? Credo;" (ib. i. 570.) The "Old Gallican form" was more doctrinal: "Credis Patrem et Filium et Spiritum Sanctum unius esse virtutis? Credo:" two other similar interrogatories following. The "Gallican Sacramentary" addressed the triple interrogatory to the sponsors, and followed exactly the wording of the Apostles' Creed. The Sarum form agrees with the old Roman, only adding "Catholicam, Sanctorum communionem," and "vitam æternam post mortem." (Maskell, Mon. Rit. i. 23.) Distinct responsive acceptance of at least the main articles of the faith was "thought so necessary," that it was never dispensed with "even in 'clinic' baptism, when men were baptised upon a sick bed:" Bingham, xi. 7. 8. For the solemn and public character of this final profession, see ib. xi. 7. 9, on the case of Victorinus.

143. Leo here seems to assume that the Roman or "Apostles'" Creed will be familiar to Eastern readers; but in Ep. 165, writing to the Eastern emperor, he brings forward the original form of the Nicene Creed. Observe that here the best authorities read "*et*," not "*ex* Maria."

144. Here, and in Ep. 165. 3, Leo uses the Nicene phrase, "God from God," which had been omitted in the "Constantinopolitan" recension of the Creed, as involved in "very God from very God," but which the Western Church gradually restored, e.g. the great Council of Toledo in 589 has "Deum ex Deo."

145. He lays stress on the importance of the Genealogies in Ep. 31. 2, "Nihil autem prodest Dominum nostrum 'verum perfectumque hominem' dicere, si non illius generis ac seminis homo creditur, cujus in evangelio prædicatur; dicit enim Matthæus, Liber generationis Jesu Christi, filii David, filii Abraham." Then, after a reference to the pedigree traced up by S. Luke to Adam, "ut Adam primum et Adam novissimum ejusdem ostendat esse substantiæ," so as to prevent the Incarnation from being resolved into a mere Theophany; (of the Theophanies Leo takes the older view, rather than that of S. Augustine.) So also Ep. 139. 3, where S. Matt. i. 1 is combined with Rom. ix. 5. So in

The Personal Union.

Ep. 72, "ut non confundaris de evangelio generationis Domini," &c. Theodoret, in his second Dialogue, insists against "Eranistes" that our Lord ought to be recognised as "the Son of David." (Op. iv. 97.)

146. "Magni consilii Angelus," the old Latin reading representing the LXX. of Isa. ix. 6, is here united with the Vulgate "Consiliarius."

147. That is, he should not have fallen into the absurdity of putting an unreal sense on "became flesh," or "became man." Leo is here supposing, as in Ep. 124. 2, and Ep. 165. 2, that Eutyches "tertium Apollinaris dogma delegit," i.e., the opinion that Christ's manhood was formed out of a divine substance. The "first" and "second" Apollinarian dogmas, in his reckoning, were that He had not a human ψυχή, and, that He had not a human νοῦς. See Ep. 59. 5.

148. Here the Tome begins to be more explicitly theological. The first words of the passage are quoted by Hooker, v. 53. 2, as in entire accordance with the language of Hilary, adduced by Leo at the end of his Ep. 165. " Ipse ex unitis in idipsum naturis naturæ utriusque res eadem est, ita tamen ut neutro careret in utroque ; ne forte 'Deus' esse, homo nascendo, desineret, et 'homo' rursus, Deus manendo, non esset," de Trin. ix. 3 ; and of Cyril, whose words, in one of his letters to Successus, Hooker paraphrases fairly enough, and presents as clearly incompatible with Eutychianism: the "Salva igitur" is also cited in Liddon's Bamp. Lect. p. 267. Compare Serm. 8, c. 1, "quod ... in unam personam concurrat proprietas utriusque substantiæ ;" and de Pass. 3. 1, "ut in Redemptorem nostrum duas noverimus convenisse naturas." When the Tome was being read in the Council of Chalcedon, some bishops of Illyricum and Palestine questioned the orthodoxy of the latter part of the sentence in the text. (Mansi, Conc. vi. 972.) Aetius, deacon of the church of Constantinople, met this doubt by reading a passage from Cyril's second letter to Nestorius : " Since His own body, by God's grace, as Paul says, tasted death for all, therefore is *He* said to have suffered death for us : not as if, so far as pertained to His

nature (φύσιν) He had experienced death, (for it were insane to say this,) but because, as I said just now, it was *His* flesh that tasted death." Such a defence of Leo's orthodoxy on the crucial point of Nestorianism—as if in reply to the misgiving, "Is not Leo abandoning the ground secured by Cyril? does he not press the distinction between the natures into a severance of the one personality?"—may be compared with Ephraim of Antioch's contention, as described by Photius, Biblioth. n. 228: "Leo loudly proclaims τὸν αὐτὸν Υἱὸν τοῦ Θεοῦ καὶ ἀληθῶς Υἱὸν ἀνθρώπου γένεσθαι . . . . anathematises Nestorius for saying that Mary was not Mother of God but of a man," and assigns alike both "forms" and the several natural "energies" to "one and the same Son." Compare Tertullian adv. Prax. 27.

149. "In integra ergo veri hominis perfectaque natura." This illustrates the stand made at Chalcedon by Leo's legates for the phrase "in two natures," rather than "of two natures." Already at the Council of Constantinople, after Flavian the president had used "of two natures," Basil of Seleucia had acknowledged the "one Lord as existing *in* two natures," although he afterwards, at the "Robbers' Synod," retracted this speech through fear; Mansi,'vi. 680, 685, 828; Evagrius, ii. 18. And long afterwards, Ephraim of Antioch contended that "one nature incarnate" and "in two natures" were phrases not opposed to each other, but respectively guarding two aspects of one truth. See above, note 35. So de Pass. 3, c. 1, "Tota est in majestate humilitas, tota in humilitate majestas;" Ep. 35. 2, "unus in utroque est;" Ep. 59. 41, "in ea scilicet natura quæ nostri et sanguinis esset et generis." Compare "totus in suis, totus in nostris," with Serm. xiv. c. 5. And see the conclusion of Proclus's Tome, where it is urged that Rom. ix. 5 brings out the personal identity of the Christ Who had become truly man with Him Who was "over all, God, blessed for ever." Mansi, v. 425. Theodoret represents his Eranistes as admitting ἐκ δύο φύσεων, but denying δύο φύσεις. Dial. ii. (Op. iv. 101.)

150. This remark as to the nature of the "self-emptying," which recurs in Serm. 2, c. 2, Serm. 14, c. 5, may be compared with a passage in Ep. 165. 8 (so also substantially in Ep. 124. 7,)

"et idem ipse est, sicut apostolus prædicat, et dives et pauper." (He is thinking of 2 Cor. viii. 9, a text also insisted on by Cyril.) Then, after explaining the "riches" and the "poverty" by S. John i. 1—3, 14, he asks, "Quæ autem est ejus exinanitio, quæve paupertas, nisi formæ servilis acceptio, per quam, Verbi majestate velata, dispensatio humanæ redemptionis impleta est?" So Cyril, in "Quod unus sit Christus" (Op. vii. 373;) " Wherein consisted the κένωσις; in the fact of His taking flesh, and being in the form of a servant, and being made like to us, whereas in His proper φύσις He was not as we are:" and adv. Theod. 4, "it is κένωσις for God the Word . . . . . . to act or speak at all humanly." When Leo says that "what was Divine was not lessened," as again in the very same words in Serm. 2, c. 2, or in Serm. 14, c. 5, "male sentiunt . . . minuendo quod est Deitatis:" or again, as further on in the Tome, that the Word "did not depart from the Father's glory," he does not, of course, mean that our Lord did not forego the *full* exercise of Divine prerogatives, for that He did so is involved in that very assumption of "our nature" on which Leo insists, and in His consequent acceptance of its limitations and infirmities; but that He "did not lose what belonged to Him," ("ut . . . . potenter propria non amitteret," de Quadr. 8, c. 1,) or in other words, that He did not, because He could not, cease to be Himself, the Divine Son; so in Nativ. 7, c. 2, "nunquam destitit esse Deus verus," exactly as Cyril says (Epist. p. 148,) οὐ τὸ εἶναι Θεὸς ἀφεῖς. See Oosterzee, Image of Christ, pp. 143, 181, E. T.

151. With this compare "Idem est qui factus est inter omnia, et per quem facta sunt omnia," de Pass. 17, c. 1; and "Idem est in forma Dei qui formam suscepit servi," &c. de Nativ. 10, c. 4.

152. "Tenet enim sine defectu proprietatem suam utraque natura." The Monophysite writers, Timotheus and Severus, afterwards attacked this (in its Greek version) as Nestorian. Eulogius, Catholic patriarch of Alexandria, (A.D. 579,) as quoted by Photius, Biblioth. n. 225, replied by quoting c. 2, "Idem . . . unigenitus . . . . natus est de Spiritu Sancto . . . . Quæ nativitas temporalis illi nativitati divinæ . . . . nihil minuit," and adding, "Did this ever come into the mind of Nestorius?"

The distinction of the Natures.

153. " De prævaricatoris consortio . . . . . solatium." This passage, with the first few lines of the next chapter, is given, within brackets, in the Ballerini's text of Leo's Serm. in Nativ. 2. Compare Paradise Lost, ix. 126;

> " Nor hope to be myself less miserable
> By what I seek, but others to make such
> As I, though thereby worse to me redound,
> For only in destroying I find ease," &c.

154. "Incomprehensibilis voluit comprehendi." Compare de Pass. 17, c. 1. "Idem est qui impiorum manibus comprehenditur, et qui nullo fine concluditur." And in Epiph. 7, c. 1, "genitricis gremio continetur, qui nullo fine concluditur." This "antithesis" has been grandly expressed in Milman's " Martyr of Antioch,"—

> " And Thou wast laid within the narrow tomb . . .
> Whom heaven could not contain,
> Nor the immeasurable plain
> Of vast infinity enclose or circle round."

155. " Nullum est in hac unitate mendacium ;" i.e. the manhood is as real as the Godhead. Compare Ep. 165. 9, that the whole mystery of faith is blurred and obscured, " si lux veritatis sub mendacio putatur latuisse phantasmatis." But the Monophysites objected to the next words, " dum invicem sunt et humilitas hominis et altitudo Deitatis :" and Eulogius in reply quoted from c. 3, " ut quod nostris remediis congruebat, unus atque idem Mediator . . . homo Jesus Christus, et mori posset ex uno, et mori non posset ex altero." Another objection to the words next following, " sicut Deus non mutatur miseratione, ita homo non consumitur dignitate," is met by Ephraim by reference to the language of " Ignatius, Julius, Athanasius, the Gregories, and Basil," &c. Leo's meaning is well illustrated by his own words, de Pass. 3, c. 1, " Nihil ibi ab invicem vacat, tota est in majestate humilitas, tota in humilitate majestas . . . Aliud est passibile, aliud inviolabile : et tamen ejusdem et contumelia, cujus et gloria ; ipse est in infirmitate, qui et in virtute."

156. "Agit enim utraque forma." This passage, down to "injuriis," (which occurs also in de Pass. 3, c. 2,) was questioned by the Illyrian and Palestinian bishops. Evidently it seemed to them Nestorianising in tendency. Aetius, therefore, produced a sentence from the great anti-Nestorian champion's second letter to Succensus, "Some expressions there are which are in the highest degree appropriate to Deity; others, again, are appropriate to manhood; and others hold a sort of middle rank, exhibiting the Son of God as being at once God and Man." (Cyr. Epist., p. 148.) It is to be observed that Cyril is here explaining the formulary of reunion between himself and the "Easterns," which concluded with the words, "We know that theologians have treated some of the expressions concerning our Lord as common, as referring to one Person, and have distinguished others as referring to two natures, and have taught us to refer to Christ's Godhead those which are appropriate to Deity, and to the Manhood those which imply humiliation." Cyril explains that the Easterns had no thought of distributing these expressions between two personalities,—the idea censured in his fourth anathema; so that the point for which he had been contending was secure. He proceeds to specify S. John xiv. 9, 10, and x. 30 as samples of the expressions called θεοπρεπεῖς, S. John viii. 40 as a sample of the ἀνθρωποπρεπεῖς, and Heb. xiii. 8, 1 Cor. viii. 6, and Rom. ix. 5 of those which "stand midway." The distinction between these classes of texts had been recognised in his Apol. adv. Orient. 4, after he had definitely excluded such a partition of the natures, in the Incarnate, as would imply two separate persons. It is evident that the phrase "two distinct natures" might have a heterodox meaning in the mouth of a Nestorianiser, but that, if it were used with express recognition of the unity of the "ego," it would convey no more than Cyril repeatedly acknowledged. Dorner, indeed, makes out an antagonism between Cyril and Leo on this point, as if Cyril had "characterised all Christ's acts and sufferings as divine-human, while Leo apportioned miracles to the divine nature, sufferings to the human nature, even after the Unio." But the difference is superficial. Cyril's rejection of all "fusion" guards the point which Leo had in mind; and as Theodoret in his third Dialogue, while insisting that the properties of both natures must be severally recognised, fully owns that "to be wearied and not wearied belonged to the same Person," (compare also Theodoret, Ep. 104 and 130,) so Leo fully acknowledges to Cyril. Repeatedly does Cyril, in his pleas against τὸ μερίζειν or διαιρεῖν τὰς φύσεις, explain that what he means to exclude is a "division of the one Christ into two," whereby some expressions would be predicated of the Logos, and others assigned ἀνθρώπῳ παρὰ τὸν ἐκ Θεοῦ Λόγον ἰδικῶς νοουμένῳ. So Proclus, in his admirable Tome, Mansi, v. 429: "That He might assure us that being God... and remaining what He was, He became flesh, and an infant, and man, while the mystery is not outraged by any changes, He, the selfsame, both works miracles and suffers; by the miracles indicating that He was what He was (before); by the sufferings giving evidence that He had become what He (originally) had framed." The words of Leo in the text lay stress on the close intercommunion of the two natures; and compare Ep. 124. 7, "in tantam unitatem ... deitate et humanitate connexa, ut nec sine homine divina, nec sine Deo agerentur humana." A certain inaccuracy, indeed, may be noted in this use of "Verbum" here for Godhead, analogous to the use of "homo" for Manhood. But the general meaning is quite clear, and should remove all doubt that might be suggested by the verb "agit," as applied to each nature. The Monophysite criticism on this passage was met by Eulogius with a reference to the following passage, "Unus .... idemque est .... vere Dei Filius et vere hominis Filius," &c. Ephraim observes that Leo did not say ὁ μὲν, ὁ δέ, but τὸ μὲν, τὸ δέ, Photius, Bibl. 229. See John Damascene, iii. 19, on the joint action, called "theandric," of the Divine and the human "energy;" and Aquinas, Sum. iii. 19. 1, quoting "Agit utraque," and asserting according to the Sixth Council, "two activities" in the one Christ. With "coruscat miraculis," compare de Quadrag. 8, c. 2, "quædam in Domino nostro ... subjecta injuriis, quædam illustrata miraculis."

157. This passage on the Voice at the Baptism was objected to by Monophysites. Eulogius quotes, in reply, the opening words of this chapter. "Ingreditur ergo," &c.

158. "Esurire, sitire, lassescere," &c. See above, Serm. 9, c. 4; 10, c. 4; 11, c. 4; and de Quadr. 8. 2, "Veri est hominis, fatigationem corpoream somni quiete relevare; sed veri Dei est, vim sævientium procellarum præcepti increpatione compescere.

quinque panibus et duobus piscibus quinque millia virorum, exceptis mulieribus et parvulis, satiare, quis negare audeat opus esse Deitatis?" So more briefly in the last of his series of Sermons, the "Tractatus contra hæresim Eutychis," c. 2 : "Humanum quippe est esurire, et sitire, et dormire . . . metuere, flere, tristari . . . mori . . . sed divinum est super mare ambulare, aquas in vina convertere, mortuos suscitare . . . ut qui hoc credunt dubitare non possint quid humanitati ascribere, quid debeant assignare Deitati, quoniam in utroque unus est Christus." So Proclus had said in his Tome : "If some are scandalised by the swaddling clothes, and by His being laid in the manger, and by His growing up, according to the flesh, in a period of time, or by His sleeping in the boat, and sitting down weary after a journey, and feeling hunger at times, and by all that is incident to one really born Man, let them know that if they mock at the sensations (πάθη), they deny the nature ; and if they deny the nature, they do not believe in the 'economy' (the Incarnation); and if they do not believe in the economy, they forfeit their salvation." They were both, in effect, following Athanasius, Orat. iii. 32 ; and the words in the Tome are translated in Newman's Notes on that chapter, Ath. Treat. ii. 445.

159. So in Quadr. 8. 2 ; "Nostra tibi innotescat affectio, cum mortuo amico fletus impenditur; divina potentia sentiatur, cum idem post quatriduanam jam fœtidus sepulturam solo vocis imperio vivificatus erigitur." Compare S. Athanasius, Orat. iii. 32 ; "In the case of Lazarus, He uttered a human voice, as man, but divinely, as God, did He raise Lazarus from the dead," &c. And in his Tom. ad Antioch. 7, "Nor was He Who raised up Lazarus one, and He Who inquired about him another ; but it was the same Who said humanly, 'Where is Lazarus laid ?' and Who divinely raised him up ;" and to the same effect, de Sent. Dionys. ii. 9. And S. Gregory Nazianzen, arguing against the Apollinarians from their own admissions ; "They clearly make a distinction between the things which belong to Christ,—they assign to what is human the facts that He was born, was tempted, hungered, thirsted, was weary, and slept ; and they set down to the Godhead the facts that He was glorified by Angels, that He overcame the tempter, and fed the people in the wilderness—and fed them in the way He did.—and walked on the surface of the

sea; and they consider the question, 'Where have ye laid Lazarus?' to be within our sphere (ἡμέτερον,) and the loud cry, 'Lazarus, come forth,' and the raising up one who had been dead four days, to be above it," &c. Epist. 102.

160. "Quamvis in Domino ... divinitas." Again, in spite of the words, "there is *one* Person," the Illyrian and Palestinian bishops objected : and this time it was Theodoret—in former years a vehement opponent of "the Egyptian"—who stood up and read "a parallel passage from the blessed Cyril, to this effect: 'Who was made man, and yet did not lay aside what was proper to Him, for He remained what He was ; for it is clearly understood that one thing is dwelling in another thing, that is, the Divine nature in the human elements.'" (Schol. 27, where the text reads, "in humanity ;" see the last words so quoted at the end of Leo's Ep. 165.) The clause " Quamvis" is amplified in Ep. 165. 5. The Monophysites afterwards renewed the objection thus met : and Eulogius adduced, in reply, the passage in the next chapter, ending with "ut unum Dei Filium et Verbum confiteamur et carnem."

161. This passage is adopted, with very slight variations, from S. Augustine, c. Sermon. Arian. c. 8 ; see above, note 5. Leo brings in the word "consempiternus," c. 2, and de Quadr. 8, c. 3. S. Augustine had been saying, "Ipse namque unus Christus et Dei Filius semper natura," (compare the Athanasian use of οὐσία specifically for our Lord's divine nature, Newman, Athan. Treat. ii. 345, and Cyril's use of κατὰ φύσιν ἰδίαν for "as He is originally in Himself," i.e. as the Divine Word ;) "et hominis Filius qui ex tempore assumptus est gratia," (meaning, not "by the Father's adopting grace," but, "by His own condescension,") "nec sic assumptus est ut prius creatus post assumeretur, sed ut ipsa assumptione crearetur" (i.e. His manhood had never existed except as assumed by His Divine Person. See Hooker, v. 52. 3.) The Monophysites attacked the words adopted by Leo. Eulogius points to the words in c. 3, "In integra veri hominis ... natura verus natus est Deus."

162. "Me utique qui sum Filius hominis." Compare Liddon,

Bamp. Lect. p. 6; "This question involves an assertion, namely, that the Speaker *is* the Son of Man. . . . The point of His question is this, what is He besides being the Son of Man? . . . what is He in the seat and root of His being?" &c. On the answer of S. Peter see also de Nat. ips. 4, c. 2. Our Lord is in both passages described as *the* Rock. Here "principali" means evidently (as often in the Latin version of S. Irenæus) "original, archetypal;" there Leo paraphrases, "Cum ego sim inviolabilis petra, ego lapis angularis . . . ego fundamentum . . . tamen tu quoque petra es, quia mea virtute solidaris, ut quæ mihi potestate sunt propria sint tibi mecum participatione communia," &c. See above, note 64. In this passage of the Tome, Leo emphasises the distinct advance from the recognition of the "Christ" to the recognition of "the Son of God." That "Son of God" is not here used in a "theocratic" or in an "ethical" sense, see Liddon, Bamp. Lect. pp. 10, 193, 235, 249.

163. "Proprietas divinæ humanæque naturæ individuæ." Here is the sense of ἀδιαιρέτως and ἀσυγχύτως. "Et ita sciremus," i.e., when contending against Eutyches, we must not give any encouragement to Nestorianism. See above, note 34.

164. "Quo fidei sacramento . . . . vacuus." "Sacramentum fidei" is here a "sacred truth received by faith." In Ep. 35, c. 1, he says that "unless a true human nature is recognised in Christ, redemptionis nostræ sacramenta vacuantur," &c.; and Ep. 59, c. 4, "Quicunque in Christo non confitetur corpus humanum, noverit se . . . nec ejus sacramenti habere consortium quod apostolus prædicat," referring to Eph. v. 32, "sacramentum hoc magnum est;" and Ep. 31. 4, "sacramentum salutis."

165. "Qui solvit Jesum." So he reads 1 S. John iv. 3, and the same reading recurs in Ep. 164. 3. Tertullian combines it with the received reading in adv. Marc. v. 16, "negantes Christum in carne venisse, et solventes Jesum :" and in the Latin translation of S. Irenæus the verse is quoted, "omnis spiritus qui solvit Jesum non est ex Deo," iii. 16. 8 : and S. Augustine in his commentary, after first quoting the received text, goes on to quote "qui solvit Christum" or "Jesum." Socrates,

"the only Greek authority for λύει," (Westcott, Epistles of S. John, p. 156,) says that Nestorius "did not know that in the old copies it is written, τὸ πνεῦμα ὃ λύει τὸν Ἰησοῦν . . . *for* those who were minded to separate the Godhead from the Man of the Economy" (i.e. Jesus) "removed this thought from the old copies : wherefore also the old interpreters noted this very fact, that there were some who had tampered with the epistle, λύειν ἀπὸ τοῦ Θεοῦ τὸν ἄνθρωπον θέλοντες," vii. 32. Westcott remarks that Socrates does not say that he had ever seen the reading in any Greek copy ; that λύει τὸν Ἰησοῦν would not naturally, of itself, convey the idea of breaking up the single personality of our Lord ; yet that S. John may have sometimes spoken against οἱ λύοντες τὸν Ἰησοῦν Χριστόν, and that this phrase, abridged, may have become first a gloss, and then a Latin reading.

166. " Et a prædicatione evangelii suum non avertit auditum." The thought is still more clearly brought out in de Quadr. 8. 1, " Quidam erubescentes evangelium crucis Christi, ut audentius evacuerent susceptum pro mundi redemptione supplicium," &c.

167. He again refers to the piercing of our Lord's side in Epiph. 4, c. 4, where, denouncing the Manicheans, he says, " Negent de ejus latere, lancea vulnerato, sanguinem redemptionis et aquam fluxisse baptismatis." The Monophysite objection to this passage is met by Eulogius with a quotation of words preceding, " naturam nostram in Unigenito Dei."

168. It need hardly be observed that he ignores the verse about " the Heavenly Witnesses ;" and in the context before us he interprets the water as symbolic of Baptism, (compare the passage last quoted, and Ep. 59. 4, " sacramentum . . . regenerationis") and the blood as significant of redemption, and of redemption as specially assured or made over by the Eucharistic reception of the Lord's blood, which he indicates by the word " poculo," (compare Sermon 8, c. 3.) This exposition is not entirely coherent ; for while the blood is made to represent the spiritual fact of redemption as realised in the Holy Eucharist, the water is made to point immediately to Christian Baptism or " the laver." The Sacramental reference ought surely to be

mediate in both cases, if in either. And any interpretation which would comprehend the whole thought of this mysterious passage must begin by placing in the foreground three events, (1) our Lord's baptism, (2) His precious bloodshedding on the cross before His death, (3) and the flow of blood and water from His side after death. Of these events (3) is regarded as recalling (1) and (2) at once, and as it were recapitulating them. But both (1) and (2) are seen in the light of the facts of cleansing and propitiation : and S. John could not forget that water had been perpetuated as the sacramental medium of the former ; that the blood, in which was centred the latter, was imparted through the cup of "the new covenant ;" and that the testimony of those ordinances to a living and working Christ was the testimony of that Spirit by whom they were made effectual. See Bishop Alexander's comment on the Apostle's words. Leo's conclusion, associating this text with the union of true Godhead and true Manhood in Christ, may seem rather far-fetched : but to his mind "the Spirit" suggests the thought of Christ's Divine life as a Person of the Trinity, while the "water and blood" represent functions of His humanity.

169. He means that the Synod of Constantinople had not met this statement with a direct refutation. Eutyches had, indeed, been condemned on the strength of it : but it had not received an argumentative reply. Leo seems to suggest that Eutyches, by confessing our Lord to have been "of two natures before the Incarnation," actually attributed to the manhood an objective existence in the heavenly world before the actual nativity. Thus in Ep. 35. 3 ; "Arbitror enim talia loquentem hoc habere persuasum, quod anima quam Salvator assumpsit prius in cœlis sit commorata quam de Maria Virgine nasceretur, eamque sibi Verbum in utero copularet,"—where he repeats that the human nature of Christ was created when it was assumed, and proceeds to denounce the Origenistic theory of the pre-existence of souls. Probably, also, he remembered that Apollinarians, whose heresy he always thought of as having reproduced itself in Eutychianism, had sometimes spoken of Christ's flesh as existing from eternity in the Son (cf. Greg. Nyssen, Antirrheticos, 13 ; Greg. Naz. Ep. 202 :) language which has indeed

been explained to mean only that in the Divine Word there was always latent the potency of Incarnation, but which in that age seemed to assert the consubstantiality of the Lord's flesh with Godhead. Compare Theodoret's second Dialogue, where "Orthodox" first leads "Eranistes" to own that Christ's flesh had no pre-existence, and then infers that before the "union" there were not two natures in existence, but one only. Eutyches' admission above mentioned seems only to have meant that abstractedly, apart from Incarnation, Godhead and Manhood were two natures,—a mere truism. See Later Treatises of S. Athanasius, p. 197.

170. Here he shows that he had learned from the "acts" or minutes that Eutyches had been brought to admit our Lord's human consubstantiality, in deference to authority.

171. "Quantacunque." Probably even restoration to his rank as presbyter, or his abbacy. Stern as Leo is toward "heretics," the Tome ends with an expression of trust that Eutyches will be divinely aided to retract and to be saved. Comp. Ep. 291, "Si resipiscens ... pro venia supplicaret, sacerdotalis ei benevolentia subveniret;" and Ep. 34, "Ut si ... plena satisfactione corrigitur, sententia qua obstrictus est relaxetur."

172. Julius, bishop of Puteoli; not Julian, bishop of Cos, whom Leo afterwards commissioned to act with the second set of legates sent by him to the Council of Chalcedon. If Julius did not acquiesce in the violent proceedings at the "Robbers' Synod," "it is certain," says Neale, "that he offered no vigorous resistance," (Hist. Patr. Alex. i. 297.) Leo says generally that his legates protested, (Ep. 44, c. 1, Ep. 45, c. 2;) but Neale thinks that this use of the plural does not prove any activity on the part of Julius. Renatus died in the isle of Delos before he could reach Ephesus. Hilarus was archdeacon of Rome; he was present at the "Robbers' Synod," and met the proposal to depose Flavian with a sturdy "Contradicitur." Leo says of him, "vix, ne subscribere per vim cogeretur, effugit," Ep. 44, c. 1. He wrote to Pulcheria that he had "kept himself clear from the guilt of Flavian's condemnation," and managed to return to

Rome, "per incognita et invia loca," and report proceedings to Leo, Ep. 46, c. 2. He lived to sit, during seven years, in Leo's place, and to carry on the tradition of his policy. Dulcitius was a mere clerk, or secretary, in attendance on the actual legates.

173. Here, at the end of this great dogmatic letter, it will be well to observe that although the Tome was suppressed at Ephesus, it received the adhesion, by signatures, of the bishops who formed the "Home Synod" (ἐνδημοῦσα) at Constantinople in the autumn of 450, (Mansi, vii. 92;) Maximus, patriarch of Antioch, sent it round to the prelates of the "East" (i.e., of the region dependent on Antioch, Leo, Ep. 88. 3:) and thus very many prelates of the Eastern empire had signed it before the Council of Chalcedon. At the second session of that Council, October 10, 451, many voices declared that they wanted no new exposition of the faith; one prelate observed that they had all signed Leo's letter, and asked that both the Nicene Creed and the letter might be read. Accordingly the Creed was read in its original form and in its "Constantinopolitan" recension; then Cyril's second letter to Nestorius, and his letter to John of Antioch, containing the formulary of "re-union:" then acclamations arose, "So do we all believe: so does Pope" or "Archbishop Leo believe." An imperial secretary, Veronicianus, proceeded to read the Tome: and the applauding bishops cried out, "Peter has uttered this through Leo!" (meaning, "Leo is true to the teaching of Peter:") "Leo and Cyril have taught alike: why was not this read at Ephesus!" (Mansi, vi. 972.) But exceptions were taken during the reading (as we have seen) to three passages, and were met by the production of three passages from Cyril, as parallel. The imperial commissioners then asked, "Has any one any further doubts?" "No one doubts," was the general answer. But Atticus, bishop of Nicopolis, stood forward, as virtually representing the prelates of Epirus, Macedonia, Thessaly, Greece, and Crete, who, like the Palestinian bishops, were very sensitive as to any appearance of Nestorianism; and requested an adjournment, that time might be obtained for comparing Leo's letter with Cyril's *third* letter to Nestorius (the letter to which were appended the twelve anathematisms.) With some difficulty, the Council was

induced by the commissioners to assent: Anatolius, bishop of Constantinople, was to name a committee to confer with those bishops who were not yet satisfied as to the full anti-Nestorian orthodoxy of the Tome. It seems that this conference removed all disquietude by proving that Anatolius and Leo rejected all notions of a "severance" of the Personal Union, i.e., were essentially in accord with Cyril. And in the fourth session, on October 17, the assembled prelates, one after another, declared that they accepted the Tome of Leo as agreeing with received authorities, as the Nicene Creed, or the Nicene and Constantinopolitan Creeds, or the decisions of the Council of Ephesus in 431, or the teaching of Cyril, or his "epistle" or "epistles," meaning the second to Nestorius and the epistle to John. Theodoret mentions "the epistles." Many bishops take pains to express a personal judgment on the Tome, after due examination and comparison with the above-named standards: "I have ascertained," or "am convinced," or "have found that it agrees, &c." The Greek phrases, in their curious variety, are significant: ἔγνων, γνωρίζω, εὑρήκαμεν, ἐδοκιμάσαμεν, πεπληροφόρημαι, ἔκρινα, εὑρών, δρῶν, κατὰ τὴν ἐμὴν κατάληψιν, ὡς συνιδεῖν ἠδυνήθην, ὅσον κατὰ διάνοιαν. Some speak more briefly: "It agrees, and I sign it as being orthodox," or, "I assent to it." (Mansi, vii. 945.) The spokesmen of the Illyrian and Palestinian bishops profess that their "doubts" had been removed, and their "objections" met. Ib. vii. 32, 33. But the long list of signatures in the "acts" of Chalcedon is most impressive as to the fact, that this solemn and deliberately promulgated utterance of the Roman see on a doctrinal question of the first importance was accepted by a great Œcumenical Council, not simply on the authority of that see, but as intrinsically satisfying the tests of orthodoxy which were applied to it. Leo, in 453, professed his satisfaction that some "doubts" had been expressed, "ne aliarum sedium ad eam quam cæteris omnium Dominus statuit præsidere consensus *assentatio* videretur," Ep. 120. 1; but there can be no doubt that the proceedings at Chalcedon are an absolute negative, so far as the Church of the fifth century is concerned, to the claim of infallibility for Papal decisions, *ex cathedra*, on matters of faith.

Flavian and the Fourth Council. 241

It may be desirable to present to the reader, in further illustration of the Tome, the doctrinal statement contained in a profession of faith drawn up by Flavian in the spring of 449 at the request of Theodosius, (Mansi, vi. 541,) and the statement contained in the "Definition of Faith" adopted by the Council of Chalcedon in its fifth session, Oct. 22, 451, (Mansi, vii. 116.) The latter, it will be seen, was largely modelled on the former, but was at once more full and more precise.

Flavian.	Council of Chalcedon.
... "We preach our one Lord Jesus Christ, Who was begotten of God the Father before ages, without a beginning, as to the Godhead, but at the end of days, the Same, for us and for our salvation, of Mary the Virgin as to the Manhood; perfect God and perfect Man, the Same, by the assumption of a reasonable soul and a body; consubstantial with the Father as to Godhead, and the Same consubstantial with His Mother as to Manhood. For, confessing Christ to be of[1] two natures after He took flesh of the holy Virgin, and became Man, in one hypostasis and in one person, we confess one Christ, one Son, one Lord; and we do not refuse to say 'one φύσις of God the Word,	... "Following, therefore, the holy Fathers, we all teach with one accord that men should confess one and the same Son, our Lord Jesus Christ, the Same perfect in Godhead and the Same perfect in Manhood, truly God, and truly Man, the Same, of a reasonable soul and a body; consubstantial with the Father as to the Godhead, and the Same consubstantial with us as to the Manhood; in all things like unto us, apart from sin; Who was begotten of the Father before ages as to the Godhead, but at the end of days, the selfsame, for us and for our salvation, of Mary the Virgin, the Mother of God, as to the Manhood; one and the same Christ, Son, Lord, Only-begotten, ac-

[1] The Greek reads ἐν δύο φύσεσιν. But this is apparently an after-alteration. Liberatus, in his Breviarium, c. 11, (Galland. Bibl. Patr. xii. 139,) reads "Ex duabus itaque naturis." So the Catholics, at a conference with the Severians at Constantinople in 533, cite the words as "of two natures," Mansi, viii. 823. And so Eulogius cites them, Photius, Bibl. n. 230 (p. 271, Bekker.)

but one which was incarnate, and became man;' because our Lord Jesus Christ is one and the same from both. But those who assert that there are two Sons, or two hypostases, or two persons, and not one and the same Lord Jesus Christ, the Son of the living God, we anathematise, and judge to be alien from the Church. And first of all, we anathematise Nestorius," &c.

knowledged (as) in[1] two natures, without confusion, change, division, or separation; the difference of the natures having been in no wise annulled because of the union,[2] but rather the properties of each nature being preserved, and (both) combined into one person and one hypostasis;—not (as) parted or divided into two persons, but one and the same Son and Only-begotten, God the Word, the Lord Jesus Christ; even as the prophets from the beginning (spake) of Him, and our Lord Jesus Christ Himself instructed us, and the Creed of the Fathers has handed down."

It may here be added that the arrangement of the Ballerini has been followed in regard to the correspondence of Leo and Flavian during the first half of the year 449. Hefele, indeed, considers that the second letter of Flavian, Ep. 26, is referred to by Leo in his letter of May 21, Ep. 27, and in the Tome, of which undoubtedly Ep. 27 was the forerunner. But the Tome clearly refers to the first information received from Flavian (c. 1,) and Ep. 36 to some later letter of Flavian's, which may reasonably be identified with Ep. 26. If the first

---

[1] Here the Greek has ἐκ δύο φύσεων, but ἐν δύο φύσεσιν was ultimately adopted. See the contemporary testimony of Euthymius in Mansi, vii. 776; also Evagrius, ii. 4; Rusticus, in Galland. xii. 69; and other authorities cited in Hefele, Hist. Councils, b. xi. s. 193. In fact, this appears from the discussion in Mansi, vii. 105, where the commissioners and the legates contend that "*of* two natures" is insufficient, and prevail on the Council to appoint a committee to revise the draft. The result was evidently the adoption of "*in* two natures."

[2] From Cyril's second Epistle to Nestorius. See note 35.

letter was long on its way, the second, although, as the Ballerini and Hefele agree, probably written in March, may have been similarly and unaccountably delayed. It is certain that Leo had received the invitation to the proposed General Council at Ephesus on May 13, (Ep. 31. 4,) that is, eight days before he wrote Ep. 27, and a month before he dated the Tome.

INDEX.

Abraham, Christians true children of, 14, 47.
Acts, the test of inward state, 34.
Adam, effect of sin of, 21, 54, 59.
Adoption, Christians children of God by, 14, 50, 61.
Agony, the, of Christ, 37, 173.
All men, Christ died for, 44, 182.
Angels, joy of, in the Incarnation, 4; ministry of, to Christ, 95.
Apollinarianism, 22, 156.
Apostles, doubts of, why helpful, 88; personal testimony borne by, 53.
Arianism, 6, 22, 139; idolatrous, 153.
Ascension, the, our interest in, 63, 82, 90, 206.
Atonement, the, implies Christ's true Divinity, 134; and Humanity, 55.

Baptism, effects of, 4, 50, 61, 68, 147; need of watchfulness after, 198.
Blood, efficacy of Christ's, 43, 120.
Body of Christ, Christians made a, 4, 10.

Cerinthus, 150.

Change, impossible for Divine nature, 54, 81, 84, 204.
Charity, a help against temptation, 96.
Christian calling, dignity of the, 4, 15.
Christian life, a struggle, 70.
Christian ordinances, 60, 186.
Church, the one, from all nations, 50.
Coequality in the Trinity, 5, 41, 99, 105, 212.
Coeternity of the Son, 19, 84, 110.
Coinherence, the Divine, 85, 108, 190.
"Communicatio idiomatum," 117, 130, 178.
Conception of Christ, 12, 57, 112, 177.
Condescension, the Divine, in the Incarnation, 8, 13, 41.
Confession of sins, 34.
Confirmation, 193.
Conformity to Divine will, 17.
Consubstantiality in the Trinity, 7, 46, 54, 108, 117.
Contrasts in the Incarnation, 3, 12, 28, 42, 85, 115.
Creator, Christ the, 5, 54, 114.

Index. 245

Creed, the, 41, 86, 110, 225.
Cross, attraction of the, 56, 191; hopes centred in the, 35, 62; to be borne by Christians, 13, 68, 84.
Crucifixion, God's will wrought out in the, 43, 66.
Cyril, the point contended for by, 161, 231; not Monophysite, 163.

David, Christ's descent from, 2, 20, 111.
Death, Christ's, our participation in, 51; removes fear of death, 81.
Degrees of Godhead, impossible, 22, 84, 100, 106, 205.
Delay of the first Advent, purpose in, 9.
Denial of Christ in act, 34.
Despair, the final sin of Judas, 44.
Docetism, 22, 152.
Doxology, forms of the, 135.

Easter, practical lessons of, 74, 78; vigil of, 200.
Ebionites, 151.
Emmanuel, prophecy of the, 6, 112.
Epiphany, festival of, 26, 166.
Eternal death, 65.
Eternity, retribution in for acts done in time, 74.
Eucharist, the Holy, effects of, 52, 189; sacrifice of, 145.
Eutyches, 23, 109, 121, 162, 221.
Evil spirits, hostility of, 71.
Exaltation of Christ's manhood, 85.

Example, our Lord's, 4, 48, 63, 80, 143, 185.

Faith, "the Catholic," 21, 57, 171, 192; necessity of true, 57, 61; revealed, 108; professed at baptism, 51, 61.
Faith, as a principle, justifying, 56, 59, 92; power of, to realise Gospel facts, 65; strong in spite of difficulties, 67; victories of, 93.
Fasting, seasons of, 73, 102, 217.
Feelings, human, in Christ, 48, 63, 116, 185.
"Firstborn of all creation," 17, 184.
Firstfruits of our nature in Christ, 61.
Flavian, 163, 221, 241.
Flesh, Christ really took our, 22, 53, 112; bodily needs of His, 57.
Fleshly impulses to be resisted, 16, 34, 69.
"Form of God," or "of a servant," 7, 19, 84, 115.
Free-will, 104, 219.

Genealogy of Christ, 111.
Gifts of the Magi, symbolism of, 28, 31, 167.
"Gloria in excelsis," the, 12, 146.
God and Man, the Redeemer must be, 3, 36, 56, 113.
Good works, result of a Divine gift, 51.
Grace, doctrine of, 17, 148, 219.

Habits, sinful, hard to conquer, 34.

Headship of Christ, 4, 10, 13, 47, 63, 86.
Healings, physical and spiritual, by Christ, 44.
Heathens' contempt for Christian belief, 37.
Heaven, our aims to be directed towards, 18, 77.
Heresies, connection of diverse, 23, 158.
Heretics, 18, 84.
Herod, 27, 57, 167.
Holy Spirit, the, a Person of the Trinity, 99; relation of to the Father and the Son, 100; offices of, 102, 121, 216; Christians' relation to, 18.
Holy Week services, 175.
"Homo" used for manhood, 165.
Human nature must itself act in redemptive work, and how, 36, 46.
Human terms inadequate as to Divine truth, 210.
Humanity, mere, ascribed by some to Christ, 22, 150.
"Hypostatic union," 131, 163.

Identity of Christ in Divine and human spheres, 25, 41, 114, 131.
Immersion, triple, 68, 197.
"In two natures," 129, 164, 228, 231, 242.
Incarnation, the, why it took place, 21, 54, 104, 217; our interest in, 13; our duty in consequence of, 4.
"Inferior to the Father," the Son as Man, 6, 57, 107, 117, 140.
Infinity, the Divine, 106.
Infirmities, assumed by Christ, 81.

Innocents, the Holy, 28, 32, 168.
Intercession of Christ, 62.

Jesus, significance of Name of, 82.
Jews, literalism of, 60; prayer for conversion of, 66, 196.
Judas, death of, 44, 183.
Justice, in the work of redemption, 2, 21, 36.

Kingdom of Christ, the, not temporal, 27.

Law, types and symbols in the, 49, 60.
Legates, the, of Leo, 123, 238.
Lent, utility of, 73, 201.
Longsuffering of God, not to be abused, 34.
Love, Divine, original design of, 59, 114.

Macedonianism, 101, 214.
Magi, the, 26, 57, 166.
Manhood of Christ, real, 86, 185.
Martyrs, 32, 51, 93.
Mary, the B. V., 5, 12, 112, 126.
Mary Magdalene, 94, 208.
Mediator, the one, 3, 113.
Membership in Christ, 10.
"Merit," 188.
"Mingled," sense of the term, 138.
Monophysites, 163, 174, 232.
Monothelites, 174.
"Mother of God," title of, 2, 126.

Nativity of Christ, miraculous, 9; spotless, 2; a source of special joy, 5, 19.

Index. 247

Natures, the two, in the one Christ, 3, 21, 24, 113, 163, 231.
Nestorius, 23, 128, 160.
New creation, the, in Christ, 4, 52.
Newness of life, 78.

"Of two natures," 121, 228, 241.
Old Testament, Saints of the, 47, 59, 144.
Omnipresence of the Son, 5, 115.
"One nature only in Christ," result of asserting, 24.
"Original sin," 2, 21, 54, 59, 81, 125.

"Pagans," 18, 148.
Paradise, re-opened, 62.
"Pascha," meaning of, 85, 199.
Passion, Christ's, efficacy of, 39; no words adequate to express, 40; realised by reading of, 65; in what sense perpetuated, 70.
Peace with God, 15.
Pentecostal festival, 97; gift of the Holy Spirit, 98.
Persecution, in some form perpetual, 70.
Person, our Lord's, one, 6, 41, 56, 81, 85, 113, 128; properly Divine, 25, 137, 150.
Persons, distinction of, in the Trinity, 99, 103.
Peter, S., 42, 50, 96, 118, 178.
Pilgrimage, life a, 96.
Poor, Christ relieved in the, 70.
Power, mere, not exerted by God for man's rescue, 20, 36, 54.
Prayer, sometimes made ignorantly, 38; for spiritual help, always heard, 34.
Preaching, a bishop's duty, 40, 79.

Proclus, "Tome" of, 222, 232.
Properties of two Natures in Christ, 6, 19, 57, 116, 233.
Propitiation, 218.

Quiet times, spiritual perils of, 33.

Readings from Scripture in church, 30, 58, 65, 169.
Reasonableness of Christians' belief, 67, 196.
Reconciliation, 36, 61, 172.
Redemption, doctrine of, 8, 181.
Regeneration, 13, 51, 68, 147.
"Remaining what He was," 3, 19, 46, 128.
Renunciations in baptism, 51, 187.
Restoration, excels creation, 59, 80, 192.
Resurrection of Christ, literal, 61; proofs of reality of, 75, 88, 118; spiritual "imitation" of, 78.
Robber, the penitent, 62, 193.

Sabellianism, 22, 154.
"Sacerdos," title of, 203.
"Sacramentum," meaning of, 136.
Sacrifice, Christ our, 39, 61.
Saints, could not save their fellow-men, 55.
Satan, Incarnation hidden from, 42, 180; dominion of, how "lost," 55; manifold hostility of, 31.
Scriptures, the Holy, free from falsehood, 58.
"Self-emptying," the, of our Lord, 8, 85, 114, 228.
Self-love, the true, 71.
Self-mortification, 69.
Shepherd, Christ the good, 51.

Sinlessness of Christ, absolute, 8, 54, 113, 142.
Son of God, the, truly God, 84; equal with the Father, 5, 24, 37, 67, 94, 104, 115.
Soul, a reasonable, in Christ, 23, 113.
"Subordination" of the Son, 213.
"Substances," two, in Christ, 6, 36, 41, 57, 113.
"Sursum corda," 209.

Temperance, what it consists in, 77.
Temporal things, how to pass through, 96.
Temptation, manifold, 16.
"Theandric energy," 232.
Theodore, 159.
"Third day, the," sense of, 75.
Thomas, S., 92.
"Tome," the, when written, 224; accepted at Chalcedon, 239.
Tongues, the fiery, 98.

Trinity, unity of the, 7, 105, 108; joint and distinct action of Persons in the, 54, 100, 103, 190.

Uncertainties of non-Christian opinion, 8.

Victim, Christ a, 8.
Virginity, the Perpetual, 112, 137.

"Water and blood," the, 120, 236.
"Way, Truth, and Life," Christ the, 80.
Will, the Divine, one in the whole Trinity, 103; our wills to be united to, 15.
Wills, Divine and human, in Christ, 37, 173.
Word, the, 3, 22, 57, 115.
Works, Divine and human of Christ, to be distinguished, 56, 115.
Worldly wisdom, opposed to faith, 13, 88.

ERRATA.

Page 225, line 15, insert "de" before "humilitatis."
,, 240, ,, 22, for "945" read "9—45."

December, 1885.

NEW BOOKS, AND NEW EDITIONS,

PUBLISHED BY

J. MASTERS & Co., 78, NEW BOND ST.,
LONDON.

EIGHTEEN SERMONS OF S. LEO THE GREAT ON THE INCARNATION, AND THE TWENTY-EIGHTH EPISTLE, OR THE "TOME." Translated, with Notes, by the Rev. W. BRIGHT, D.D., Regius Professor of Ecclesiastical History, and Canon of Christ Church, Oxford. Second edition. Crown 8vo.

THE POLITY OF THE CHRISTIAN CHURCH OF EARLY, MEDIÆVAL, AND MODERN TIMES. By ALEXIUS AURELIUS PELLICCIA. Translated from the original Latin by the Rev. J. C. BELLETT, M.A. 8vo., cloth, 15s.

"It is not in the discussion of controverted questions whether of doctrine or discipline, but its copious and detailed exposition of Christian ritual in the widest sense of the term that the distinctive excellence and interest of Pelliccia's book is to be sought. And here the student will find a vast supply of trustworthy and to ordinary readers not easily accessible information. To liturgiological and theological students the volume will prove a most valuable aid, the more so from its compressing into a very moderate compass so large and varied a repertory of information."—*Saturday Review.*

GOD'S WITNESS IN PROPHECY AND HISTORY. Bible Studies on the Historical Fulfilments of the Prophetic Blessings on the Twelve Tribes contained in Gen. xlix. With a Supplementary Inquiry into the History of the Lost Tribes. By the Rev. J. C. BELLETT, M.A. Crown 8vo., cloth, 6s.

"We sincerely commend this interesting and instructive volume to the perusal of our readers. It is a scholarly production of a cultivated and devout writer whose studies have been energetically devoted to the understanding of the Inspired Word. It is calculated especially to benefit junior ministers, and will have a special claim for Bible classes and Sunday School Teachers."—*Ecclesiastical Gazette.*

OUTLINES OF CHURCH TEACHING. A Series of Instructions for the Sundays and Chief Holy Days of the Christian Year. By C. C. G. With Preface by the Rev. FRANCIS PAGET, M.A., Regius Professor of Pastoral Theology in the University of Oxford, and Canon of Christ Church. Crown 8vo., cloth, 4s. 6d.

SIMPLE READINGS ON THE MINOR PROPHETS. By M. C. HYETT. With Preface by the Rev. W. WALTERS, M.A., Vicar of Pershore, Hon. Canon of Worcester. Crown 8vo., cloth, 3s.

OUTLINES OF PLAIN INSTRUCTIONS FOR BIBLE CLASSES. Edited by the Rev. J. R. WEST, Canon of Lincoln and Vicar of Wrawby. Fcap. 8vo., 9d.

IN TIME OF NEED, or, Words in Season for the Use of District Visitors and others. By JESSIE E. CARTER. Edited by the Rev. CHARLES BODINGTON, Vicar of Christ Church, Lichfield. Super royal 32mo., 1s. 6d.; roan, 2s. 6d.

A small book of convenient size to carry in the pocket, containing short passages from the Bible, suitable for different occasions, with references to longer ones, and also corresponding Prayers and Hymns, with some blank pages for private notes.

PLAIN CHURCH TEACHING FOR WEEKDAYS THROUGHOUT THE YEAR; or, Readings from the Collect, Epistle, and Gospel of each Sunday and Holyday. Third edition. Cloth limp, 3s.; cloth boards, red edges, 4s.

THE COPTIC MORNING SERVICE FOR THE LORD'S DAY.
Translated into English by JOHN, MARQUESS OF BUTE, K.T. With the Original Coptic of those parts said aloud. Crown 8vo., cloth, 6s.

ALL THE DAYS OF OUR LIFE. Short Readings for Daily Life and for the Church Seasons. By C. H. B. Second edition. 32mo., cloth, 1s. 6d.

NOTES ON THE ANGELS. Based on the Writings of S. Thomas Aquinas. Edited by a Priest, and dedicated by permission to the Rev. A. D. WAGNER, M.A. Compiled for School Teaching, by the Lady in Charge of S. Mary's School for the Daughters of the Clergy and others, Queen-square, Brighton, and inscribed also to the Pupils who have attended this School for the last thirty years. Cloth, 1s. 6d.

CONSIDERATIONS ON THE SPIRITUAL LIFE. Suggested by Passages in the Collects for the Sundays in Lent. By the Rev. G. S. HOLLINGS, Sub-Warden of the House of Mercy, Bovey Tracey, author of "Meditations on the Divine Life," &c. Crown 8vo., cloth, 2s. 6d.

CONSIDERATIONS ON THE WISDOM OF GOD. By the Rev. G. S. HOLLINGS. Crown 8vo., cloth, 4s.

MEDITATIONS ON THE DIVINE LIFE AND THE BLESSED SACRAMENT, together with Considerations on the Transfiguration. By the Rev. G. S. HOLLINGS. Crown 8vo., cloth, 3s. 6d.

THE EVENING OF LIFE; or, Meditations and Devotions for the Aged. By the Rev. W. E. HEYGATE, M.A., Rector of Brighstone, Isle of Wight. Third Edition. Crown 8vo., cloth, 4s.

CHRISTUS CONSOLATOR. Short Meditations for Invalids, from the Writings of Dr. PUSEY, selected by a Lady. With a Preface by GEORGE E. JELF, M.A., Canon of Rochester. 2s.; roan, 3s.

A GRAMMAR OF THEOLOGY. Being a Manual of Instruction in Churchmanship for Adults and the more intelligent Youths: to be used either before or after their Confirmation. By the Rev. F. C. EWER, S.T.D., New York. Fourth edition. Fcap. 8vo., 1s. 6d.

HELPS TO MEDITATION. Sketches for Every Day in the Year. By the Rev. A. G. MORTIMER, Rector of S. Mary's, Castleton, New York. With Introduction by the Bishop of Springfield. Vol. I. Advent to Trinity, 220 Meditations. 8vo., cloth, 7s. 6d. Third Edition. Vol. II. Trinity. Second Edition. 7s. 6d.
*** The object of this work is to supply Material for Meditation and Outlines of Sermons.

HELPS TO MEDITATION FOR BEGINNERS. By a Priest of the Church of England. Edited by the Rev. CANON BODY. 18mo., 3d.

SUGGESTIONS ON THE METHOD OF MEDITATION. By the Rev. W. B. TREVELYAN. With a Preface by the LORD BISHOP OF ELY. 2d.

ON THE NATURE AND CONSTITUTION OF THE PRESENT KINGDOM OF HEAVEN UPON EARTH. By the Rev. J. R. WEST, M.A., Canon of Lincoln, and Vicar of Wrawby. Fcap. 8vo., cloth, 2s. 6d.

COLLECTS, EPISTLES, AND GOSPELS, suggested for use on certain special occasions and Holy-Days. With a Preface by the Rev. T. T. CARTER, M.A., Hon. Canon of Christ Church, Oxford, and Warden of the House of Mercy, Clewer. Dedicated by permission to the Lord Bishop of Oxford. Crown 8vo., 1s. 6d.

AN ACT OF SPIRITUAL COMMUNION. By the Rev. James SKINNER, M.A. With Notice by the Rev. T. T. CARTER, M.A., Superior General of the Confraternity of the Blessed Sacrament. Royal 32mo., cloth, 6d.

78, *New Bond Street.* 3

SPRING BUDS: Counsels for the Young. From the French.
By the Translator of "Gold Dust." With a Preface by CHARLOTTE M. YONGE. Imp. 32mo., cloth, 2s.; limp cloth, 1s. 6d.; roan, 3s. 6d.; calf or morocco, 6s.

GOLD DUST SERIES.

GOLD DUST: a Collection of Golden Counsels for the Sanctification of Daily Life. Translated from the French. With Preface by CHARLOTTE M. YONGE. In Two Parts. Price of each Part, cloth gilt, 1s.; wrapper, 6d.; roan, 1s. 6d.; limp calf, 2s. 6d.

*** Parts I. and II. in one Volume, limp roan, 2s. 6d.; limp calf, 3s. 6d.

GOLD DUST. (In larger type.) Translated from the French.
Edited by C. M. YONGE. Complete in 1 Vol., Imp. 32mo., cloth, full gilt sides, 2s. 6d.; roan, 3s. 6d.; calf or morocco, 6s.

GOLDEN TREASURES. Counsels for the Happiness of Daily Life. Translated and abridged from the French. Edited by the Author of "The Divine Master." Uniform with "Gold Dust," cloth gilt, 1s.; roan, 1s. 6d.; calf, 2s. 6d.

"This little book has been drawn from the same source as 'Gold Dust,' and will be found to possess all the rare qualities which won so favourable a reception for its predecessor."

SPARKS OF LIGHT FOR EVERY DAY. Collected by Madame GUIZOT DE WITT; done into English by the Translator of "Gold Dust." Edited by CHARLOTTE M. YONGE. Cloth gilt, 1s.; wrapper, 6d.; limp roan, 1s. 6d.; limp calf, 2s. 6d.

With Twelve Photographs, extra cloth, gilt edges, 5s.; morocco, 10s.
HYMNS FOR LITTLE CHILDREN. By Mrs. C. F. Alexander.
Fifty-sixth Edition, handsomely printed on thick toned paper, with red border lines, 16mo., cloth, 2s. 6d.

"This well known collection has certainly never before appeared in so attractive a form as in the beautiful little book before us. The poems need no words at this day to enhance the value they have so long possessed, but the volume in which they are now embodied is really a work of art from the exquisite photographs with which it is adorned, and the perfect taste with which the whole is arranged."—*Churchman's Companion.*

With Eighty-five Engravings, small 4to., reduced from 6s. to 3s. 6d.
MORAL SONGS. By Mrs. C. F. Alexander. A New Illustrated Edition, with eighty-five engravings on wood from original drawings by E. M. Wimperis, R. P. Leitch, W. H. J. Boot, P. Skelton, W. Rainey, and other Artists. The illustrations have been arranged and engraved by James D. Cooper.

NEW ILLUSTRATED EDITION.
SACRED ALLEGORIES. By the late Rev. E. Monro, M.A.
Complete in 1 vol. With Eight Illustrations engraved on wood by Mr. J. D. Cooper. Crown 8vo., cloth, 7s. 6d.; morocco, 16s.

THE DARK RIVER.	THE REVELLERS, THE	THE JOURNEY HOME.
THE VAST ARMY.	MIDNIGHT SEA. AND	THE DARK MOUNTAINS.
THE COMBATANTS.	THE WANDERER.	

Also, in fcap. 8vo., 2 vols., 3s. 6d. each, bound in cloth; or in Six Parts, separately, in limp cloth, 1s. each Part, with Illustrations.

THE CHANGED CROSS. With Illuminated borders from original Designs, with new and elegant design on cover. Words by L. P. W. Illuminations by K. K. Square 16mo., cloth, 6s.

HEROES OF THE CROSS. A Series of Biographical Studies of Saints, Martyrs, and Christian Pioneers. By W. H. DAVENPORT ADAMS. Crown 8vo., 488 pp., cloth, 7s. 6d.

"This is a handsome volume containing biographical sketches of men and women notable for their heroic conduct in the struggle to uphold the standard of the religion of CHRIST. Mr. Adams presents a fair and impartial picture of the heroes selected for delineation. A catholic tone pervades the whole book, and Mr. Adams has provided his readers with a valuable and worthy series of studies from the lives of great men and women."—*Church Times.*

CURIOSITIES OF SUPERSTITION AND SKETCHES OF SOME UNREVEALED RELIGIONS. By W. H. DAVENPORT ADAMS, author of "Heroes of the Cross," &c. Crown 8vo., cloth, 5s.

THOUGHTS ON HOLINESS, Doctrinal and Practical. By W. A. COPINGER. Fcap. 8vo., cloth, 2s. 6d.

"The aim of this little book, which is full of spiritual life and light, is to set the highest privileges, responsibilities, and duties of the professing Christian in fresh lights and uncommon surroundings."—*Liverpool Mercury.*

HOMEWARD BOUND. The Voyage and the Voyagers; the Pilot and the Port. By the Rev. F. E. PAGET, M.A., Rector of Elford. Third edition. Crown 8vo., cloth, 4s.

"It is a review of the cares, the duties, the troubles of life; the consolations that enable souls to bear, the principles upon which it behoves them to act, the hopes that brighten the darkest prospects of the traveller through the world. It is no unworthy gift to the Church from one who has served her so well by his pen in past time."—*Literary Churchman.*
"No one can read it without being the better for it."—*Church Bells.*

A STUDENT PENITENT OF 1695. Diary, Correspondence, &c., of a Student, illustrating Academical Life at Oxford. By the Rev. F. E. PAGET, M.A., Rector of Elford. Crown 8vo., cloth, 4s. 6d.

"The Diaries are very remarkable for their beauty, truth, and sound moral and spiritual perceptions. The whole book is a gem. But it is the latter part of it which charms us most. It is full of suggestiveness, and that of a very delicate and beautiful kind. For sick persons or for those who have much (or indeed anything) to do with the sick it will be most valuable."—*Literary Churchman.*

FIVE PLAIN SERMONS ON THE SACRAMENT OF THE ALTAR. By the Rev. W. H. CLEAVER, M.A. Fourth Edition. Fcap. 8vo., 1s.

SIX PLAIN SERMONS ON PENITENCE. By the Rev. W. H. CLEAVER, M.A. Fourth Edition. Fcap. 8vo., 1s.

THE LIFE OF PEACE. By the Rev. R. C. Lundin Brown, M.A., late Vicar of Rhodes, Manchester. Fcap. 8vo., cloth, 2s. 6d.

"This is a work of unusual beauty and spiritual worth. It is one that we can recommend to our readers to be put upon the shelf beside their Thomas à Kempis and 'Holy Living and Dying' for periodical use. We have had few works before us of late with which we have been so pleased."—*Literary Churchman.*

THE DEAD IN CHRIST. A Word of Consolation for Mourners. By the Rev. R. C. LUNDIN BROWN, M.A., late Vicar of Rhodes, Manchester. Third Edition, super-royal 32mo., cloth boards, 1s. 6d.; cloth limp, 1s.

ANCIENT EPITAPHS from A.D. 1250 to 1800. Collected and set forth in chronological order by T. F. RAVENSHAW, M.A., F.S.A., Rector of Pewsey, Wilts. 8vo., cloth, 7s. 6d.

A FEW PRACTICAL HINTS ON CHURCH EMBROIDERY. With six plates. 1s.

KALENDAR OF THE IMITATION: Sentences for every day of the year from the "Imitatio Christi." Translated from the edition of 1630. Edited by the late Rev. J. M. NEALE, D.D. New edition, royal 32mo., cloth, 1s.

PEARLS RE-STRUNG: Stories from the Apocrypha. By Mrs. MACKARNESS, author of "A Trap to Catch a Sunbeam," &c. 16mo., cloth, 2s. Illustrated.

"An elegant and successful treatment of some of the more marked narratives of the Apocryphal writings. Nothing could be more attractive and winning than the way in which these stories are presented here, and children will be sure to appreciate them in the new garb in which Mrs. Mackarness has clothed them."—*Literary Churchman.*

POCKET BOOK OF DEVOTIONS AND EXTRACTS FOR INVALIDS. By C. L. Edited by the Ven. ALFRED POTT, B.D., Archdeacon of Berkshire, Vicar of Clifton Hampden. Super royal 32mo., cloth, 1s. 6d.

CHURCH CHOIRS; containing a Brief History of the Changes in Church Music during the last Forty or Fifty Years, with Directions for the Formation, Management, and Instruction of Cathedral, Collegiate, and Parochial Choirs; being the result of thirty-six years' experience in Choir Training. By FREDERICK HELMORE. Fourth Edition, Crown 8vo., 1s.

"The hints and directions on the formation, management, and instruction of Church Choirs are simply invaluable."—*Church Times.*

SPEAKERS, SINGERS, AND STAMMERERS. With Illustrations. By FREDERICK HELMORE, author of "Church Choirs," "The Chorister's Instruction Book," &c. Crown 8vo., cloth, 4s. 6d.

"It will prove invaluable to all who are preparing to enter professions, whether music, the bar, or the pulpit."—*Public Opinion.*

"We know many manuals of elocution, and we are bound to say that this is the best we have ever seen. We perceive at once that we are in the hands of a master. There is a most valuable chapter on 'Voice Training' of which we must express a very high appreciation. This is a book which should not be left unnoticed by those who have in their charge the training of our young clergy."—*Literary Churchman.*

VILLAGE CONFERENCES ON THE CREED. By the Rev. S. BARING-GOULD, M.A., Vicar of Lew Trenchard, Devon; author of "Origin and Development of Religious Belief," &c. Third Edition. Crown 8vo., cloth, 3s. 6d.

ONE HUNDRED SKETCHES OF SERMONS FOR EXTEMPORE PREACHERS. By the Rev. S. BARING-GOULD, M.A., author of "Origin and Development of Religious Belief," &c. Fourth Edition. Crown 8vo., cloth, 6s.

CHRIST IN THE LAW; or, the Gospel foreshadowed in the Pentateuch. Compiled from various sources. By a Priest of the Church of England. Third Edition. Fcap. 8vo., cloth, 3s. 6d.

"The author has apprehended, as it seems to us, the real spirit and the only true moral value of the Old Testament."—*Saturday Review.*

CHRIST IN THE PROPHETS. Joshua, Judges, Samuel, Kings. By the Author of "CHRIST in the Law." Fcap. 8vo., 4s. 6d.

"The compiler of that capital book, 'CHRIST in the Law,' has now issued a continuation under the title of 'CHRIST in the Prophets.' This volume is a worthy companion to its predecessor, and that is no small praise. We strongly advise clergymen to give both volumes of R. H. N. B.'s work to their school teachers, impressing upon them at the same time the duty of studying them carefully and of reproducing what they learn from them in the lessons they give the children."—*Church Times.*

GENESIS AND MODERN SCIENCE. By the Author of "Christ in the Law," &c. An Explanation of the First Chapter of the Bible in accordance with observed facts. Fcap. 8vo., 1s. 6d.

"A most useful little work, well suited for these times. It is very suitable reading for any whose faith in revelation is in danger of being undermined by the plausible assertions of modern unbelief."—*National Church.*

Published by J. Masters and Co.,

BY THE REV. T. T. CARTER, M.A.,
LATE RECTOR OF CLEWER, HON. CANON OF CHRIST CHURCH, OXFORD, AND WARDEN OF THE HOUSE OF MERCY, CLEWER.

HARRIET MONSELL. A Memoir. With Portrait, engraved on steel by Stodart. Second Edition. Imperial 16mo., cloth, 5s.

PARISH TEACHINGS. The Apostles' Creed and Sacraments. Crown 8vo., cloth, 4s. 6d.

SERMONS. Third Edition. 8vo., 9s.

SPIRITUAL INSTRUCTIONS. Crown 8vo., cloth.
1. THE HOLY EUCHARIST. Fifth Edition. 3s. 6d.
2. THE DIVINE DISPENSATIONS. Second Edition. 3s. 6d.
3. THE RELIGIOUS LIFE. 3s. 6d.
4. THE LIFE OF GRACE. 3s. 6d.

LENT LECTURES. Four Series in 1 Vol. Crown 8vo., cloth, 6s.

THE IMITATION OF OUR LORD. Fifth edit. Demy 8vo., 2s. 6d.

THE DOCTRINE OF THE PRIESTHOOD IN THE CHURCH OF ENGLAND. Third Edition. 4s.

THE DOCTRINE OF CONFESSION IN THE CHURCH OF ENGLAND. Third Edition. Crown 8vo., 5s.

THE DOCTRINE OF THE HOLY EUCHARIST, drawn from the Holy Scriptures and the Records of the Church of England. Third Edition. Fcap. 8vo., 9d.

VOWS AND THE RELIGIOUS STATE. Crown 8vo., 2s.

FAMILY PRAYERS. Sixth Edition. 18mo., cloth, 1s.

EDITED BY THE REV. T. T. CARTER.

A BOOK OF PRIVATE PRAYER, FOR MORNING, MID-DAY, NIGHT, AND OTHER TIMES, with Rules for those who would live to God amid the business of daily life. Eleventh Edition. Limp cloth, 1s.; cl., red edges, 1s. 3d.; roan, 1s. 6d.; French morocco, 2s.; limp calf, 3s. 6d.

THE DAY OF PRAYER. Short Prayers for every Hour of the Day. Second edition. 3d.

LITANIES, and other Devotions. Second Edition. 1s. 6d.

MEMORIALS FOR USE IN A RELIGIOUS HOUSE. Second Edition Enlarged. 6d.

NIGHT OFFICE FOR CHRISTMAS. 6d.

THE FOOTPRINTS OF THE LORD ON THE KING'S HIGHWAY OF THE CROSS. Devotional Aids for Holy Week. Fcap. 8vo., cloth, 1s.

FOOTSTEPS OF THE HOLY CHILD, being Readings on the Incarnation. Part I., 1s. Part II., 2s. 6d. In One Vol., 3s. 6d. cloth.

MANUAL OF DEVOTION FOR SISTERS OF MERCY. In Eight Parts, or Two Vols., cloth, 10s.

SIMPLE LESSONS; or, Words Easy to be Understood. A Manual of Teaching. Three Parts in one Volume. Third Edition. 18mo., cloth, 3s.

CHILDREN'S SERVICES.

A PLEA FOR CHILDREN'S SERVICES. By the Rev. Theodore Johnson, Curate of Warkton, Northamptonshire. 2d.

SIX METRICAL LITANIES FOR CHILDREN. By the same Author. 1d.; or 7s. per 100.

LITANY FOR CHILDREN, with Music. ½d., or 2s. 6d. per 100.

THE ORDER FOR A CHILDREN'S SERVICE. With Music. Compiled by Henry Ditton-Newman, Organist of S. John's, Torquay. With Pointing for both Gregorian and Anglican usage. 3rd edition. 2d., or 14s. per 100; cloth, 4d.

Published with the approval of the Archbishops of Canterbury and Dublin, and authorised for use in the Dioceses of Durham, Winchester, Ely, Peterborough, Lincoln, Bath and Wells, and Oxford.

BIBLE TRUTHS IN SIMPLE WORDS. Short Addresses to Children. By the Rev. J. E. Vernon, M.A., Vicar of Olveston, Almondsbury. Fcap. 8vo., 3s.

"As sermons the addresses are excellent, and there are very few so well suited to children as these."—*Literary Churchman.*

"We quite think that sermons such as these would be listened to by children with understanding and profit."—*Church Bells.*

Second Edition, with Two new Stories. 16mo., cloth, 2s.

SERMON STORIES FOR CHILDREN'S SERVICES AND HOME READING. By the Rev. H. Housman, author of "Readings on the Psalms."

"Having read the Easter Day Sermon story to a large congregation of children, we can speak from experience of the interest excited by this touching allegory, which appears to be the gem of the book."—*Church Bells.*

"Will be found very helpful in children's services, readings at school, and even in some of those Cottage Lectures which require to have some life and interest in them."—*The Guardian.*

SUNDAY AFTERNOONS AT AN ORPHANAGE. Sermonettes for Children. By the late Rev. J. M. Neale, D.D. Third Edition. 18mo., cloth, 2s.

BY THE RIGHT REV. J. R. WOODFORD, D.D.,
Late Lord Bishop of Ely.

ORDINATION SERMONS preached in the Dioceses of Oxford and Winchester, 1860—72. 8vo., 6s. 6d.

"Sermons all of them striking, all of them models of careful conscientious thought and composition, and many of them very forcible and original. It is a valuable volume."—*Literary Churchman.*

"A noble volume of Sermons which are such as very few living preachers could equal."—*Church Review.*

"Pre-eminently good Sermons, well-reasoned, well wrought, happy in illustration, rich in reflection, eloquent in expression."—*Scottish Guardian.*

SERMONS PREACHED IN VARIOUS CHURCHES OF BRISTOL. Second Edition. 8vo., 7s. 6d.

OCCASIONAL SERMONS. Two Vols; Second Edition. 8vo. 7s. 6d. each.

Published by J. Masters and Co.,

BY THE REV. J. M. NEALE, D.D.,
LATE WARDEN OF SACKVILLE COLLEGE, EAST GRINSTED.

SERMONS PREACHED IN SACKVILLE COLLEGE CHAPEL. Second Edition. Four Vols. Crown 8vo., cloth.

Vol. I. Advent to Whitsun Day. 7s. 6d.
II. Trinity and Saints' Days. 7s. 6d.
Vol. III. Lent and Passiontide. 7s. 6d.
IV. The Minor Festivals. 6s.

"Among the several volumes of writings by the late Dr. Neale which have been recently published, we must assign the foremost place as regards general utility to the *Sermons preached in Sackville College Chapel*, which hold, as we conceive, the very highest rank amongst modern Sermons intended to instruct and comfort the unlearned and suffering, by reason of the mingled clearness and beauty, the deep teaching and the practical application with which these admirable discourses abound."—*Church Times.*

"Charming volumes."—*Literary Churchman.*

READINGS FOR THE AGED. Selected from "Sermons preached in Sackville College Chapel." By the late Rev. J. M. NEALE, D.D., Warden of the College. Crown 8vo., cloth, 6s.

"One of the most useful books probably ever issued for parochial use is the late Dr. Neale's READINGS FOR THE AGED. Being also, as it deserves to be, one of the best known books among us, it needs no recommendation at our hands."—*Literary Churchman.*

SERMONS PREACHED IN A RELIGIOUS HOUSE. Second Series. Two Vols. Fcap. 8vo., cloth, 10s.

SEATONIAN PRIZE POEMS. Fcap. 8vo., 3s. 6d.

MEDIÆVAL HYMNS AND SEQUENCES, translated by the Rev. J. M. NEALE, D.D. Third Edition, with numerous additions. Royal 32mo. 2s.

HYMNS FOR CHILDREN. Three Series in One Vol. Tenth Edition. 18mo., cloth, 1s.

HYMNS FOR THE SICK. Fourth Edition. 6d.; cloth, 1s.

BY THE REV. W. H. HUTCHINGS, M.A.

Second Edition, enlarged and revised. Crown 8vo., cloth, 4s. 6d.

THE LIFE OF PRAYER. A Course of Lectures.

"Nothing can be more delightful than the way in which the author of these Lectures has treated a devotional subject of the very first rank and absolutely needful for every Christian."—*Church Quarterly.*

"It is eminently wise and pious. We do not know any work at once so full and so concise, so sympathetic and so systematic."—*Literary Churchman.*

Third Edition, revised and enlarged. With an Index, crown 8vo., cloth, 4s. 6d.

THE PERSON AND WORK OF THE HOLY GHOST. A Doctrinal and Devotional Treatise.

"Readers of Mr. Hutchings' valuable work will welcome this new and improved edition. From a Course of Lectures it has become a Treatise. We may hope that it will become of permanent use to the Church."—*Church Quarterly.*

Second Edition, crown 8vo., cloth, 4s.

SOME ASPECTS OF THE CROSS.

"A thorough and profound treatise on this subject written with great power of analysis and with a noteworthy combination of soberness and depth."—*Guardian.*

COMMENTARIES.

Fourth Edition, Four Vols., Post 8vo., cloth, 10s. 6d. each.

A COMMENTARY ON THE PSALMS, from the Primitive and Mediæval Writers; and from the various Office-Books and Hymns of the Roman, Mozarabic, Ambrosian, Gallican, Greek, Coptic, Armenian, and Syriac Rites. By the Rev. J. M. NEALE, D.D., and the Rev. R. F. LITTLEDALE, LL.D.

⁎ A new edition of Vol. IV. is now ready, containing, besides the Index of Texts, a new INDEX OF SUBJECTS for the whole work.

The INDEX OF SUBJECTS may be had separately. Price 1s. in paper cover.

"This truly valuable and remarkable Commentary is a work which *stands almost, if not entirely, alone in the theology of England*; and one to which we may *fairly challenge Christendom at large to produce anything precisely corresponding*. It will be found by those who have any taste at all for such studies a rich and valuable mine to which they may again and again recur without running the slightest risk of digging out the contents too hastily."—*Guardian*.

THE PSALM OF THE SAINTS: a Gloss upon Psalm CXIX. Extracted from NEALE and LITTLEDALE'S Commentary on the Psalms. Crown 8vo., cloth, 3s. 6d.

MISERERE: the Fifty-first Psalm, with Devotional Notes. Reprinted, with additions, from "Neale's Commentary on the Psalms." Wrapper, 6d.; cloth, 1s.

A COMMENTARY ON THE SONG OF SONGS. By the Rev. R. F. LITTLEDALE, LL.D., D.C.L. 12mo., antique cloth, 7s.

A COMMENTARY ON THE PRAYER BOOK, for the use of Pastors and Teachers in the Church and School. By the Rev. RICHARD ADAMS, M.A., Vicar of Lever Bridge, Bolton. Fcap. 8vo., cloth, 4s.

"The younger clergy, theological students, Sunday School teachers, and in fact teachers of all grades, will find it a most serviceable manual. It gives just the matter wanted for Lessons on the Prayer Book; and for this reason any one using it will get more help from it than from any book we know."—*Literary Churchman*.

COTTAGE COMMENTARY.
Vol. I. S. Matthew, limp cloth, 2s. 6d.
II. S. Mark, limp cloth, 1s. 9d.
III. S. Luke, 2s. 6d.
Vol. V. The Epistles to the Hebrews, S. James, S. Peter, S. John, and S. Jude, 2s. 6d.

READINGS ON THE PSALMS, with Notes on their Musical Treatment, originally addressed to Choristers. By the Rev. H. HOUSMAN. Fcap. 8vo., cloth, 3s. 6d.

THE ACTS OF THE APOSTLES. An Exposition of the Leading Events recorded in that Book. Cloth, 1s.

THE BOOK OF GENESIS. An Exposition of the Leading Events recorded in it. Cloth, 1s.

THE EPISTLE TO THE ROMANS. With Short Notes, chiefly Critical and Doctrinal. By the Rev. CANON CHAMBERLAIN. Fcap. 8vo., cloth, 2s.

A COMMENTARY ON THE TE DEUM. From Ancient Sources. By the BISHOP OF BRCHIN. 1s.

A COMMENTARY ON THE CANTICLES USED IN THE PRAYER BOOK. By the BISHOP OF BRECHIN. 1s.

A COMMENTARY ON THE SEVEN PENITENTIAL PSALMS. From Ancient Sources. By the BISHOP OF BRECHIN. Royal 32mo., cloth, 1s.

CHAPTERS ON THE TE DEUM. By the Author of "Earth's Many Voices." 16mo., cloth, 3s.

BOOKS FOR THE USE OF THE CLERGY.

Sixth Edition, much enlarged.

THE PRIEST'S PRAYER BOOK, with a brief Pontifical. Containing Private Prayers and Intercessions; Offices, Readings, Prayers, Litanies, and Hymns, for the Visitation of the Sick; Offices for Bible and Confirmation Classes, Cottage Lectures, &c.; Notes on Confession, Direction, Missions, and Retreats; Remedies for Sin; Anglican Orders; Bibliotheca Sacerdotalis, &c., &c.
One Vol. cloth . . . 6s. 6d.   Two Vols. cloth . . . 7s. 6d.
One Vol. calf or morocco 10s. 6d.

Reprinted from "The Priest's Prayer Book,"
RESPONSAL TO THE OFFICES OF THE SICK. For the Use of Attendants. Cloth, 1s.
PAROCHIAL OFFICES. 1d.   SCHOOL OFFICES. 1d.
OFFICE FOR A RURIDECANAL SYNOD OR CLERICAL MEETING. 1d.
ANGLICAN ORDERS. A Summary of Historical Evidence. 1d.
OFFICE FOR THE ADMISSION OF A CHORISTER. 1d.
ITINERARY. Devotions for those who are about to journey. ½d., or 3s. 6d. per 100.

EMBER HOURS. By the Rev. W. E. HEYGATE, M.A., Rector of Brighstone, Isle of Wight. Third Edition Revised, with an Essay on RELIGION IN RELATION TO SCIENCE, by the Rev. T. S. ACKLAND, M.A., Vicar of Newton Wold, author of "Story of Creation," &c. Fcap. 8vo., cloth, 3s.

MEMORIALE VITÆ SACERDOTALIS; or, Solemn Warnings of the Great Shepherd, JESUS CHRIST, to the Clergy of His Holy Church. From the Latin of Arvisenet. Adapted to the Use of the Anglican Church by the late BISHOP OF BRECHIN. Third edition, Fcap. 8vo., cloth, 3s. 6d.; calf, 8s.

MEMORANDA PAROCHIALIA, or the Parish Priest's Pocket Book. By the Rev. F. E. PAGET, M.A., Rector of Elford. 3s. 6d., double size 5s.

THE BOOK OF COMMON PRAYER OF 1662, according to the *Sealed Copy* in the Tower. Printed in red and black, fcap. 8vo., cloth, 2s. 6d., originally published at 12s. 6d.

THE CHURCHMAN'S DIARY: an Almanack and Directory for the Celebration of the Service of the Church. 4d.; interleaved, 6d.; cloth, 10d.; roan tuck, 2s.

SERMONS REGISTER, for Ten Years, by which an account may be kept of Sermons, the number, subject, and when preached. Post 4to., 1s.

REGISTER OF SERMONS, PREACHERS, NUMBER OF COMMUNICANTS, AND AMOUNT OF OFFERTORY. Fcap. 4to., bound, 4s. 6d. (The Book of Strange Preachers as ordered by the 52nd Canon.)

REGISTER OF PERSONS CONFIRMED AND ADMITTED TO HOLY COMMUNION. For 500 names, 4s. 6d. For 1000 names, 7s. 6d. half-bound.

THE LITANY, TOGETHER WITH THE LATTER PART OF THE COMMINATION SERVICE NOTED. Edited by RICHARD REDHEAD. Handsomely printed in red and black. Demy 4to., wrapper, 7s. 6d.; imitation morocco, 18s.; best morocco, 24s.; morocco panelled, &c., 30s.

THE LITTLE HOURS OF THE DAY, according to the Kalendar of the Church of England. Complete Edition, crown 8vo., cloth, 3s. 6d.; wrapper, 2s. 6d.

HORARIUM; seu Libellus Precationum, Latinè editus. 18mo., cl. 1s.

THE CLERGYMAN'S MANUAL OF PRIVATE PRAYERS. Collected and Compiled from Various Sources. A Companion Book to "The Priest's Prayer Book." Cloth, 1s.

THE PRIEST IN HIS INNER LIFE. Fcap. 8vo., cloth, 1s.

DEVOTIONAL BOOKS.

BENEATH THE CROSS. Readings for Children on our LORD'S Seven Sayings. By FLORENCE WILFORD. Edited by CHARLOTTE M. YONGE. 18mo., cloth boards, 1s. 6d.; limp cloth, 1s.

THE LOVE OF THE ATONEMENT, a Devotional Exposition of the Fifty-third chapter of Isaiah. By the Right Rev. R. MILMAN, D.D., Bishop of Calcutta. Fifth Edition. Fcap. 8vo., cloth, 3s. 6d.; calf, 6s.

MEDITATIONS ON THE SUFFERING LIFE OF OUR LORD. Translated from Pinart. Adapted to the use of the Anglican Church by A. P. FORBES, D.C.L., Bishop of Brechin. Fifth Edition. Fcap. 8vo., cloth, 5s.; calf, 10s.

NOURISHMENT OF THE CHRISTIAN SOUL. Translated from Pinart. Adapted to the use of the Anglican Church by A. P. FORBES, D.C.L., Bishop of Brechin. Fourth Edition. Fcap. 8vo., cloth, 5s.; calf, 10s.

THE MIRROR OF YOUNG CHRISTIANS. Translated from the French. Edited by A. P. FORBES, D.C.L., Bishop of Brechin. With Engravings, 2s. 6d.; morocco antique, 7s.

THE DIVINE MASTER: a Devotional Manual illustrating the Way of the Cross. With Ten steel Engravings. Eleventh Edition. 2s. 6d.; morocco, 5s. Cheap Edition, in wrapper, 1s.

THE SHADOW OF THE HOLY WEEK. By the Author of "The Divine Master." 18mo., cloth, 1s.

THE PSALTER, or Seven Ordinary Hours of Prayer, according to the Use of the Church of Sarum. Beautifully printed and illustrated. Fcap. 4to., antique binding. Reduced to 15s.

THE DIVINE LITURGY: a Manual of Devotions for the Sacrament of the Altar. For those who communicate. FOURTH EDITION, revised, with additional Prayers and Hymns, limp cloth, 1s. 6d. A superior edition printed on toned paper, cloth boards, red edges, 2s. 6d.; calf, 6s.

A FEW DEVOTIONAL HELPS FOR THE CHRISTIAN SEASONS. Edited by Two Clergymen. Two Vols., cloth, 5s. 6d.

THE KALENDAR OF THE IMITATION: Sentences for every day of the year from the "Imitatio Christi." Translated from the edition of 1630. Edited by the Rev. J. M. NEALE, D.D. New edition, royal 32mo., cloth, 1s.

THE GREAT TRUTHS OF THE CHRISTIAN RELIGION. Edited by the Rev. W. U. RICHARDS, M.A. 6th edition. Fcp. 8vo. cloth, 3s.; calf, 8s.

MEDITATIONS ON THE MOST PRECIOUS BLOOD AND EXAMPLE OF CHRIST. By the Rev. J. S. TUTE, M.A., Vicar of Markington, Yorkshire. Fcap. 8vo., cloth, 1s.

SPIRITUAL VOICES FROM THE MIDDLE AGES. Price 3s. 6d.

PRAYERS AND MAXIMS. In large type. Fourth Edition. Crown 8vo. cloth, 2s. 6d.

THE HOUR OF DEATH. A Manual of Prayers and Meditations intended chiefly for those who are in Sorrow or in Sickness. By the Rev. J. B. WILKINSON. Royal 32mo., 2s.

MEDITATIONS ON OUR LORD'S PASSION. Translated from the Armenian of Matthew, Vartabed. 2s. 6d.

TWELVE SHORT AND SIMPLE MEDITATIONS ON THE SUFFERINGS OF OUR LORD JESUS CHRIST. Edited by the Very Rev. DEAN BUTLER. 2s. 6d.

THE FOOTPRINTS OF THE LORD ON THE KING'S HIGHWAY OF THE CROSS. Devotional Aids for Holy Week. Edited by the Rev. T. T. CARTER. Fcap. 8vo., cloth, 1s.

SELECTIONS, NEW AND OLD. With a Preface by Bishop
Wilberforce. Fcap. 8vo., 4s. 6d.
THE HIDDEN LIFE. Translated from Nepveu's Pensées Chrétiennes.
Fourth Edition, enlarged. 18mo., 2s.
FOOTSTEPS OF THE HOLY CHILD, being Readings on the Incarnation. Edited by the Rev. T. T. Carter. Part I., fcap. 8vo., 1s. Part II., 2s. 6d.
In One Vol. cloth, 3s. 6d.
COMPANION FOR LENT. Being an Exhortation to Repentance, from the Syriac of S. Ephraem; and Thoughts for Every Day in Lent, gathered from other Eastern Fathers and Divines. By the Rev. S. C. Malan, M.A. 1s. 3d.
THE CHRISTIAN'S DAY. By the Rev. F. E. Paget, M.A. Royal 32mo., 2s. cloth.
MEDITATIONS FOR EVERY WEEK IN THE CHRISTIAN YEAR. By the Compiler of "Plain Prayers," with an Introduction by the Very Rev. W. J. Butler, M.A., Dean of Lincoln. Second Edition. 18mo., cloth, 1s. 6d.
THE SEVEN WORDS FROM THE CROSS. A Devotional Commentary. By Bellarmine. Second Edition. 1s. 6d.
THE THREE HOURS AGONY: Meditations, Prayers, and Hymns on the Seven Words from the Cross of our Most Holy Redeemer, together with Additional Devotions on the Passion. 4d.
EUCHARISTIC MEDITATIONS FOR A MONTH ON THE MOST HOLY COMMUNION. Translated from the French of Avrillon. Limp cloth, 2s. 6d.
DAILY MEDITATIONS: from Ancient Sources. Advent. Cloth, 1s.
DAILY MEDITATIONS FOR A MONTH, on some of the more Moving Truths of Christianity; in order to determine the Soul to be in earnest in the love and Service of her God. From Ancient Sources. Cloth, 1s.
A TREATISE OF THE VIRTUE OF HUMILITY, abridged from the Spanish of Rodriguez; for the use of persons living in the world. Cloth, 1s.
CONSIDERATIONS ON MYSTERIES OF THE FAITH, newly Translated and Abridged from the Original Spanish of Luis de Granada. 2s. cloth.
SPIRITUAL EXERCISES: Readings for a Retreat of Seven Days. Translated and Abridged from the French of Bourdaloue. 1s. 6d.

AIDS TO CATECHISING.

CATECHISINGS ON THE PRAYER BOOK. By the Ven. W. Lea, M.A., Archdeacon of Worcester. Third Edition. 18mo., cloth, 1s.
A CATECHISM ON THE BOOK OF COMMON PRAYER. By the Rev. Alexander Watson. 18mo., cloth, 2s.
A CATECHISM OF THEOLOGY. Second Edition, revised. 18mo., cloth, 1s. 6d.; wrapper, 1s.
THE CHURCH CATECHISM DEVELOPED. By Walter Hilmay Pierssy. 18mo., 4d.
A CATECHISM ON THE CHURCH. By the Rev. J. R. West, M.A., Vicar of Wrawby. New Edition. 4d.
CATECHISM OF THE CHIEF THINGS WHICH A CHRISTIAN OUGHT TO KNOW AND BELIEVE TO HIS SOUL'S HEALTH. Edited by several Clergymen. New Edition. 2d.
THE EVENING MEETINGS; or, the Pastor among the Boys of his Flock. By C. M. S. Fcap. 8vo., 2s.

MANUALS OF PRAYER.

THE DAY HOURS OF THE CHURCH OF ENGLAND, newly Translated and Arranged according to the Prayer Book and the Authorised Translation of the Bible. Fifteenth Thousand. Crown 8vo., wrapper, 1s.; cloth, 1s. 6d.; calf or morocco, 7s.
An Edition on large toned paper. Wrapper, 2s.; cloth, 2s. 6d.

THE ORDER FOR PRIME, TERCE, SEXT, NONE, AND COMPLINE, ACCORDING TO THE USE OF THE CHURCH OF ENGLAND. Newly revised. 9d. in wrapper.
This is printed in a form suitable for binding with the various editions of the Prayer Book from 24mo. to crown 8vo.

THE SERVICE FOR CERTAIN HOLYDAYS. Being a Supplement to "The Day Hours of the Church of England." Crown 8vo., 2s.

THE DAY OFFICE OF THE CHURCH, according to the Kalendar of the Church of England; consisting of Lauds, Vespers, Prime, Terce, Sext, None, and Compline, throughout the Year. To which are added, the Order for the Administration of the Reserved Eucharist, Penance, and Unction; together with the Office of the Dead, Commendation of a Soul, divers Benedictions and Offices, and full Rubrical Directions. A complete Edition, especially for Sisterhoods and Religious Houses. By the Editor of "The Little Hours of the Day." Crown 8vo., 4s. 6d.; cloth, red edges, 5s. 6d. SUPPLEMENT TO THE DAY OFFICE, 9d.

THE CHURCHMAN'S GUIDE TO FAITH AND PIETY. A Manual of Instruction and Devotions. Compiled by ROBERT BRETT. Fifth Edition. Cloth, 3s. 6d.; antique calf or plain morocco, 8s. 6d. Two Vols., cloth, 4s.; limp calf, 11s.; limp morocco, 12s.

THE PRIMER, set forth at large with many Godly and Devout Prayers. Edited, from the Post-Reformation Recension, by the Rev. GERARD MOULTRIE, M.A., Vicar of South Leigh. Fourth Thousand. 18mo., cloth, 3s.

THE HOURS OF THE PRIMER. Published separately for the use of individual members of a household in Family Prayer. 18mo., cloth, 1s.

MANUAL OF DEVOTION FOR SISTERS OF MERCY. Edited by the Rev. T. T. CARTER, M.A. In Eight Parts. Two Vols. cloth, 10s.; calf or mor. 17s.

A BOOK OF PRIVATE PRAYER FOR MORNING, MID-DAY, NIGHT, AND OTHER TIMES, with Rules for those who would live to GOD amid the business of Daily Life. Edited by the Rev. T. T. CARTER. Eleventh Edition. Limp cloth, 1s.; cloth, red edges, 1s. 3d.; roan, 1s. 6d.; French morocco, 2s.; limp calf, 3s. 6d.

THE MANUAL: a Book of Devotion. By the Rev. W. E. HEYGATE. Twenty-first Edition. Cloth limp, 1s.; boards, 1s. 3d.; leather, 1s. 6d.; French mor. 2s.; limp calf, 3s. 6d. Cheap Edition, 6d. A Superior Edition, 12mo., cloth, 1s. 6d.

SURSUM CORDA: Aids to Private Devotion. Collected from the Writings of English Churchmen. Compiled by the Rev. F. E. PAGET. 2s. 6d. cloth.

THE MANTLE OF PRAYER; a Book of Devotions, compiled chiefly from those of Bishop Andrewes. By A. N. With a Preface by the Very Rev. W. J. BUTLER, M.A., Dean of Lincoln. Fcap. 8vo., cloth, 1s. 6d.; roan, 2s. 6d.

CHRISTIAN SERVANT'S BOOK of Devotion, Self-Examination, and Advice. Sixth Edition. Cloth, 1s.

POCKET MANUAL OF PRAYERS FOR THE HOURS, &c., with the Collects from the Prayer Book. New Edition. Royal 32mo., cloth, 1s.; limp roan, 2s.; calf, 3s.
This popular Manual has been revised by several clergymen, and important additions have been made for the purpose of rendering it more suitable for private use, and especially for Retreats.

THE POCKET BOOK OF DAILY PRAYERS. Translated from Eastern Originals. By the Rev. S. C. MALAN, M.A. Suited for the Waistcoat Pocket. Cloth, 6d.; roan, 1s.
DEVOTIONS FOR DAILY USE. With Preface by the Hon. and Rev. Canon COURTENAY. Royal 32mo., cloth extra, 1s.
A MANUAL OF PRIVATE DEVOTIONS, containing Prayers for each Day in the Week, Devotions for the Holy Communion, and for the Sick. By BISHOP ANDREWES. 6d.
A COLLECTION OF PRIVATE DEVOTIONS FOR THE HOURS OF PRAYER. By BISHOP COSIN. 1s.
THE CHRISTIAN'S PLAIN GUIDE. By the Rev. WALTER A. GRAY, M.A., Vicar of Arksey. 32mo., cloth boards, 1s. Cheap Edition, wrapper, 6d.
THE DEVOUT CHORISTER. Thoughts on his Vocation, and a Manual of Devotions for his use. By THOMAS F. SMITH, B.D. 32mo., cloth, 1s.
A MANUAL OF DEVOTIONS FOR SCHOOL-BOYS. Compiled from various sources. By R. BRETT. 6d.
PRAYERS FOR LITTLE CHILDREN AND YOUNG PERSONS. By R. BRETT. 6d.; cloth, 8d. Part I. 2d., cloth 4d.; Part II. 4d., cloth 6d.
THE YOUNG CHURCHMAN'S MANUAL. Second Edition. 6d.

FAMILY PRAYERS.

FAMILY PRAYERS. By the Rev. CANON CARTER. Sixth Edition. 18mo., cloth, 1s.
BOOK OF FAMILY PRAYERS, collected from the Public Liturgy of the Church of England. By E. G., Minor Canon of Durham. 2s.
PRAYERS FOR A CHRISTIAN HOUSEHOLD, chiefly taken from the Scriptures, from the Ancient Liturgies, and the Book of Common Prayer. By the Rev. T. BOWDLER. Fcap. 8vo., cloth, 2s. 6d.
FAMILY DEVOTIONS FOR A FORTNIGHT. Compiled from the Works of BISHOP ANDREWES, KEN, WILSON, KETTLEWELL, NELSON, SPINCKES, &c. (Suited also for private use.) New Edition. Fcap. 8vo., cloth, 1s. 6d.
PRAYERS AND LITANIES, taken from Holy Scripture, together with a Calendar and Table of Lessons. Arranged by the Rev. J. S. B. MONSELL, LL.D. 16mo., cloth, 1s.
FAMILY PRAYERS adapted to the course of the Ecclesiastical Year. By the Rev. R. A. SUCKLING. Sixth Edition. 6d.; cloth, 1s.
PRAYERS FOR FAMILY USE. From Ancient Sources. With Preface by the Archdeacon of S. Alban's. Fcap. 8vo., cloth, 1s.

By the Author of "The Churchman's Guide to Faith and Piety."

DEVOTIONS FOR THE SICK ROOM, PRAYERS IN SICKNESS, &c. Cloth, 2s. 6d.
COMPANION FOR THE SICK ROOM: being a Compendium of Christian Doctrine. 2s. 6d.
OFFICES FOR THE SICK AND DYING. Reprinted from the above. 1s.
LEAFLETS FOR THE SICK AND DYING; supplementary to the Offices for the same in "The Churchman's Guide to Faith and Piety." First Series. Price per set of eight, 6d.; cardboard, 9d.

VOLUMES OF SERMONS AND LECTURES:

ASHLEY, REV. J. M.—THE VICTORY OF THE SPIRIT: a Course of Short Sermons by way of Commentary on the Eighth Chapter of S. Paul's Epistle to the Romans. Fcap. 8vo., cloth, 2s.

——— THIRTEEN SERMONS FROM THE QUARESIMALE OF QUIRICO ROSSI. Translated from the Italian. Edited by J. M. Ashley, B.C.L. Fcap. 8vo., cloth, 3s. 6d.

BAINES, REV. J.—SERMONS. Fcap. 8vo., 5s.

BRECHIN, THE LATE BP. OF.—ARE YOU BEING CONVERTED? Sermons on Serious Subjects. Third Edition. Fcap. 8vo., 2s.

——— SERMONS ON AMENDMENT OF LIFE. Second Edition. Fcap. 8vo. 2s.

——— SERMONS ON THE GRACE OF GOD, and other Cognate Subjects. 3s. 6d.

BRIGHT, REV. CANON.—EIGHTEEN SERMONS OF S. LEO THE GREAT ON THE INCARNATION, AND EPISTLE XXVIII., OR THE "TOME." Translated, with Notes. Crown 8vo.

CHAMBERLAIN, REV. T.—THE THEORY OF CHRISTIAN WORSHIP. Second Edition. 3s. 6d.

——— THE SEVEN AGES OF THE CHURCH as indicated in the Messages to the Seven Churches of Asia. Post 8vo., 3s.

CHANTER, REV. J. M.—SERMONS. 12mo., 3s. 6d.

CODD, REV. E. T.—SERMONS addressed to a Country Congregation, including Four preached before the University of Cambridge. Third Series. 6s. 6d.

CURRIE.—SERMONS AND LECTURES, FOR SUNDAYS AND HOLY DAYS. By the Rev. James Currie, M.A., late Rector of West Lavington. Demy 8vo. Vol. I. Advent to Trinity, 7s. 6d. Vol. II., Trinity Season, &c., 7s. 6d.

DAVIDSON, REV. J. P. F.—THE HOLY COMMUNION. A Course of Sermons. Second Edition. Fcap. 8vo., cloth, 1s. 6d.

EVANS, REV. A. B., D.D.—CHRISTIANITY IN ITS HOMELY ASPECTS: Sermons on Various Subjects. Second Series. 12mo., 3s.

FLOWER, REV. W. B.—SERMONS FOR THE SEASONS OF THE CHURCH, translated from S. Bernard. 8vo., 3s. 6d.

GALTON, REV. J. L.—ONE HUNDRED AND FORTY-TWO LECTURES ON THE BOOK OF REVELATION. In Two Vols. Fcap. 8vo., 18s.

——— NOTES OF LECTURES ON THE BOOK OF CANTICLES OR SONG OF SOLOMON, delivered in the Parish Church of S. Sidwell, Exeter. 6s.

HAMILTON, REV. L. R.—PAROCHIAL SERMONS. Fcap. 8vo. 3s. 6d.

HILL, REV. H.—SHORT SERMONS ON SOME LEADING PRINCIPLES OF CHRISTIAN LIFE. 6s.

IRONS, REV. W. J., D.D.—THE PREACHING OF CHRIST. A Series of Sixty Sermons for the People. In a Packet, 5s.; cloth, 6s.

——— THE MIRACLES OF CHRIST: being a Second Series of Sermons for the People. Second Edition. 8vo., 6s.

LEA, THE VEN. ARCHDEACON.—SERMONS ON THE PRAYER BOOK. Fcap. 8vo., 2s.

LEE, REV. F. G., D.C.L.—MISCELLANEOUS SERMONS, by Clergymen of the Church of England. Edited by F. G. Lee. Crown 8vo., 3s. 6d.

Published by J. Masters and Co., 78, New Bond Street.

MILLARD, REV. F. M.—S. PETER'S DENIAL OF CHRIST.
Seven Short Sermons to Boys. Fcap. 8vo., 1s. 4d.

NEWLAND, REV. H.—POSTILS; Short Sermons on the Parables, &c., adapted from the Fathers. Second Edition. Fcap. 8vo., 3s.

NUGEE, REV. G.—THE WORDS FROM THE CROSS AS APPLIED TO OUR OWN DEATHBEDS. Second Edition. Fcap. 8vo., 2s. 6d.

PAGET, REV. F. E.—SERMONS ON THE SAINTS' DAYS. 12mo., 3s. 6d.

——— SERMONS FOR SPECIAL OCCASIONS. Crown 8vo., 3s. 6d.

POTT, THE VEN. ARCHDEACON.—CONFIRMATION LECTURES delivered to a Village Congregation in the Diocese of Oxford. 3rd Edition. 2s.

PRICHARD, REV. J. C.—SERMONS. Fcap. 8vo., 4s. 6d.

PRYNNE, REV. G. R.—PLAIN PAROCHIAL SERMONS. Second Series. 8vo., 10s. 6d.

——— PAROCHIAL SERMONS (New Volume.) 8vo., 10s. 6d.

SERMONS BY VARIOUS CONTRIBUTORS ILLUSTRATING THE OFFICES OF THE PRAYER BOOK. 8vo., 3s. 6d.

SMITH, REV. C. F.—SERMONS PREACHED IN HOLY WEEK. 6s.

THOMPSON, REV. H.—CONCIONALIA. Outlines of Sermons for Parochial Use throughout the Year. FIRST SERIES. Third Edition. Fcap. 8vo., 7s. 6d. SECOND SERIES. 6s. 6d.

TOMLINS, REV. R.—SERMONS for the Greater Cycle of High Days in the Church's Year, with Sermons for Special and Ordinary Occasions. Second Edition. 12mo., 5s.

——— ADVENT SERMONS. Second Edition. First and Second Series, in One Vol., cloth, 3s. 6d.

WATSON, REV. A.—THE SEVEN SAYINGS ON THE CROSS. 8vo., 3s. 6d.

WEST, REV. J. R.—SERMONS ON THE ASCENSION OF OUR LORD. Fcap. 8vo., 3s. 6d.

——— PARISH SERMONS FOR THE ADVENT AND CHRISTMAS SEASONS. Fcap. 8vo., 3s.

——— PARISH SERMONS ON THE HOLY EUCHARIST. Fcap. 8vo., cloth, 4s. 6d.

WILKINSON, REV. J. B.—MISSION SERMONS. Third Series. Fcap. 8vo., 6s.

WINDSOR, REV. S. B.—SERMONS FOR SOLDIERS preached at Home and Abroad. Fcap. 8vo., 3s. 6d.

WOOD, REV. S. THEODORE.—THE REVOLT OF MAN FROM GOD. An Advent Course of Four Sermons, Addresses to Men. 1s.

WOODFORD, RT. REV. BISHOP.—SERMONS PREACHED IN VARIOUS CHURCHES OF BRISTOL. Second Edition. 7s. 6d.

——— OCCASIONAL SERMONS. Vol. I., 7s. 6d. Vol. II., 7s. 6d.

——— ORDINATION SERMONS PREACHED IN THE DIOCESES OF OXFORD AND WINCHESTER, 1860—1872. 8vo., 6s. 6d.

LONDON: J. MASTERS & CO., 78, NEW BOND STREET.

www.ingramcontent.com/pod-product-compliance
Lightning Source LLC
Chambersburg PA
CBHW052214240426
43670CB00037B/442